STATUS INTEGRATION AND SUICIDE

Status Integration
and Suicide

A Sociological Study

---

by JACK P. GIBBS, *Professor of Sociology*
University of Texas

and WALTER T. MARTIN, *Professor of Sociology*
University of Oregon

UNIVERSITY OF OREGON ꓭBOOKS

Eugene, Oregon 1964

PREFACE

MORE THAN sixty years have passed since Emile Durkheim's volume on suicide was first published. During these decades, *Le Suicide* has remained the foremost sociological treatment of the subject, respected not only as a penetrating analysis but perhaps even more as a model of sociological theory and investigation. The research reported in this volume, divergent as it may at times seem, is a direct outgrowth of Durkheim's work, and the debt the writers owe to him is both obvious and incalculable.

There are other debts, too, more easily acknowledged. Compilation of the New Zealand data was made possible by a Fulbright fellowship awarded to Jack P. Gibbs, and a grant from the National Science Foundation made possible the organization of all data reported here. For this assistance and for the ready cooperation of the New Zealand Department of Justice and the New Zealand Educational Foundation, the authors are grateful beyond measure.

The first comprehensive statement of the theory of status integration, some procedures for measurement, and initial tests appeared in a doctoral dissertation written by Jack P. Gibbs under the direction of Walter T. Martin at the University of Oregon in 1957. Much of the original work is incorporated in the present report.

Careful and competent statistical work was done by Robert Blauner, Ruth Chertok, Stella G. Estes, Stephen Forstein, Nona Glazer, Robert G. Holloway, Connie Panagakis, and James M. Rollins. Completion of the manuscript was greatly facilitated by the services of excellent typists: Mary Ellen Henderson, Sevilla Jesse, Marcella King, Marlene McCormick, and Beverly Schroeder. The Department of Sociology, University of Oregon, provided valuable clerical assistance in the final stages of manuscript preparation.

Limitations of space prohibited publication of much of the data utilized in the tests of the theory; in those cases where only summary results are presented, the original tables may be obtained from the American Documentation Institute, 1719 N St., N.W., Washington 6, D.C.

J. P. G.

W. T. M.

CONTENTS

LIST OF TABLES

LIST OF FIGURES

PART ONE

The Sociological Analysis of Suicide and the Theory of Status Integration

CHAPTER ONE

The Sociological Analysis of Suicide

THE DIFFERENCES in suicide rates of nations and other populations have long intrigued observers and have led to a great deal of speculation regarding causation. The proffered explanations notwithstanding, the differences remain as perplexing today as they ever were. Why, for example, is the suicide rate of Denmark 23.3 per hundred thousand population, while Ireland's is only 2.0?[1] If this is a matter of religious differences, why is the suicide rate of Italy three times as high as that of Ireland? If, again, this is a result of climatic differences, why is the rate for Norway, which is even closer to the Arctic Circle, only one-third that of Denmark? Or, to take another example, why do white males in the United States have a rate three times that of nonwhite males? If this is the result of an inherent racial tendency on the part of whites, why is the rate for white females lower than the rate for nonwhite males? Why does the suicide rate for white males increase consistently from childhood to old age? If this results from the tribulations of aging, why does the rate among white females decline in the later years of life? Most puzzling of all, why do these differences in suicide rates persist consistently for decades and even centuries?

From a recognition of the extent and consistency of the variations

---

[1] The rates in this section are all from recent years and are drawn from the World Health Organization, *Epidemiological and Vital Statistics Report,* IX, No. 4 (1956), pp. 243-287.

in suicide rates of compared populations,[2] emerge two theoretical questions of particular significance to sociology: Is it possible to formulate a theory of social structure, a *sociological* theory, that will correctly predict differences in the suicide rates of populations? Can this sociological theory be a *general* one, in that it correctly predicts differences among all types and categories of populations? The present study evolved from consideration of these questions; it is concerned with a theory that is both sociological and general in nature.

The theory of status integration was not developed to explain individual cases of suicide, but to account for variations in the suicide rates of populations. It is a sociological theory, in that it looks to a mensurable characteristic of the social structure as a source of explanation, a line of investigation well established by Emile Durkheim. It is a general theory, in that it provides a basis for predicting the rank of the suicide rates of any populations or population categories for which the necessary data are available. That is, the theory of status integration is a sociological formulation that is not limited to any particular social class or society; it is equally appropriate for predicting suicide rates by occupation, race, sex, marital status, religion, state, or nation. It has not been possible, in this single volume, to apply the theory to every possible type of population, and indeed, we are aware that the results have not been uniformly satisfactory in every case of application. Every attempted application is reported, however, and the reader may evaluate the results and make additional tests himself.

The authors also recognize that many readers will hesitate to accept that a single sociological theory can account for variation in suicide rates, particularly since suicide appears to be such a private behavior involving the deepest and most powerful of human emotions. However, the theory of status integration, incorporating, as it does, much of the theory of status, role, and role conflict, is broadly conceived, so that although a single theory is advanced, no single variable or specific cluster of variables is proposed as always accounting for the suicide rate.

It is, in addition, most important to stress that the theory of status integration is concerned with differences between suicide rates and not their exact magnitudes; that is, given two populations, the theory makes possible a prediction of which population has the higher or the lower rate. This is, of course, a simple task compared to predicting

---

[2] A population, for the purposes of this study, is an aggregate of people, specifically a socially recognized aggregate in the sense of a political society, a political division of a society, or an aggregate of individuals who have in common one or more of the social statuses in a society.

the magnitudes of suicide rates or actual quantitative differences between them, and although with further elaboration of the theory and necessary data it might be possible to construct formulas capable of predicting the suicide rate of any given population, it appeared more feasible to first test, under a great variety of conditions, the theory's ability to predict qualitative differences. The criterion of adequacy in this testing is the ability of the theory to arrange populations in rank order according to the magnitude of their suicide rates.

There has always been, and continues to be, lively interest resulting in extensive research on the subject of suicide; indeed, it is probably, among the more isolated and specific forms of behavior, the one which has received the most scholarly attention. K. G. Dahlgren estimated in 1945 that there were approximately four thousand published works on the subject.[3] This literature provides an extensive backlog of facts and cases, but begins with the individual and moves to the philosophical or speculative. It provides certain clues and insights regarding the causes of suicide, but sociological explanations are not explored in depth, and the various works are not oriented toward the development of a general theory.[4] For this reason, we shall concern ourselves mainly with the work of Emile Durkheim and those scholars who have followed after the great French sociologist, and through examination of these sociological studies trace the development of the theory of status integration.

Durkheim's *Suicide*[5] made two outstanding contributions toward the theoretical explanation of the phenomenon in terms of social or cultural variables. He first demonstrated that differences in the suicide rates of European populations could not be accounted for by several previously suggested variables of an extrasocial nature (pages 41-42). Then, concluding from his evidence that the determinant of variability in suicide rates lies in the realm of social phenomena, Durkheim carried out an elaborate analysis of European countries and other populations throughout the nineteenth century. Through his observations of low suicide rates among Catholics, Jews, the married, parents, the uneducated, and countries at war, to mention a few, he was led to postulate the existence of a common denominator: "Suicide varies inversely with the degree of integration of the social groups" (page

---

[3] Karl Gustav Dahlgren, *On Suicide and Attempted Suicide* (Lund, 1945), p. 1.

[4] A review of selected theoretical approaches to suicide is contained in Jack P. Gibbs, "A Sociological Study of Suicide" (unpublished doctoral dissertation, University of Oregon, 1957), Chap. II.

[5] Emile Durkheim, *Suicide,* trans. by John A. Spaulding and George Simpson (Glencoe, Ill., 1951). All subsequent references will be to this edition; page numbers in parentheses follow the references in the text.

209). If Durkheim had remained content with this general conclusion, it would have been much easier to evaluate his work. The later introduction of the idea that suicide rates also are influenced by the prevalence of altruism (pages 217-240) and anomie (pages 241-276) presents us with three theories rather than one. The difference between the concepts involved warrants consideration. A careful reading of Durkheim indicates that altruism is not a separate concept but rather a special case of social integration—excessive integration, to be specific (pages 217 and 221). This means that the suicide rate varies inversely with social integration until the latter reaches a high point, and that, after this, increases in social integration are accompanied by increases in suicide. Consequently, the empirical referents of social integration may apply to altruism as well. This appears to be the only solution, since Durkheim gave little attention to measurement. In treating the concept of altruism in this manner, we have only to remember that Durkheim has implied that beyond a certain point social integration varies directly with the suicide rate.

Too much faith should not be placed in Durkheim's assertion. In the first place, the reports of suicide being prevalent among primitive peoples, which led him to employ the concept, are now open to serious question. In addition, Durkheim's belief that being bound up too closely in the collective life of a society is inherently conducive to suicide led him to assume that the content of collective life is irrelevant. However, an actual test of his claim must await specification of empirical referents for social integration and its measurement in a wide variety of populations.

Durkheim's concept of anomie is far more difficult to analyze than altruism, because he implies that anomie is a phenomenon independent of social integration. In discussing the difference between anomic and egoistic suicide (that type caused by lack of social integration), Durkheim distinguished between the types as follows: "It [anomic type] differs from [egoistic type] in its dependence, not on the way in which individuals are attached to society but on how it regulates them" (page 258). Though this suggests a certain distinction between anomie and social integration, the difference, as Sainsbury notes,[6] is a slender one. This is particularly true when one attempts to specify the empirical referents for the two in such a way as to make them clearly independent. For example, Durkheim regards widowhood, divorce, economic crises, and certain occupations as in some way indicative of anomie (pages 241-246, 259-276), but these

---

[6] Peter Sainsbury, *Suicide in London* (New York, 1955), p. 22.

phenomena may be equally symptomatic of a lack of social integration. Nor can it be said that Durkheim was consistent in his distinction; in discussing egoistic suicide, he made the following observation regarding the effect of a low degree of social integration on individual behavior (page 209) :

The more weakened the groups to which he belongs the more he consequently depends on himself and recognizes no other rules of conduct than what are founded on his private interests.

. . . .

When society is strongly integrated, it holds individuals under its control, considers them at its service and thus forbids them to dispose wilfully of themselves.

Such statements indicate that social integration has a regulating function, but Durkheim later describes the concept of anomie in terms of regulation also.

In view of the difficulties involved in attempting to distinguish clearly between these three concepts, we have decided to concentrate our efforts on social integration, the concept central to Durkheim's general conclusion. Contending with social integration is difficult enough without considering anomie: indeed, nearly all the properties Durkheim ascribes to anomie can be subsumed under the concept of social integration. And, even if the two concepts are taken to be completely independent, an evaluation of Durkheim's theory of inverse relationship between social integration and suicide need not necessarily also encompass the assertion of a relationship between anomie and suicide. Finally, as indicated above, the relationship between social integration and suicide is the fundamental part of his theoretical formulation and, as such, is more deserving of consideration.

Durkheim's critics have attacked his study on metaphysical grounds[7] and his admirers have accepted his findings as constituting strong support for the theory, but both parties have overlooked an important fact: Durkheim's theory has never been subjected to a formal test— nor is it testable. Durkheim does not present an explicit connotative definition of social integration, much less an operational definition, nor, consequently, does he correlate a measure of social integration with suicide; rather, he presents differential suicide rates and states that the differences observed are due to variability in social integration. Durkheim, indeed, seems sometimes to identify some characteristic of a population as indicative of a high degree of social integration after the establishment of the population's low suicide rate. Lack-

---

[7] Gustavo Tosti, "Suicide in the Light of Recent Studies," *American Journal of Sociology,* III (1898), 464-478.

ing the specification of the empirical referents for the concept and the operations for measuring its prevalence, his proposition is supported, not by its predictive power, but by his forceful argumentation.

It may be argued, of course that Durkheim's findings on differential suicide rates point directly to the appropriate referents for the concept of social integration. This would mean that an index of social integration could be prepared for any population by basing it on the proportion of Catholics, Jews, married persons, married persons with children, and illiterates in the population. However, such an index would involve no theory beyond the assumption that certain statuses in a society provide invariable immunity. But this is not the case, as Durkheim's own data show. Consider the suicide rate of Catholics in Baden; the mean annual rate was 17.0 per hundred thousand Catholics during the years 1878-1888, a rate over twice as high as that (8.0) of Protestants in Austria for 1852-1859. It is also of interest to note that the rate of suicide among Jews in Austria stood at 2.1 for 1852-1859, while in Baden it was 21.0 for 1878-1888 (page 154). Even if these three religions provided an invariable degree of immunity to suicide, an index based on them could not be applied to non-European populations where none of the three prevails. What has been said about the variable immunity to suicide provided by religious affiliation applies equally well to the other statuses included in Durkheim's analysis of differential suicide rates.

Such an attempt to reduce the concept of social integration to a simple index of demographic composition would be not only very unpromising but also an injustice to Durkheim. What he sought was not an actuarial explanation of differential suicide rates but a common denominator which is associated with a low suicide rate in whatever population it is found. That he was able to conceptualize the common denominator and make statements about its nature, however vaguely, is the heart of his contribution.

Durkheim does indeed make some attempt to describe the nature of the phenomenon advanced as the common denominator; in his observations on social integration there are suggestions as to its empirical properties, though these are not specific enough for purposes of measurement. Although Durkheim seems consistently to identify it with the degree of consensus in a population (pages 158-162), consensus is a nebulous concept, and Durkheim specifies neither which types of consensus constitute social integration nor the operations to be performed in their measurement.

Though the majority of Durkheim's statements about the nature of social integration pertain to the concept of consensus, there are some exceptions. In one instance, he links social integration to family density (pages 199-202). Logical connections in these extraconsensual properties are not well defined and one is often left with the impression that social integration is defined in terms of anything that correlates inversely with suicide.

If we accept Durkheim's suggestion that social integration is some form of consensus, serious questions arise regarding the adequacy of the theory. Consensus, whatever type is selected and however measured, will not adequately account for the extreme differences in suicide rates by sex and age in the same society. Since Durkheim based his case for the most part on forceful argumentation, it is particularly significant that his argument is weakest in the case of suicide differentials by age and sex. The widow endures her condition better than the widower, says Durkheim, because, "As she lives outside of community existence more than man, she is less penetrated by it; society is less necessary to her because she is less impregnated with sociability" (page 215). A somewhat similar explanation is that of the disparity in the suicide rates of divorced males and females (page 272):

This consequence of divorce is peculiar to man and does not affect the wife. Women's sexual needs have less of a mental character because, generally speaking, her mental life is less developed. These needs are more closely related to the needs of the organism, following rather than leading them, and consequently find in them an efficient restraint. Being a more instinctive creature than man, woman has only to follow her instincts to find calmness and peace.

Although Durkheim does not treat the differences in the suicide rates of males and females independent of marital status, a fact that is of considerable theoretical significance, the statements quoted above are indicative of the reasoning he consistently followed in any reference to sexual variation. This suggests that the female is immune to suicide because she is less caught up in collective life, an explanation inconsistent with the general theory that the suicide rate varies inversely with the degree of social integration. The lower suicide rate for females thus appears to be explained more on a biological than a sociological level, a deviation from Durkheim's otherwise consistent rejection of reductive explanations.

Similarly, regarding suicide increasing with increasing age, Durkheim says, "Just as suicide appears more or less early depending on the age at which men enter into society, it grows to the extent that they are more completely involved in it" (page 102). Thus, while egoistic suicide is said to grow out of individuals becoming detached from social life (page 209), Durkheim suggests that suicide tends to increase with increasing age because of increasing involvement in social life.

Another question about the consensual nature of social integration relates to the *content* of collective beliefs, which should, in our opinion, be considered as well as the degree of consensus. There is in Durkheim's theory, particularly in his discussion of altruistic suicide (pages 217-228), an implicit denial that content has anything to do with the amount of suicide; but the possibility cannot be ignored that certain values may dispose the individual to suicide, and that, in societies where these values are a part of the prevailing belief system, suicide would vary directly with the degree of consensus and not inversely.

If the above criticisms seem vigorous, we can only say that they imply neither a rejection of Durkheim's theory nor a denial of the value of his work. They should, however, indicate that the theory remains, and will remain, untested until empirical referents for social integration have been established. Above all, it is not suggested that the concept is to be dismissed as useless because the empirical referents for it were left unspecified. Durkheim's statements about social integration are vague, yet provide a firm basis for subsequent research. Indeed, quite a few important studies have built upon Durkheim's foundation; yet, while all of them have contributed to our knowledge about suicide, they all share his problem: the empirical referents of the independent variable are not so specified that a measure could be developed.

Halbwachs' study of suicide[8] is in essence a continuation of Durkheim; his treatment of statistical data is similar, though his interpretation of variability in suicide rates is much more psychologically oriented. Halbwachs' study also differs in its single explanation for all suicide: social isolation, the detachment of the individual from collective life. There seems to be little difference between this theory and that of social integration, and the two seem equally untestable for the same reasons.

Merton's analysis of the relationship between social structure and conformity,[9] which constitutes a general theory of deviant behavior, represents a broad application of the concept of anomie. Anomie is described as a disproportionate accent on cultural goals at the expense of a de-emphasis of the institutionally approved means for reaching

---

[8] Maurice Halbwachs, *Les Causes du Suicide* (Paris, 1930).
[9] Robert K. Merton, "Social Structure and Anomie," *American Sociological Review,* III (1938), 672-682.

the goals. Every social structure is supposedly characterized by some degree of anomie, and it is this degree which fixes the over-all level of deviant behavior. Merton's theory will not receive extended consideration here because he has failed to specify the operations which yield a measure of anomie; and, because of the difficulty of differentiating between means and goals or ends, the concept may well defy operationalization.[10] To further complicate matters, anomie cannot be defined as violation of institutionally accepted means without the relationship between anomie and deviant behavior becoming tautological.

The difficulties encountered in the use of Durkheim's concept of social integration are illustrated in the conclusions reached by Straus and Straus in their study of suicide and homicide rates in Ceylon,[11] particularly among ethnic groups: "Reasoning from the characteristics of loosely as opposed to closely integrated social structures has led to the expectation that the suicide rate will vary directly, and the homicide rate inversely, with the degree to which a society is closely structured."[12] This conclusion appears to be incompatible with Durkheim's statement of a general inverse relationship between suicide and integration; though it agrees with his assertion of a direct relationship in the case of "altruistic" suicide. In either case, Straus and Straus do not define "closeness" or "looseness" in such a way as to make measurement possible.[13]

A recent monograph by Henry and Short is an imaginative effort to develop a general theory to explain variations in both suicide and homicide rates. It proceeds on the basis of three assumptions:

(1) Aggression is often a consequence of frustration; (2) business cycles produce variation in the hierarchial ranking of persons and groups; (3) frustrations are generated by interference with the "goal response" of maintaining a constant or

---

[10] Recent published works extending this line of conceptual analysis do not deal with the problems of moving from highly abstract concepts to empirical referents. See three articles in the *American Sociological Review*, XXIV (1959): Robert Dubin, "Deviant Behavior and Social Structure: Continuities in Social Theory," 147-164; Richard A. Cloward, "Illegitimate Means, Anomie, and Deviant Behavior," 164-176; and Robert K. Merton, "Social Conformity, Deviation, and Opportunity-Structures: A Comment on the Contributions of Dubin and Cloward," 177-189. For a recent attempt to utilize the concept anomie specifically in connection with suicide rates, see Elwin H. Powell, "Occupation, Status, and Suicide: Toward a Redefinition of Anomie," *American Sociological Review*, XXIII (1958), 131-139. Also, see Gibbs and Martin "On Status Integration and Suicide Rates in Tulsa," *American Sociological Review*, XXIV (1959), 392-396.

[11] Jacqueline H. Straus and Murray A. Straus, "Suicide, Homicide, and Social Structure in Ceylon," *American Journal of Sociology*, LVIII (1953), 461-469.

[12] Straus and Straus, p. 469.

[13] The theory developed in this study is applied to Ceylon suicide data in Gibbs and Martin, "Status Integration and Suicide in Ceylon," *American Journal of Sociology*, LXIV (1959), 585-591.

rising position in a status hierarchy relative to the status position of others in the same status reference system.[14]

From these assumptions flows the general hypothesis, "the reactions of both suicide and homicide to the business cycle can be consistently interpreted as aggressive reactions to frustration generated by the flow of economic forces."[15] The nature of the aggressive reaction is a function of the individual's "status position"[16] (rank-status) and a variable called "strength of the relational system" ("the degree of involvement in social or cathectic relationships with other persons"). Two general propositions emerge: (1) a positive relation is anticipated between suicide and rank-status, and a negative relation between suicide and strength of the relational system; and (2) a negative relation is anticipated between homicide and rank-status and a positive relation between homicide and strength of the relational system.[17]

Later, an additional variable, "strength of external restraint" ("the degree to which behavior is required to conform to the demands and expectations of other persons") is introduced along with an additional proposition: "suicide varies negatively and homicide positively with the strength of external restraint over behavior."[18]

Although Henry and Short have not limited their efforts to conceptual analysis, they have not yet designated empirical referents for "strength of the relational system" and "strength of external restraints over behavior," and so present no measures of these variables, stating only that certain population categories rank higher in these ways than others.

We have not tried to present a comprehensive balanced review of the studies discussed above, meaning only to indicate how Durkheim's work has inspired contemporary sociologists further to develop theories of deviant behavior. We have attempted to show how the investigators, including Durkheim, have been handicapped in their analyses by abstract concepts to which no empirical referents are assigned and for which no concrete measures can be devised.

We have two main aims in this study—to build upon the work of Durkheim in the development of a general theory to account for varia-

---

[14] Andrew F. Henry and James F. Short, Jr., *Suicide and Homicide* (Glencoe, Ill., 1954), p. 14.

[15] Henry and Short, pp. 14-15.

[16] As used by Henry and Short, "status" refers to standing or rank in a hierarchy of social positions, a use not to be confused with ours.

[17] Henry and Short, pp. 16-17.

[18] Henry and Short, p. 17.

tions in suicide rates, and to ground explanatory concepts firmly in the empirical world so that concrete measures may be developed and used in testing the hypotheses that flow from the theory.

CHAPTER TWO

Status Integration and Variability in Suicide Rates

IT IS FOR good reason that many students have looked to Durkheim as a source of explanation for the empirical facts of suicide. His work offers the most promising point of departure for anyone interested in developing a theory concerned with differences in suicide rates. This is especially true of his statement that suicide rates vary inversely with the degree of social integration. Indeed, the sole objection to this assertion as a theoretical statement is that the concept of social integration is not clearly defined and consequently cannot be measured. By specifying the empirical referents of integration in terms subject to measurement, Durkheim's statement would be transformed into an empirical proposition capable of being subjected to a variety of tests. This appears to be the logical next step in advancing beyond Durkheim's work, and it is to this problem that this chapter is devoted.

TYPES OF INTEGRATION

The concept of integration has come to have a general meaning, but there is as yet no commonly accepted specific meaning. The highly abstract nature of the general meaning poses difficulties for the researcher attempting to deal with specific empirical variables and leads to consideration of various types of integration.

Virtually everyone who has subjected the term "integration" to conceptual analysis has concluded that several different variables are involved. Gillin, for example, suggests four kinds of integration: relatedness, functional linkage, consistency, and balance among the components of a culture system.[1] Landecker also describes four types of integration: cultural (consistency among the standards of a culture); normative (conformity of the conduct of the group to cultural standards); communicative (exchange of meanings throughout the group); and functional (interdependence among group members through the division of labor).[2]

An analysis of types of integration does not facilitate the testing of Durkheim's theory. In the first place, assuming that the types are exhaustive and mutually exclusive, there is no suggestion as to which is the crucial one for differences in suicide rates. This problem might not be serious if we knew that there was a high intercorrelation among the different types of integration, but there is no concrete evidence of this.

The problem of selecting one type of integration as opposed to another for a test of Durkheim's theory is posed in any suggestion which links the concept to empirical variables. Linton's classification of cultural traits suggests a definition of integration: "While the Universals and Specialties within any culture normally form a fairly consistent and well-integrated unit, the Alternatives necessarily lack such consistency and integration."[3] According to Landecker, Linton's observation provides a rationale for measurement: "Thus cultural integration can be measured by determining the proportion of alternatives in relation to universals and specialties. The lower the proportion of alternatives, the higher the degree of cultural integration."[4]

Assuming that it is possible to gauge cultural integration in the manner suggested by Landecker, there is still no suitable theoretical rationale for expecting it to be related to differences in suicide rates. The same may be said, of course, for almost all of the types of integration that have been suggested. Types of integration without solid connection to substantive theory appear to offer limited usefulness for testing Durkheim's theory.

It is most important, when using Durkheim's theory as a point of departure, to make a careful selection of the type of integration and the empirical variables for its measurement; the selection of the type and the operations for its measurement should be governed by, or at least linked to, Durkheim's observations.

---

[1] John Gillin, *The Ways of Men* (New York, 1948), pp. 515-531.

[2] Werner S. Landecker, "Types of Integration and Their Measurement," *American Journal of Sociology,* LVI (January, 1951), 340.

[3] Ralph Linton, *The Study of Man* (New York, 1936), p. 282, quoted in Landecker, p. 333.

[4] Landecker, p. 333.

Landecker's normative integration (conformity of the conduct of the group to cultural standards) was considered on the grounds that it reflected Durkheim's emphasis on the consensual nature of integration; but it was rejected in view of the prior observation that suicide rates have been known to vary independently of other forms of deviant behavior, and because it appeared to be limited in its ability to explain age and sex differentials within a society. In addition, empirical observations arising from the extensive research of Robert C. Angell[5] seem to cast doubt on normative or consensual integration as the key to differences in suicide rates. In preparing an index of integration for selected American cities, Angell used empirical variables that, according to Landecker, are measures of normative integration. Through component measures based on the incidence of selected types of crimes and contributions to community welfare drives, Angell arrived at a composite index of both the degrees of conformity and consensus on values. Although Angell's measure was in many respects crude, one would expect his index of integration to bear some relationship to suicide rates; however, such is not the case. Porterfield notes that "suicide rates are in no way correlated with [Angell's] indices of social integration;"[6] and though it would be foolhardy to cite this as conclusive proof that suicide is not linked to the normative or consensual dimension of integration, it is one reason why we have concentrated on a different conception of integration, which we call "status integration."

INTEGRATION AND SOCIAL RELATIONSHIPS

Throughout Durkheim's comments on the nature of integration there is a constant suggestion that it has to do, in the final analysis, with the strength of the ties of individuals to society. In formal terms, then, it may be said that the stronger such ties are, the lower will be the suicide rate for a society. However, this proposition is only of heuristic value—one does not see individuals tied to a society in any physical sense. To create a testable proposition, it is necessary to establish the equivalent of a physical tie in social life. Such an equivalent is found in social relationships, and the strength of physical ties finds its counterpart in the degree to which these relationships are stable and

---

[5] See Robert C. Angell, "The Social Integration of American Cities of More Than 100,000 Population," *American Sociological Review*, XII (June, 1947), 335-342; "The Moral Integration of American Cities," *American Journal of Sociology*, VII, Part II (July, 1951), 1-140.
[6] Austin L. Porterfield, "Indices of Suicide and Homicide by States and Cities," *American Sociological Review*, XIV (August, 1949), 489.

durable. Thus, the first postulate of the theory of status integration reads: *The suicide rate of a population varies inversely with the stability and durability of social relationships within that population.*

THE DETERMINANT OF THE STABILITY AND DURABILITY OF SOCIAL RELATIONSHIPS

The first postulate is potentially testable in a direct approach. Since social relationships come into being only through social interaction, it is conceivable that the behavioral patterns of each individual in a population could be analyzed in terms of the frequency of interaction with others, the length of time spent in interaction with others, the regularity of the interaction with others, and the length of the individual's life spent in his present pattern of interaction.[7]

Two problems, however, make a direct test of the first postulate impossible at the present time: the present state of sociological knowledge, concepts, and theory regarding social relationships is not adequate for an attempt to make a direct measure of such dimensions as stability and durability; and the amount and type of data needed for measurements of this sort are beyond the scope of existing sources. In the face of these problems, a choice was made not to attempt a direct measure of the stability and durability of social relationships. If the first postulate is accepted, it follows that a statement of the conditions under which the stability and durability of social relationships will be at a maximum is in turn a statement of the conditions under which the suicide rate will be at a minimum.

In Weber's analysis of social relationships, it is suggested that the fundamental condition for the maintenance of a social relationship is the requirements of conformity to the demands and expectations of others.[8] Though Weber's insight deserves recognition, his orientation in the direction of voluntaristic nominalism is not conducive to generalizations about the conditions under which the stability and durability of social relationships will be at a maximum. For the observation to be fruitful, it must be coupled with Durkheim's social realism, which stresses the source of the demands and expectations individuals place on each other and the authority that underlies the requirement for conformity.

---

[7] All of these attributes of interaction are taken to be the variables in terms of which the stability and durability of social relationships would be defined in operational terms.

[8] Max Weber, *The Theory of Social and Economic Organization,* trans. A. M. Henderson and Talcott Parsons (New York, 1947), pp. 118, 126.

Although social relationships are observed and experienced in the form of interaction, on a higher level of abstraction they typically are governed by an authority independent of the particular individuals involved in them. The demands and expectations to which persons must conform if they are to maintain social relationships exist for the most part independently of the will of individuals; unless demands and expectations are sanctioned by an impersonal authority external to the interacting parties, the necessity for conformity is fortuitous. The social sanctions governing social relationships come into being through social identification of the interacting parties in terms of the status occupied by each. The predominant type of social relationship found in a population is thus one in which the status of an individual, his social identification, determines the demands and expectations to which he must conform in order to maintain interaction and his rights (the demands and expectations his society permits him to make of others).

With the above comments serving to emphasize the social character of human relationships, Weber's observation is converted into the second postulate of the theory : *The stability and durability of social relationships within a population vary directly with the extent to which individuals in that population conform to the patterned and socially sanctioned demands and expectations placed upon them by others.*[9]

CONFORMITY TO DEMANDS AND EXPECTATIONS AND ROLE CONFLICT

Although there is little or no relevant evidence, it seems likely that there is considerable difference among populations in the extent to which persons conform to patterned and socially sanctioned demands and expectations. Assuming this to be true, an attempt will be made to postulate the conditions that determine the extent of such conformity in a population.

In sociological terms, the rights of persons occupying a certain status and the demands and expectations that can be placed upon them by others constitute the roles of the status. In other words, along with the social identification of a person's status in a society there is associated a certain configuration of rights, duties, and obligations. These con-

---

[9] This postulate contains a fundamental departure from Durkheim. Whereas Durkheim appeared to stress the consensual nature of the ties of the individual to social life, the present theory holds that the ties of the individual to social life are to be found in actual behavior that creates and/or maintains social relationships. In short, consensus and behavior are not identical, and it is the latter which in final analysis determines the existence and maintenance of social relationships.

stitute the roles to which an individual with a particular status must conform if he is to maintain stable and durable social relationships.

Conformity to the roles of a particular status would not be difficult if it were not for the fact that each person in a population occupies several statuses simultaneously. Thus, a person is never simply a carpenter and nothing more—he is also a single, married, widowed, or divorced carpenter. In abstract terms, the consequences of this is that a person's social relationships do not stem from his occupancy of only one status. It is the fact that individuals occupy several statuses simultaneously, each of which has numerous roles that bring him into contact with other persons, which binds him to social life.

Social roles are the institutionally proper ways for an individual to participate in his society and thus satisfy his needs and wants. But roles are also *demands* upon the individual, norms which prescribe certain acts and forbid others. These demands come from the various groups in which the individual holds membership: his family, peer group, social class, occupational group, and so on.[10]

A man may have numerous social relationships as a consequence of his occupation, but conformity to the roles of his occupational status alone will not maintain his social relationships with his wife and children; the latter can only be maintained by conforming to the roles of husband and father. Conformity to the roles of one status alone is not ordinarily difficult. It is only when conformity to the roles of one status tends to interfere with conformity to the roles of one or more of the other statuses that the individual finds it difficult to maintain his social relationships.

The extent of variability in the stability and durability in social relationships as anticipated by the postulates may best be explained through a consideration of individuals attempting to conform to conflicting roles. For large and consistent differences in this respect to be present among populations, there must be something in the nature of social life other than purely individual choice. We thus arrive at the third postulate of the theory: *The extent to which individuals in a population conform to patterned and socially sanctioned demands and expectations placed upon them by others varies inversely with the extent to which individuals in that population are confronted with role conflicts.*

Ideally, a theory should tie in whenever and wherever possible with existing theory and research findings. Considering that the concept of role is central to sociology, one would expect to find that it has received

---

[10] Jackson Toby, "Some Variables in Role Conflict Analysis," *Social Forces,* XIX, (March, 1952), 323.

a great deal of attention. Although this is to some extent true, it has unfortunately played a surprisingly small part in the generation of testable, empirical propositions. As Neiman and Hughes remark, "There are few, if any, predictive studies of human behavior involving the concept role. If predictive ability is one measure of a scientific construct, this is a telling criticism of the construct."[11] Equally unfortunate is the failure of sociologists taking a macroscopic approach to social life and society to bring the concept into play either directly or, as it is used here, inferentially.

Actually, the concept of role has received considerable attention from sociologists. As Neiman and Hughes' survey of the literature shows, the concept has been subjected to analysis by many sociologists, not to mention anthropologists and social psychologists, but this attention notwithstanding, "The concept role is at present still rather vague, nebulous and nondefinitive."[12]

The major difference in opinion about empirical referents for "role" lies in whether the term refers to actual behavior or, as we believe, to norms that prescribe or proscribe behavior, and which take the form of patterned and socially sanctioned rights, duties, and obligations. The fact that norms are not palpable makes it difficult to deal with roles directly, but does not prevent dealing with them on an inferential level.

A rather surprising amount of theory and research has been devoted to role conflict, a dimension of role central to the present study, and there seems to be general agreement as to what is involved. Laulicht, in his definition, amplifies Seeman's (partially quoted):

A role conflict situation is one in which a person occupying a given social position is exposed to "incompatible behavioral expectations. Though an apparent incompatibility may be resolved, avoided, or minimized in various ways, the conflicting demands cannot be completely and realistically fulfilled."[13]

Getzel and Guba also agree: "Role conflicts ensue whenever an actor is required to fill two or more roles whose expectations are in some particular inconsistent."[14]

---

[11] Lionel J. Neiman and James W. Hughes, "The Problem of the Concept of Role—A Re-Survey of the Literature," *Social Forces,* XXX (December, 1951), 149.

[12] Neiman and Hughes, p. 149.

[13] Jerome Laulicht, "Role Conflict, the Pattern Variable Theory, and Scalogram Analysis," *Social Forces,* XXXIII (March, 1955), 250. The portion within quotation marks is from Melvin Seeman, "Role Conflict and Ambivalence in Leadership," *American Sociological Review,* XVIII (August, 1953), 373.

[14] J. W. Getzel and E. G. Guba, "Role, Role Conflict, and Effectiveness: An Empirical Study," *American Sociological Review,* XIX (April, 1954), 166.

Despite a consensus as to the nature of role conflict, the theory and research that have been devoted to it are not suggestive regarding a crucial question: under what conditions will a large proportion of a population be confronted with a conflict in roles? The failure of existing theory and research to provide an answer to this question lies in a psychological orientation to the phenomenon and the manner in which it has been analyzed. For the most part, studies have dealt with real or alleged conflicts among particular roles: military chaplains,[15] women in the United States,[16] leaders, [17] and military instructors.[18] Related observations, though not dealing directly and explicitly with role conflict, may be found in Cottrell's study of the adjustment of the individual to his age and sex role[19] and Parsons observations on the roles associated with age and sex in the United States.[20] The methods employed to identify role conflict, the techniques used to analyze the phenomenon once isolated, and the conclusions reached in these studies do not lend themselves to a theory concerning the conditions which determine or reflect the amount of role conflict that will prevail in a population. It is not even correct to say that studies have produced a testable theory about role conflict as a general phenomenon, on a population level or otherwise. The same may be said for the more experimental studies, in which individuals are called upon to resolve alleged role conflicts in hypothetical situations.[21]

By and large, it would appear that most studies have concentrated less on the prevalence of role conflict within populations than on particular role conflicts, the perception of norms by the individual, conceptual analysis of the different types of role conflict, and the manner or means by which role conflicts can be resolved.[22] A notable exception

---

[15] Waldo W. Burchard, "Role Conflicts of Military Chaplains," *American Sociological Review,* XIX (October, 1954), 528-535.

[16] Mirra Komarovsky, "Cultural Contradictions and Sex Roles," *American Journal of Sociology,* LII (November, 1946), 184-189; "Functional Analysis of Sex Roles," *American Sociological Review,* XV (August, 1950), 508-516.

[17] Seeman, pp. 373-380.

[18] See note 14 above.

[19] See Leonard S. Cottrell, Jr., "The Adjustment of the Individual to His Age and Sex Role," *American Sociological Review,* VII (October, 1942), 617-620.

[20] See Talcott Parsons, "Age and Sex in the Social Structure of the United States," *American Sociological Review,* VII (October, 1942), 604-616.

[21] As examples, see Samuel A. Stouffer, "An Analysis of Conflicting Social Norms," *American Sociological Review,* XIV (December, 1949), 707-717; Samuel A. Stouffer and Jackson Toby, "Role Conflicts and Personality," *American Journal of Sociology,* LVI (March, 1951), 395-405; and Laulicht (note 13 above).

[22] With reference to the manner or means by which role conflicts can be resolved, the most typical manner or means suggested in observations on the question would appear to involve the termination of social relationships. See Stouffer, Toby, and Getzel and Guba.

is Warren's attempt to link role conflict to the concept of social disorganization.[23] However, since he links the two only on a conceptual level without specifying empirical referents for social disorganization, his study does not lend itself to a statement about conditions indicative of a high level of role conflict.

Investigations of role conflict among particular groups of people have, however, overlooked a significant point. Most investigations have concentrated, not on conflicts between the several roles of one status (intra-status roles), but rather on those conflicts arising between a role of one status and another role or roles of one or more other statuses. In Getzel and Guba's study, where the concept of status is ignored, the real or alleged role conflicts encountered by military instructors seem to arise from the fact that they are at once officers and teachers. Similarly, it would appear from Komarovsky's description that the real or alleged role conflicts of college women arise from the fact that the women must conform simultaneously to the roles of student and unmarried female,[24] and the role conflicts of military chaplains as described by Burchard may be attributed to the chaplains' attempts to conform to the various roles of military officer and spiritual leader. An awareness of inter-status role conflicts is implicit in the above investigations; our intent is only to make it explicit.

STATUS INCOMPATIBILITY AND ROLE CONFLICT

We have suggested that the conditions which determine the prevalence of role conflict in a population remain unknown. An approach to the problem necessitates a shift in current emphasis on the psychological dimension of role to its societal correlates. From the sociological point of view, the concept of role is inseparably bound up with the concept of status: "There is an increasing trend toward associating the concept role with that of status. Here perhaps is the most definitive use of the concept, and the one about which there is most consensus."[25]

A role was previously referred to as a socially sanctioned right, obligation, or duty that determines what demands and expectations will be placed upon a person and what demands and expectations that person can make of others. The question as to whom such rights, duties, and obligations apply is largely a question of status. The more commonly accepted definitions of status, while not necessarily contradictory or

---

[23] Roland L. Warren, "Social Disorganization and the Interrelationship of Cultural Roles," *American Sociological Review*, XIV (February, 1949), 83-87.

[24] Komarovsky, "Cultural Contradictions and Sex Roles."

[25] Neiman and Hughes, p. 149.

inconsistent, never go beyond linking the term with the concept of position. Linton says, "A status, in the abstract, is a position in a particular pattern,"[26] and Hiller defines it as "a place or position in the scheme of social relations."[27]

These definitions capture the general or commonly accepted meaning of "status" but, unfortunately for precise communication, position is a far broader concept than status.[28] For research purposes, we have found it more useful to conceive of a status as a social identification. Every person in a society is socially identified by inclusion in recognized categories to which particular descriptive terms are applied. The status of an individual is thus not revealed by his position in a pattern of social relations (which is first and foremost a highly abstract idea in the mind of a sociologist), but by statements of persons who have knowledge of the individual from interaction with him; these statements to the effect that the person is a man, a barber, a married man, a Negro, a father, are designations of his statuses. All statements, however, which identify him with a recognized category are not status designations, because status implies socially sanctioned rights, duties, and obligations. Thus, a status is a recognized category of persons to which particular socially sanctioned rights, duties, and obligations apply; and these rights, duties, and obligations are the roles of the status.[29]

One crucial assumption made in the present theory is that in any society, given a collection of statuses and their corresponding roles, there is always the potential of conflict among the roles. The roles of any status are such that success in conforming to these roles is contingent upon the nature of the roles of the other statuses that a person occupies. If conforming to the roles of one status interferes with conforming to the roles of another status, an individual is confronted with an incompatibility in statuses. It is of particular importance to note that while this changes the referent of the present analysis from role to status, two statuses are incompatible only in the sense that conformity to one or more roles of one status interferes with conformity

---

[26] Linton, *The Study of Man,* p. 113.

[27] E. T. Hiller, *Social Relations and Social Structure* (New York, 1947), p. 235.

[28] See Emile Benoit-Smullyan, "Status, Status Types, and Status Interrelations," *American Sociological Review,* IX (April, 1944), 151.

[29] The definition of concepts is always at least partially relative to the problem at hand, and the present problem does not call for either a psychological or a hierarchial conception of status. Role and role conflict are dealt with inferentially so that our definition of these terms need not go beyond a general statement of what is involved. For a more elaborate conceptual analysis and classification that treats these concepts somewhat differently see Neal Gross, Ward S. Mason, and Alexander W. McEachern, *Explorations in Role Analysis* (New York, 1958).

to one or more roles of the other status. Consequently, two statuses with conflicting roles are incompatible from the behavioral point of view only when they are occupied simultaneously. For example, to pose a hypothetical situation, the fact that conformity to role A of status X tends to interfere with conformity to role B of status Y poses no problem as long as the two statuses are not occupied simultaneously by one and the same individual.

This reasoning results in the fourth postulate of the present theory: *The extent to which individuals in a population are confronted with role conflicts varies directly with the extent to which individuals occupy incompatible statuses in that population.*

STATUS INTEGRATION AND STATUS INCOMPATIBILITY

Since two statuses with conflicting roles are incompatible only insofar as individuals attempt to occupy them simultaneously, the incompatibility of statuses cannot be analyzed directly. What is needed is an observable and mensurable phenomenon that reflects the extent to which the occupancy of incompatible statuses prevails in a population. As with role conflict, existing theory and research on status have concentrated on other problems. Although Adams' study of status congruency,[30] Slotkin's on the status of the marginal man,[31] Gold's on the status of the janitor,[32] Schuetz's on the status of the stranger,[33] and Devereaux and Weiner's on the status of nurses[34] all in one way or another touch on the idea of incompatibility,[35] none of them is primarily concerned with that problem.

The inability to closely link the idea of status incompatibility to other studies stems from the fact that sociologists have come to have a somewhat narrow conception of status. It would appear, particularly in American sociology, that there is implicit in the concept an hierarchial connotation which dominates current research and theory. In its con-

---

[30] Stuart Adams, "Status Congruency as a Variable in Small Group Performance," *Social Forces*, XXXII (October, 1953), 16-22.

[31] J. S. Slotkin, "Status of the Marginal Man," *Sociology and Social Research*, XXVIII (September-October, 1943), 47-54.

[32] Ray Gold, "Janitors Versus Tenants: A Status-Income Dilemma," *American Journal of Sociology*, LVII (March, 1952), 486-493.

[33] Alfred Scheutz, "The Stranger: An Essay in Social Psychology," *American Journal of Sociology*, XLIX (May, 1944), 499-507.

[34] George Devereaux and Florence R. Weiner, "The Occupational Status of Nurses," *American Sociological Review*, XV (October, 1950), 628-634.

[35] The same may be said for most of the studies and observations on role conflict which have been previously cited. In these studies however, the emphasis is upon roles with little treatment of the concept of status.

cern with stratification and social class, contemporary sociological theory sometimes forgets that status has a meaning independent of hierarchy.[36]

A crucial assumption made in the present theory is that the patterns formed by the occupancy of statuses are indicative of the extent to which the occupancy of incompatible statuses prevails in a population. More specifically, it is assumed that the behavior of persons moving in and out of statuses is closely related to the compatability of various combinations of statuses. In this connection, it should be obvious that the assumption is only valid when one or both of two statuses is achieved. That is, the scarcity of Chinese males in the continental United States is not assumed to result from an incompatibility between the status male and the status Chinese, but the relatively small proportion of Chinese-Americans who become government officials is assumed to be a case of status incompability.

If two statuses have conflicting roles, making them incompatible statuses when occupied simultaneously, it is assumed that they will be less frequently occupied simultaneously than will two statuses with roles that do not conflict. There are three reasons for this. In some cases, the incompatibility is recognized to the point where occupancy is socially discouraged; an example of this is the treatment afforded women who aspire to be airline pilots. In other cases, the person occupying two statuses that are incompatible will give up one or both because of dissatisfaction arising out of attempts to conform to conflicting roles (the large number of divorced bartenders suggests how the demands of an occupational status may create dissatisfaction with a particular marital status). In still other cases, inability to conform to the roles of one or both of the statuses leads to the person's being deprived of one or both statuses; an example is a person who, too old to meet the demands of his occupation, is deprived of that status.

Assuming that the actual occupancy of statuses in a society reflects status compatibility, it follows that the degree of compatibility between two statuses is directly proportional to the extent to which they are occupied simultaneously. As a simple example, consider a hypothetical population in which 75 per cent of the persons with occupation X are married, while only 35 per cent of the persons with occupation Y are married; these two figures constitute a measure of the degree to

---

[36] As examples of the scant attention given to the nonhierarchical dimension of status, see Samuel C. Ratcliffe, "Social Structure and Status," *Sociology and Social Research*, XIV (November-December, 1929), 156-162; Seymour M. Lipset and Reinhard Bendix, "Social Status and Social Structure: I, *British Journal of Sociology*, II (June, 1951), 150- 168.

which being married and having certain specified occupations are compatible.[37] For occupation Y, marriage is far less compatible than it is for occupation X. We must stress, before proceeding further, that although the extent to which two statuses are occupied simultaneously is taken to be a measure of the degree to which the two are compatible, the mere frequency of occupancy is not what makes them compatible or incompatible. Rather, the degree of compatibility is a function of the extent to which their roles conflict, and the extent to which they are occupied simultaneously follows from this.

It must be emphasized that incompatible statuses are those configurations[38] that are infrequently occupied. In terms of the examples given above, "occupation X-married" is a status configuration that is frequently occupied, while the status configuration "occupation Y-married" is one which is infrequently occupied.[39] The relative frequency with which a status configuration is occupied will henceforth be referred to as the *degree of integration* among the statuses in the configuration or simply as the degree of status integration. Thus, to return to the examples again, if 100 per cent of the persons with occupation X were married persons, there would be maximum integration between this occupational status and marital status. Since every individual occupies a status configuration, the extent to which persons occupy compatible statuses in a population is a function of the degree to which the occupied status configurations conform to a pattern. The pattern of maximum status integration would be found in a population where knowledge of one status of an individual would enable an investigator to predict with certainty all undisclosed statuses. We thus reach the fifth and final postulate of the present theory: *The extent to which individuals occupy incompatible statuses in a population varies inversely with the degree of status integration in that population.*

---

[37] It should be emphasized that the example given here is only for the purpose of illustration. As the reader will come to see in the following chapter, the example is over simplified because it tends to ignore all other statuses. In actual practice, the compatibility or incompatibility of statuses is a matter of the compatibility between one status and a configuration of statuses.

[38] A status configuration is two or more statuses that theoretically could be occupied simultaneously. An example of a status configuration in the United States would be "male-carpenter." A more complex status configuration would be "male-carpenter-married-Negro-parent."

[39] The frequency with which a status configuration is occupied is, of course, always relative. Thus, in the example given above, the status configuration "occupation X-married" is more frequently occupied than is the status configuration "occupation Y-widowed."

A REVIEW OF THE POSTULATES

Although the problem of measuring the degree of status integration in a population is a complex one, as the following chapter will show, we have in the concept something that is observable and mensurable. The set of postulates that links status integration to variability in suicide rates is reviewed below.

Postulate No. 1: The suicide rate of a population varies inversely with the stability and durability of social relationships within that population.

Postulate No. 2: The stability and durability of social relationships within a population vary directly with the extent to which individuals in that population conform to the patterned and socially sanctioned demands and expectations placed upon them by others.

Postulate No. 3: The extent to which individuals in a population conform to patterned and socially sanctioned demands and expectations placed upon them by others varies inversely with the extent to which individuals in that population are confronted with role conflicts.

Postulate No. 4: The extent to which individuals in a population are confronted with role conflicts varies directly with the extent to which individuals occupy incompatible statuses in that population.

Postulate No. 5: The extent to which individuals occupy incompatible statuses in a population varies inversely with the degree of status integration in that population.

From the above postulates there follows the major theorem: *The suicide rate of a population varies inversely with the degree of status integration in that population.* This theorem is central to the present study. In the following chapter, examples will be given of the type of hypotheses to be tested in line with the theorem, and the operations necessary for the measurement of status integration will be specified.

QUESTIONS REGARDING THE THEORY

One of the major assumptions made in the present theory is that the movement of persons in and out of statuses is indicative of the degree of role conflict in the different status configurations. Perhaps the most serious question that can be raised regarding this assumption relates to the prestige value of statuses. It is possible to conceive of two statuses with conflicting roles having such a high prestige value that individuals persist in attempting to occupy them despite their conflicting roles. The fact that these two statuses are frequently occupied simultaneously would tend to give the impression that they are compatible. If such a factor is present, it can only be assumed that a strain toward consistency is also operating in such a way as to bring about an eventual modification of the roles so as to reduce their conflict.

As a criticism of the theory, it can be suggested that the roles connected with the status of businessman conflict with the roles of the status husband in the United States, but despite this a large proportion of businessmen are married. This frequent occupancy of two allegedly incompatible statuses appears to directly contradict the assumptions of the theory. However, this high degree of integration does not indicate complete compatibility; rather, it means that, in spite of the observations of mutually interfering roles for the statuses of businessman and husband, these two statuses are more compatible than are the configurations businessman-single, businessman-widower, or businessman-divorced. That is, the measure of status integration is a *relative* measure which expresses "more" or "less" compatibility rather than all or none. Thus, the fact that businessmen are typically married does not mean a complete absence of incompatibility between these two statuses.

Another serious question regarding the theory is the obvious inability of status integration to reflect role conflicts among ascribed statuses. Since the movement of individuals in and out of statuses constitutes an underlying assumption, the theory is not applicable to configurations of ascribed statuses.[40] This would not create a problem if ascribed statuses did not have roles associated with them. Such is not the case and the possibility of a configuration of ascribed statuses being incompatible is a reality. However, it is possible that a strain toward consistency is particularly operative for ascribed statuses and that differences among populations with regard to role conflicts among ascribed statuses is negligible.

Throughout the presentation of the theory one salient fact regarding the concept of role was ignored. Conformity to roles involves a range of behavior. By this fact it can be argued that conflicting roles can be resolved (without a disturbance of the stability and durability of social relationships) through deviation from the type of behavior

---

[40] Similarly, the theory could not be expected to hold in a population where the possibility of shifting statuses is at a minimum. There is no evidence at the moment, but this basic assumption of inter-status mobility would appear to be drastically violated in the case of a population of bedridden, widowed, females all of age 85 or older. Members of this population have almost no opportunity to change their labor force, marital, occupational, educational, or parental statuses.

that represents maximum conformity to a role. Though the idea is accepted that conformity always involves a range of behavior, this does not mean that a person may behave in whatever way he pleases and still retain his statuses. It does not follow that conformity to one role interferes no more or no less with conformity to all other roles simply because a range of behavior is involved. Furthermore, since every role of a status involves a range of permitted behavior, the factor is a constant from one status to the next. If it is claimed, on the other hand, that some statuses have roles with a wider range of permitted behavior than others, the fact of the wider range is a part of the roles. This observation applies equally well to the compartmentalization of roles.

An objection to the present theory could be based on the fact that it does not explain why some roles conflict and others do not. In terms of content this is obviously always relative to the specific roles being considered. It is not necessary to single out the roles of each and every status in a population, even if this were possible, and subject them to a type of analysis that would reveal the sources of conflict. It is only necessary as far as the present theory is concerned to assume that when two statuses are infrequently occupied there is something about the two sets of corresponding roles that makes conformity to both difficult. Research in the future may reveal the nature of the conflict between particular roles; for the time being, however, the validity of the theory is not contingent upon such a demonstration.

An appropriate question in a discussion of incompatible statuses is why they come to be occupied at all. Since the present theory does not seek to establish ultimate causes, the observations that follow are at best only suggestive. In the first place, it should be made clear that the theory does not separate and label status configurations as being either compatible or incompatible; compatibility is always a matter of degree. The theory does not hold that it is a physical impossibility to simultaneously occupy statuses with highly conflicting roles; it is possible to maintain occupancy, but the consequences will entail a considerable loss as far as the stability and durability of social relationships are concerned. Thus, the answer to the question as to why some statuses are infrequently occupied must be sought elsewhere.

One very important factor lies in the problematical nature of the effectiveness of social control. Although the degree of incompatibility between two statuses may be socially recognized and their simultaneous occupancy discouraged, this does not prevent all individuals, particularly those confronted with fortuitous circumstances, from making the attempt, any more than the proscription of incest by law and mores makes incest a physical impossibility. Nor is it realistic to say that the social control system in all societies operates to discourage the occupancy of incompatible statuses to an equal degree, be the incompatibility socially recognized, ignored, or undetected. On the contrary, in a society where the value system places an emphasis on romantic marriage, material success, vertical mobility, and individual freedom, the conditions are conducive for the attempt to occupy statuses without consideration of probable consequences.

The most serious reservation regarding the theory is its failure to take into account factors of a more psychological nature. It could be argued that the consequences of a loss of social relationships is a feeling of frustration and isolation from social control, both of which could result in forms of deviant behavior other than suicide. This would mean that the degree of status integration in a population might well fix the magnitude of total deviancy in a population but not the magnitude of the suicide rate. Only research in the future, in which a measure of the degree of status integration in a population is correlated with the incidence of forms of deviancy other than suicide, can hold the answer to this question. For the purposes of this study it will be assumed that the loss of social relationships has a specific as opposed to a general consequence.[41]

METHODOLOGICAL OBSERVATIONS IN DEFENSE OF THE THEORY

The theory is obviously highly abstract, and many of the objections which can be raised against it stem primarily from the inherently vague concepts that play a role in the derivation of the major theorem. Such theories abound, however, in any science; and, providing they are capable of generating testable, empirical propositions, they are undoubtedly justifiable. As suggested by the major theorem, the present theory does lead to a testable proposition, and so has something more than argumentation to offer as evidence of validity.

The set of postulates from which the major theorem was derived may appear to be a somewhat tortuous line of reasoning; this can only be justified on the grounds that it generates a theorem which can be linked to empirical variables. However, the set of postulates does provide a means for gauging the validity of the theory apart from the major theorem. With the future development of new sources of data

---

[41] Two other possible objections to the theory will be taken into account in a later section where it can be shown that the objections are not justified on empirical grounds.

and techniques of analysis, it will be possible to test some of the postulates directly and to derive other testable theorems. If, for example, it were possible to measure the degree of stability and durability of the social relationships within a large number of populations, the first postulate could be tested directly, as well as a theorem linking status integration with stability and durability of social relationships.

Another fruitful approach would be to derive from the postulate a thorem linking status integration and role conflict. To test this theorem, reports by individuals of their experienced difficulties in conforming to roles would be linked to their status configurations. Although such reports are not conclusive proof of the presence of role conflict, the theory would expect persons in infrequently occupied status configurations to experience more difficulty in attempting to conform to their roles. The same would be true for actual failure to conform to roles.

With the fifth postulate, the theory would anticipate that individuals occupying status configurations characterized by a low degree of integration (i.e., infrequently occupied) would express a greater degree of dissatisfaction with one or all of their statuses and a greater willingness to change one or all of their statuses. The theory also anticipates that such a status configuration would be characterized by a higher rate of turnover in occupancy.

There are, in fact, numerous potentialities for future research as far as the set of postulates is concerned, and the writers are cognizant that only through the full development of these potentialities will a thorough evaluation of the theory be achieved. Such a development must of necessity await access to certain types of data, the perfection of techniques, and a sharpening of the concepts "role" and "status."

In conclusion, the set of postulates involves concepts that do not denote readily observable or mensurable phenomena; but it functions to link two phenomena, suicide rates and status integration, that do possess these characteristics, and points to the types of relationships that should hold for other phenomena once they become amenable to empirical analysis.

SUPPORT OF THE THEORY IN SUBSTANTIVE TERMS

Traditionally, most abstract theories in sociology are supported by argumentation or the citation of illustrative examples. It would be possible to cite numerous peculiarities and uniformities in suicide rates that tend to support the present theory. Such illustrations would be a poor second, however, to systematic tests of the major theorem.

Without considering specific illustrative evidence which supports the theory, there is one characteristic of variability in suicide rates that does deserve recognition. One of the most baffling aspects of this variability is that while the suicide rates of persons in different statuses do differ considerably, no status known to date provides absolute immunity to suicide[42] or a stable relative immunity within a society or among societies. Consider, for example, the immunity of the female relative to the male. In Sweden, during the period 1901-1905, there were only 21.8 female per 100 male suicides; in Bengal, for the year 1907, there were 177.1 female per 100 male suicides.[43] In the United States, 1949-1951, the mean annual suicide rate of widowed persons in the age group, 20-24, was 440 per cent higher than that of married persons, but in the age group, 70-74, the suicide rate of the widowed was two per cent less than that of the married.[44] In terms of the present theory, this becomes understandable because the degree of immunity to suicide enjoyed by persons is always a matter of status configurations and not particular statuses. In general terms, then, the present theory is in line with a fundamental characteristic of variability in suicide rates.

As for the matter of argumentation, it is obviously desirable to show wherever and whenever possible how a new theory ties in with existing knowledge. Throughout the formulation of the present theory, it was repeatedly noted that it is linked only to Durkheim's observations. This is particularly unfortunate for the assumption that the actual pattern of status occupancy is indicative of the degree of incompatibility among statuses. As evidence that the assumption is based on something more than the writers' credulity, however, the following points should be considered. First, as either general observations or formal analysis reveal, the occupancy of statuses in any society does not conform to a purely random pattern. Something beyond mere chance expectancy operates to link the occupancy of one status with another particular status. There is as yet no formal theory regarding this nonrandom pattern, much less a formal theory with empirical evidence to support it. Thus, with regard to the assumption, there is no formal evidence to the contrary. Though the assumption is not entirely justified

---

[42] Two possible exceptions are tied in with age—infancy and extreme old age.

[43] Both sets of figures from John Rice Miner, "Suicide and Its Relation to Climatic and Other Factors," *American Journal of Hygiene*, Monographic Series No. 2 (1922), pp. 30, 31.

[44] U.S. Department of Health, Education, and Welfare, *Vital Statistics—Special Reports*, No. 39 (Washington, 1956), p. 426

on the grounds of the absence of evidence to the contrary, this is no small factor in its tentative acceptance.

A second reason for considering the assumption warranted is that it is not completely alien to prior observations. In an analysis of the "dilemmas" and "contradictions" of status, Hughes notes that the occupancy of one particular status in the United States tends to be associated with the occupancy of certain other statuses (the latter being "auxiliary characteristics"). He describes certain commonly-found status configurations and how persons who do not conform to the pattern are faced with adjustment problems, citing as an example the case of a woman engineer who was excluded by her male colleagues from the social life associated with their work. Later, in commenting on the status of physicians in the United States, Hughes says:

. . . it remains probably true that the white, male, Protestant physician of old American stock, although he may easily fail to get any clientele at all, is categorically acceptable to a greater variety of patients than is he who departs, in one or more particulars, from the type.[45]

These observations, and others, led Hughes to conclude that not only is it difficult for persons who deviate from particular status configurations to reconcile their roles, but also their deviation is a problem for persons who enter into a social relationship with them; the reluctance of persons to accept the deviant is reflected in such epithets as "hen doctor," "boy wonder," "bright young man," and "brain trust." What is most important for the present theory is the fact that the status configurations which (according to Hughes) pose adjustment problems are infrequently occupied in the United States, and the reverse is true for those that are described as posing no adjustment problems. Thus, the assumption in the present theory is only an extrapolation of observations such as Hughes recorded.

It would be possible to argue further for the assumption by citing a series of instances where the actual occupancy of certain status configurations conforms to perceptions of status incompatibility on an impressionistic level. Such illustrations, however, would not constitute proof. In final analysis, only a series of studies approaching the theory from several different directions will constitute formal evidence for or against the acceptance of the assumption.

[45] Everett C. Hughes, "Dilemmas and Contradictions of Status," *American Journal of Sociology*, L (March, 1945), 354.

CHAPTER THREE

The Measurement of
Status Integration

IN RECOGNITION of the difficulties encountered in linking highly abstract concepts to empirical referents, the present chapter is devoted exclusively to the measurement of status integration and the technical problems involved. Subsequent chapters will take into consideration specific problems and questions relative to particular hypotheses, but the concern here is with an over-all description of the methods for the treatment of data.

PROBLEMS IN MEASUREMENT

The numerous problems involved in the measurement of status integration are not met with definitive solutions in the present study. Little would be gained by pretending otherwise, and the results of the tests of hypotheses in subsequent chapters may be best interpreted when the problems are made explicit.

The Problem of Inadequate Data. With specific hypotheses, the difficulties encountered in an attempt to measure the degree of status integration are by no means purely methodological in nature. The crucial problem in many instances is a purely practical one, namely, the lack of data of the type and scope required. This lack is not one peculiar to the present study, of course. It is one which plagues attempts to test almost any abstract theory in the behavioral sciences. All too often, as is true here, whatever data are at hand must of necessity be used; and they may be inadequate because their reliability has not been established or because they fail to encompass all of the variables called for by the theory.

To dispel any doubts on the matter, it must be said at the outset that there is no existing source for the type of data needed for an ideal test of the major theorem. Nor does there appear to be any hope of having such data in the immediate future. This fact has many ramifications. If the statistics used to test the major theorem are inadequate in one or more respects, there is a strong possibility that the results will be negative. If negative evidence under such circumstance is accepted for refuting the theory, it is obvious that all tests would have to be based on data with no known imperfections. This would mean that the availability of data would direct theory and not vice versa, a course of action that would lead to the ultimate in scientific sterility. Theory, of necessity, must advance beyond the limits set by available data.

Fortunately, the present theory is such that it is possible to have a fairly precise idea of the inadequacy of existing statistics. Throughout the present chapter, then, an attempt will be made to describe the type of data that would approximate the conditions for an ideal test of the theorem. In doing so, it is hoped that the reader may more readily appreciate the limitations of the tests and understand why nothing more than a moderately high inverse relationship between measures of status integration and suicide rates is expected to hold.

Dangers of Oversimplification. In the preceding chapter, status integration was described in terms of the relative frequency with which status configurations are occupied, and an illustration was given of its measurement with a simple status configuration in a hypothetical society. To make the illustration more concrete and show why such an oversimplified measure is undesirable, consideration will be given to the relationship between age and marital status in a particular country.

In 1950 in the United States, 8.73 per cent of the persons 75 years of age and over (a status[1]) were single, 33.83 per cent were married, 56.51 per cent were widowed, and 0.93 per cent were divorced.[2] Thus, the respective integration measures are .0873, .3383, .5651, and .0093. When the major theorem is applied to these measures of integration, an hypothesis is derived that the suicide rate of widowed persons 75 years of age and over would be lower than that of married persons in

---

[1] The question as to what types of categories do or do not constitute a status will be taken up in a later section of this chapter.

[2] Throughout this report, all data relating to marital status by age in the United States as of 1950 have been drawn from *U.S. Census of Population: 1950.* Vol. II, *Characteristics of the Population*, Part 1, United States Summary, Chapter C, Table 102, 179.

the same age group. Or, in general, the higher the integration measure, the lower the suicide rates for the four marital statuses.

It remains to be seen whether or not the above prediction is correct. There is an inherent danger, however, in testing the major theorem in terms of such an hypothesis or even in using it as an illustration. This is because the measures of integration are based on only two statuses—age and marital status. Suppose for the moment that more data were available. They might show that married persons were much more homogeneous[3] with respect to occupational, parental, racial, and religious statuses than the widowed. This would mean that while the widowed did have a greater integration measure with respect to this particular age status, they were less integrated as far as other statuses were concerned. In such an event, the prediction of a higher suicide rate for the married would in all probability be in error. Ideally, such a prediction should be made only when the integration measure is based on persons 75 and over with all statuses but marital status in common. Because of a lack of data needed to achieve such control, it can be assumed only that a bias in the form of other statuses is not operating to the point where the major theorem receives no support whatsoever from the oversimplified tests.

The tendency to oversimplify the measurement of status integration is a very real one because of the limitations of available data and the sheer labor involved in measurement at more complex levels. This oversimplification could easily lead to a premature rejection of the theory.

MEASUREMENT OF STATUS INTEGRATION ON A SOCIETAL LEVEL

The measurement of status integration requires at the outset reference to a hypothetical society where status integration is at a maximum. Table 1 represents a hypothetical society in which measures of integration between a particular family of statuses[4] and five status configurations are shown.

In the model society shown in Table 1, letters and numbers indi-

---

[3] The terms "homogeneity" and "homogeneous" are used herein as being synonymous with integration. If reference were made, for example, to married persons 75 and over being homogeneous with respect to occupation, this would mean that they all tend to have the same occupation. In more technical terms, there would be a high degree of integration between a particular occupational status and the status configuration designated as "married, 75 and over."

[4] By a family of statuses, we mean a collection of statuses having a common classificatory basis. Thus, the statuses of male and female make up one family of statuses, while the marital statuses of single, married, widowed, and divorced make up another.

cate particular statuses within families of statuses. Thus, for example, R1 would be a particular race, O3 would be a particular occupation, A4 would be a particular age group, S1 would be the status of male, Re2 would be a particular religious status, and P2 would be a particular parental status. The figures in the columns of the table represent the proportion of the persons occupying the status configuration represented by the column who have a specified marital status. As an example, all of the persons occupying the status configuration shown in the first column are widowed. The last row in the table shows the proportion of the population who occupy the status configuration at the head of each column. In the case of the first column, .07 of the population occupy the status configuration shown there. The part that the last row plays in the measurement of status integration will be explained in a later section of this chapter.

Table 1. THE INTEGRATION OF MARITAL STATUSES WITH SELECTED STATUS CONFIGURATIONS IN A HYPOTHETICAL SOCIETY WHERE MARITAL INTEGRATION IS AT A MAXIMUM

| Marital Status | All Occupied Status Configurations | | | | |
	R1-A1-Re1-O1-S1-P1	R2-A2-Re2-O2-S2-P2	R1-A3-Re3-O3-S1-P1	R1-A4-Re1-O4-S1-P3	R2-A5-Re3-O5-S2-P2
Single	.00	.00	.00	1.00	.00
Married	.00	1.00	.00	.00	1.00
Widowed	1.00	.00	.00	.00	.00
Divorced	.00	.00	1.00	.00	.00
ΣX	1.00	1.00	1.00	1.00	1.00
ΣX^2	1.0000	1.0000	1.0000	1.0000	1.0000
Proportion of population	.07	.43	.03	.15	.32

It should be obvious that many more columns are called for in Table 1 than are actually given. For the table to be complete, every status configuration comprised of all statuses but marital status would be shown, providing that each is occupied. This means that every conceivable combination of statuses would not necessarily be included. If Table 1 depicted a real society, it might be found, for example, that the status configuration R2-A3-Re3-O3-S2-P3 is not occupied by anyone; if this were true, there would be no column to represent this status configuration.

Not only is the table incomplete as far as columns go, but it is only one of many tables that would be used in actual practice. Only the integration of marital status is shown in this particular table. For a complete measure of status integration in a society there would be as many tables as there are families of achieved statuses, with each family

37

requiring a different set of occupied status configurations at the head of the columns.[5]

It will be noted in Table 1 that all persons occupying the status configurations shown at the top of the first column have the same marital status. In terms of the theory, no one occupies an incompatible status, the integration measure being at a maximum. The same may be said for the other columns.

For the model shown in Table 1 to be of heuristic value, it must be compared with another hypothetical case that reflects a pattern of status occupancy more like that actually found in existing societies. Table 2 has been designed for this purpose.

For the sake of comparison, the statuses shown in this table are the same as those shown in Table 1; only the figures in the cells are different.

Table 2. THE INTEGRATION OF MARITAL STATUSES WITH SELECTED
STATUS CONFIGURATIONS IN A HYPOTHETICAL SOCIETY
WHERE MARITAL INTEGRATION IS LESS THAN MAXIMUM

Marital Status	All Occupied Status Configurations				
	R1-A1- Re1-O1- S1-P1	R2-A2- Re3-O2- S2-P2	R1-A3- Re3-O3- S1-P1	R1-A4- Re1-O4- S1-P3	R2-A5- Re3-O5- S2-P2
Single	.15	.05	.00	.35	.05
Married	.05	.75	.05	.25	.90
Widowed	.60	.15	.25	.20	.05
Divorced	.20	.05	.70	.20	.00
ΣX	1.00	1.00	1.00	1.00	1.00
ΣX^2	.4250	.5900	.5550	.2650	.8150
Proportion of population	.1435	.3825	.0870	.1970	.1900

The figures shown in the columns of Table 2 represent the proportion of persons in a status configuration with a specified marital status. As an example, the proportion of single persons occupying the status configuration R1-A1-Re1-O1-S1-P1 is .15. In such a table, the proportions are computed by dividing the total in each column into the numbers in each cell within the column.

From a purely impressionistic level, it is obvious that there is far less status integration in Table 2 than in Table 1. Though we may observe that the two hypothetical societies are different in this respect, the disparity cannot be expressed mathematically unless some formula is applied to the figures. If we add the figures in the columns in both

---

[5] Since movement or the possibility of movement in and out of statuses is assumed, ascribed statuses appear only in the status configurations in the column headings and never in the rows of a table.

Table 1 and Table 2 we get 1.00 in each column and a total of 5.00 for the five columns. Thus, this formula does not differentiate the two hypothetical societies. However, if we square and sum the figures in each column (as shown in the next to the last row in Table 1 and Table 2), the products obtained do differentiate the two cases. In a society where status integration is at a maximum, the sum of the squares of the proportions in each column will always be equal to 1.00, and the total status integration measure for the society as a whole will always be equal to 1.00 multiplied by the number of columns, with each column representing a different status configuration. In the case of Table 1 the total status integration measure is 5.00 (the sum of the ΣX^2 at the bottom of each column), whereas for the hypothetical society shown in Table 2 the corresponding measure is only 2.65.

For any table, there are three types of status integration measures, each of which provides a test of the major theorem in the form of an hypothesis. For the purpose of illustration, the society shown in Table 2 will be treated as though it were a real society with the suicide rate known for any status configuration within the table and the population as a whole. One set of hypotheses would be concerned with the most simple measure of status integration, the proportions shown within each column. In the first column of Table 2, the hypothesis derived from the major theorem would constitute a prediction that the widowed persons have the lowest suicide rate and the married persons have the highest. Stated abstractly, it would call for an inverse relationship to hold between suicide rates and measures of status integration by cells within each column. These simple within-column figures will be called Type 1 measures of status integration, and they are used to test what is designated as a Type 1 hypothesis.

A second measure expresses the degree of integration between a status configuration and a family of statuses. In Tables 1 and 2 this measure is the sum of the squares of the proportions in each column.[6] Maximum integration in this case is always 1.00. If the hypothetical society shown in Table 2 were real, the hypothesis derived from the major theorem would call for an inverse relationship to hold between the ΣX^2 value at the bottom of each column and the suicide rate for all persons occupying the status configuration represented in the column. In more specific terms, the hypothesis would call for the lowest suicide rate to be found among persons occupying the status con-

---

[6] If only the ΣX^2 for a column is needed, it may be found without the labor of computing proportions, e.g., $\Sigma n_i^2 / (\Sigma n)^2$, where n_i = the frequency of a cell. This procedure, while faster, does not provide the X's (cell proportions), and this makes it impossible to compare cells not within the same column.

figuration in the last column ($\Sigma X^2 = .8150$) and the highest rate to be found among persons occupying the status configuration in the next to the last column ($\Sigma X^2 = .2650$). The between-column test described in this paragraph involves a Type 2 measure of status integration and a Type 2 hypothesis.

A question might be asked regarding the interpretation of a situation in which the proportions shown in a column are all approximately equal. The nearest approach to this in Table 2 is in column 4 where the largest proportion is .35 and the smallest is .20. To make a more extreme example, consider the interpretation if the proportions shown in this column read as follows: single .24, married .26, widowed .25, and divorced .25. Here there is no concentration of cases in one status (i.e., in no case does any status have a markedly lower proportion than the other statuses). The interpretation in such a case is that none of the marital statuses is particularly compatible with the configuration shown at the top of the column. Since the ΣX^2 for the column is now .2502, the lowest Type 2 measure shown, the theory predicts a high suicide rate for this configuration as a whole with more or less equal rates within the column.

A final hypothesis derived from the major theorem calls for the comparison of the total status integration measure of the society shown in Table 2 with a corresponding measure for other cases. The total status integration value for Table 2, as noted previously, is 2.65. If a corresponding value for another society should be less than 2.65, this society would be expected to have a higher suicide rate. This is a Type 3 hypothesis involving a Type 3 or all-columns measure of status integration.

A Weighted Total Status Integration Measure. One additional variable that is involved in the measurement of total status integration requires description. Since the total measure is nothing more than the sum of values (ΣX^2) for each column within a table, it does not take into account the possibility that a value for a given column may influence only a small proportion of the total population. To return to Table 2 for an example, the last column has a status integration measure of .8150, but only 19 per cent of the total population are influenced by this high value. For the total measure to take into account the proportion of the population influenced by the component measures the value for each column (ΣX^2) is multiplied by the proportion of the population who occupy the status configuration represented by the column. For Table 1 and Table 2 the application of this method for weighting the total status integration measure means that each ΣX^2

value shown at the bottom of the column is multiplied by the value immediately below it and the products summed. This operation yields a weighted total status integration measure of .5420 for the hypothetical society in Table 2. For Table 1, where status integration is at a maximum, the operation yields a weighted total measure of 1.00, which is the maximum value.

Although the weighted total status integration measure appears to be an improvement over the unweighted measure, the decision was made to employ both in the inter-societal tests of the major theorem that are reported in the next chapter.

PROBLEMS IN MEASURING STATUS INTEGRATION

The initial problem encountered in the measurement was, of course, the selection of a mathematical formula to express the extent to which a society or a status configuration deviates from maximum integration. It is obvious that the formula selected is only one of several that could be used. For example, the cube rather than the square of the proportions in each column could be used. Reasons for employing the above formula will be discussed later; in the meantime, it seems simpler than others and also yields meaningful measures.

Whatever technique is used in the measurement of status integration must be in some way tied in with the model of a society in which status integration is at a maximum. Only when its values express deviation from a fixed maximum or minimum is a particular measure meaningful. Consider, for example, the total status integration measure of 2.65 for the hypothetical society shown in Table 2. This value is meaningful only when it is known that the maximum value which could be obtained is 5.00.

The use of a model society and a formula for measuring deviation from it is desirable not only in that it yields meaningful results but also because it provides a means to equate measures of status integration for tables which involve an unequal number of columns or rows. This control is achieved by the fact that any measure of status integration obtained by the method described above has both an absolute upper and lower limit.

If Nr stands for the number of rows in a table, then the lower limit of a measure of status integration in a column is equal to 1.00/Nr. The lower limit of a total measure is in turn the lower limit of the columns multiplied by the number of columns. For Table 2, the lower limit of the status integration measure (ΣX^2) for each column is .25, this value being obtained by the formula 100/Nr or 100/4. The lower limit of the total status integration measure is 1.25, this value being obtained by the formula Nc(1.00/Nr), in which Nc stands for the number of columns. If Table 2 were based on five marital statuses, as a cross-cultural test might require, the lower limit for the values in each column would be .20 and the lower limit for the total measure would be 1.00. Though the tests of the major theorem in the present study do not involve a comparison of societies with an unequal number of statuses, research in the future may be confronted with the problem; and this would require total status integration measures which are relative to the upper and lower limits of each table employed.

A Question Regarding a Particular Status. One of the major problems in the measurement of status integration stems from the possibility that any one particular method may not be applicable to all types of statuses. To consider this possibility in greater detail, consideration will be given to occupations, a family of statuses with respect to which we have some doubts regarding the applicability of the above method for measuring status integration. Table 3 represents a hypothetical society in which measures of integration between seven occupational statuses and five status configurations are given.

Table 3. OCCUPATIONAL INTEGRATION IN A HYPOTHETICAL SOCIETY

| Occupation | All Occupied Status Configurations | | | | |
	R1-A1- Re1-M1- S1-P1	R2-A2- Re2-M2- S2-P3	R1-A3- Re3-M3- S1-P1	R1-A4- Re1-M4- S1-P3	R2-A5- Re3-M1- S2-P2
O1	.25	.10	.07	.23	.05
O2	.10	.15	.38	.05	.05
O3	.03	.02	.06	.01	.04
O4	.07	.50	.09	.06	.10
O5	.04	.08	.15	.35	.06
O6	.05	.10	.10	.25	.60
O7	.46	.05	.15	.05	.10
ΣX	1.00	1.00	1.00	1.00	1.00
ΣX^2	.2940	.3018	.2160	.2466	.3902

It will be noted in Table 3 that the occupational status O3 consistently has the lowest measure of integration within the five columns. Thus, if the major theorem were to be applied here, the hypotheses would call for the persons in O3 to have the highest suicide rate in each of the five columns. However, when we consider the nature of occupational specialization, it is apparent that there may be something operating here other than status incompatibility. For any occupation, there is probably a limit to the number of people who can subsist through its pursuit. If the society shown in Table 3 actually existed and occupation O3 were that of physician, the extent to which it is infrequently occupied within each of the five columns might very possibly be due to factors independent of status incompatibility. The fact that relatively few persons in a society can be physicians tends to make it an infrequently occupied status.

While limitations imposed on the present study by the availability of data have precluded experiments with occupational integration, it is all the more necessary that the problem be recognized in the course of future research. The first task of future research in this regard will, of course, be the application of the present method for measuring status integration. If measures of occupational integration do not bear an inverse relationship to the suicide rates by cells within columns, the reservations regarding this particular family of statuses will be confirmed. In such an event, two alternative methods for measurement should be employed, both of which would appear to be more capable of taking into account that some occupations are of necessity infrequently practiced. For this family of statuses it appears that a measure of integration for making predictions of differences in suicide rates within columns could be based on the extent to which the occupancy of a status configuration involving a particular occupation exceeds chance expectancy. Thus, a measure of integration between a particular occupational status and a status configuration would take the form of a ratio of the number of persons in the occupation to the number expected on the basis of chance. The highest ratio within a column of cells would then be expected to be found with the lowest suicide rate and vice versa.

Another way to take into account the possible problem posed by occupational statuses lies in the application of the present method to a second dimension of status integration. Heretofore in the illustrations only the proportions within columns have been considered. If the proportions within the rows were taken into account, the measures of status integration so obtained would be independent of the absolute number of persons who occupy a given occupational status. For example, in a table including the occupational status of physician, the measures of status integration would be based upon the proportion of physicians in a society who occupy a given status configuration and not the proportion of persons occupying a given status configuration who are physicians. Thus, the predictions of suicide rates within columns could be based on the proportions within rows. There is much that can be said for this approach to the measurement of status integration since it only involves the application of the original method to the second dimension of status integration. This second dimension should be taken into account in future research and subsequent development of the theory, and the measurement of occupational integration in the manner described above would be a step in this direction.

Though it is necessary to tentatively consider occupational integration as a special problem, it is one only insofar as predictions of suicide rates within columns are concerned. Since the factors that may possibly set limits on the occupancy of an occupational status independent of status incompatibility remain constant from one column to the next (from one status configuration to the next), predictions can be made regarding differences in suicide rates among columns without adopting a different method for measuring status integration. For Table 3, a hypothesis derived from the major theorem would call for the highest suicide rate to be found among persons occupying the status configuration shown in the middle column ($\Sigma X^2 = .2160$) and the lowest suicide rate to be found among persons occupying the status configuration shown in the last column ($\Sigma X^2 = .3902$).

Masking of Status Integration. One of the most pressing problems encountered in the measurement of status integration lies in the use of data that do not differentiate between statuses. The net results of lumping different statuses into one category are measures that underestimate the actual extent of integration. Consider, for instance, the effects of lumping three statuses into one category as shown in Table 4, which represents occupational integration in a hypothetical society.

Table 4. THE EFFECT OF FAILURE TO DISTINGUISH STATUSES WHEN MEASURING OCCUPATIONAL INTEGRATION IN A HYPOTHETICAL SOCIETY

| Occupation | Status X | | Status Y | | Status Z | | Over-all category (X+Y+Z) | |
	No.	MSI*	No.	MSI	No.	MSI	No.	MSI
O1	7,500	.75	....	.00	....	.00	7,500	.25
O2	....	.00	6,000	.60	....	.00	6,000	.20
O3	500	.05	....	.00	6,500	.65	7,000	.23
O4	....	.00	3,000	.30	1,500	.15	4,500	.15
O5	2,000	.20	1,000	.10	2,000	.20	5,000	.17
ΣX	10,000	1.00	10,000	1.00	10,000	1.00	30,000	1.00
ΣX^2		.6050		.4600		.4850		.2068

* Measure of status integration.

When the measure for the last column is computed, it gives the impression that the degree of occupational integration in the society is only slightly above the absolute minimum, but such a measure is very misleading. All three of the statuses are highly integrated with occupational status, and the low measure found in the last column is only a consequence of the three being lumped together into an over-all category.

As a general rule, when different statuses are combined into one over-all category, the integration measure for the category is very low. What makes the problem particularly difficult is the fact that such a combination does not have an invariable consequence. As an example of this, consider the high values of status integration shown in Table 4. If statuses X, Y, and Z had little occupational integration, the measure for the over-all category would be approximately the same. Consequently, the degree of integration in an over-all category can be low even when the integration measures for the individual statuses are low or high. This problem makes it essential to examine carefully the categories employed in the data which are used to test a hypothesis derived from the theorem. It is here that the nature of available data is a crucial issue, since the categories may mask more than they reveal.

Determination of Status. A test of the major theorem among societies or within any particular one requires at the outset a decision as to the categories of persons which are to be treated as statuses. Even under ideal conditions, it is often difficult to judge from an abstract definition of a status, such as that given in the preceding chapter, whether a given category does or does not qualify. This problem, which is inherent in dealing with abstract concepts, is compounded by the fact that the available data seldom leave room for discretion in the matter. Consequently, in the analysis of subsequent chapters, it should be remembered that the categories used to test hypotheses derived from the theorem may appear somewhat arbitrary and fail to correspond in one or more respects with the conceptual description of status. The claim is not made that each category corresponds precisely to the definition of status offered in the preceding chapter. In some cases, as will be noted, the categories are only approximations at best of the types that would be used under ideal conditions.

The problems encountered in an attempt to test the major theorem are by no means all of a practical nature. In some cases, it is difficult to provide a rationale for the treatment of the data in such a way as to form status categories. This is particularly true when the data pertain to the age of persons in a society where age grading is less pronounced and largely informal and implicit. It is obvious that in all societies certain demands and expectations are made of individuals as a consequence of their age, but the crucial problem here is the establishment of realistic age groups. Until we have more systematic knowledge regarding the nature and social consequences of age grading in the societies used to test the theorem, the status categories established in this respect will of necessity be somewhat arbitrary. From a methodological point of view, the chief danger lies in lumping age categories together in such a way as to mask the degree of status integration that would be found were finer distinctions made. Consequently, the policy was adopted in this study to use as many age categories as are manageable when attempting to measure this aspect of status integration.

Occupancy of Status and the Element of Time. Although not included as a variable in the formulation of the present theory, the element of time in the occupancy of statuses cannot be ignored. It is almost inconceivable to think of loss of social relationships as an instantaneous consequence of the occupancy of incompatible statuses. An ideal test of the major theorem would be based on a comparison of the suicide rates of persons who have occupied different status configurations for approximately the same length of time.

The nature of the data used in the present study precludes such control, but future research which seeks a conclusive series of tests will have to take the factor of time into account. For the present, the only alternative is to note certain hypotheses where the element of time is likely to be particularly operative.

NEED FOR EXPERIMENTATION

Observations on the measurement of status integration should leave little doubt that many practical and methodological problems are posed. For some of them, such as the element of time in the occupancy of status, the nature of existing data precludes a solution. In other cases, where a solution is within the realm of possibility, the methods employed in dealing with the problems are frankly open to some serious questions. All in all, however, answers to the many questions may lie only in extensive experimentation. In this sense, then, the study does not offer definitive tests of the major theorem because the method employed represents only one of numerous possibilities in the measurement of status integration. Experimentation on a grand scale is only justified, however, when there is some substantial reason to anticipate positive results. If crude data and somewhat arbitrary methods yield positive though imperfect results, extensive experimentation in the future will be warranted.

PART TWO

Initial Tests of the Major Theorem

in the United States

CHAPTER FOUR

Tests of the Major Theorem on Political Divisions of the United States

THE FIRST intersocietal tests of the major theorem involve the treatment of certain political divisions of the United States as societies, with the first test being conducted on the individual states. It should be noted that these units of observation have limited political autonomy, and that they do not qualify as societies if absolute autonomy is taken as an essential characteristic of a society. A test of the major theorem on a truly international scale is described in a later section.

HYPOTHESES

Two Type 3 hypotheses[1] regarding variability in suicide rates among the states in the United States have been derived from the major theorem:

Hypothesis No. 1: *There will be an inverse relationship by states between total status integration measures and suicide rates.*

Hypothesis No. 2: *There will be an inverse relationship by states between weighted total status integration measures and suicide rates.*

---

[1] See p. 40.

SELECTION OF DATA

As indicated in the preceding chapter, it is essential that the measurement of integration be based on as many statuses as possible; otherwise, the influence of those not included is left uncontrolled. The data in census reports regarding the occupancy of status configurations in individual states are typically restricted to configurations comprised of three statuses, with the maximum number of four being found in tables giving, separately, occupation and marital status by age, sex, and color. The computation of status integration measures by states, even when the tables contain a small number of cells, is very laborious. Consequently, a decision had to be made regarding the comparative importance of occupational and marital status. Occupational status was selected on the grounds that it is perhaps the major or key status of individuals in the United States[2] and, at the same time, promised to yield greater variability in total status integration measures by states than would marital status. Thus, for a test of the above hypotheses the most relevant data pertaining to status integration in individual states is occupation by age, sex, and color as of 1950.[3]

TREATMENT OF DATA

The variable of race is treated in reports by the Bureau of the Census on individual states in terms of two colors—white and nonwhite. In order to include these two categories in the status configurations, 18 of the 48 states were excluded because occupations were given only by age and sex.[4] The age categories employed by the Bureau of the Census in reporting occupations by states are as follows: 14-15, 16-17, 18-19, 20-24, 25-29, 30-34, 35-44, 45-54, 55-59, 60-64, and 65 and over.[5] For the purpose of constructing a table to measure status integration in each state, the eleven age categories shown above were reduced to four: 14-19, 20-29, 30-54, and 55 and over. Ideally, all of the categories employed in the census reports should have been used, so as to avoid, as much as possible, the masking of status integration. The resulting table for each state would have contained 484 cells and the task of preparing such a table and computing a total status inte-

---

[2] See Anne Roe, *The Psychology of Occupations* (New York, 1956), pp. 31-35.

[3] *U.S. Census of Population: 1950.* Vol. II, *Characteristics of the Population,* Parts 2-50, Chapter C, Table 76.

[4] The thirty states used in the test of the hypotheses are shown in Table 6, p. 54.

[5] It should be noted that occupations by age for the individual states were reported only for employed persons.

gration measure for each of the 30 states was beyond the resources of the study.

Though statistics by age, sex, and color are given for specific occupations in each of the 30 states, a table encompassing the hundreds of occupational titles would contain an astronomical number of cells. Once again, while such a table for each state would have been most desirable, the amount of labor involved precluded its use. The most feasible solution to the problem called for the use of the eleven major occupational groups recognized in the census reports. These groups are shown in Table 5.

Separate tables are provided for males and females in the reports of occupation by age, but not for whites and nonwhites. For each state, the figures given for nonwhites must be subtracted from the state total in order to obtain the number of whites who occupy a given status configuration. For example, to obtain in any state the number of white male laborers 14-19 years of age in 1950, the number of nonwhite male laborers 14-19 years of age must be subtracted from the total number of male laborers of this age.

The end products of the operations performed on the data for each state were recorded in a table such as Table 5, where the state of New Jersey is used as an illustration of the measurement of total status integration.

Once the numbers in the 176 cells shown in the table were established, each of them was converted into a proportion of the total in the column. This proportion, as noted previously, is the measure of integration between a status configuration and an occupational status. For a concrete example, in the case of New Jersey it was found that .0793 of the white males 20-29 years of age were laborers. After the numbers had been converted the proportion in each cell was squared and the products summed. The resulting sum of the squares constitutes the occupational status integration measure for the column. This value is shown at the bottom of each column in the next to the last row in Table 5. Thus, the occupational integration measure for the status configuration white-male 20-29 in New Jersey as of 1950 was .1651. To obtain a total status integration measure for each state the status integration measures at the bottom of the column were summed. The resulting product for New Jersey is 3.83, which constitutes the total status integration measure for the state as a whole.

The values shown in the last row of Table 5 represent the proportion of the persons in the table who occupied the status configuration shown at the top of the column. The value of .1297 at the bottom of

Table 5. OCCUPATIONAL INTEGRATION MEASURES, NEW JERSEY, 1950

	Status Configuration							
	Nonwhite Females by Age				Nonwhite Males by Age			
Occupational Group	14-19	20-29	30-54	55+	14-19	20-29	30-54	55+
Professional & technical..	.0192	.0415	.0312	.0247	.0061	.0223	.0240	.0342
Farmers, farm managers	.0009	.0002	.0006	.0022	.0027	.0016	.0044	.0172
Managers, officials, and proprietors............	.0014	.0054	.0138	.0192	.0030	.0138	.0343	.0589
Clerical................................	.0699	.0710	.0271	.0078	.0343	.0529	.0382	.0293
Sales workers..................	.0253	.0138	.0106	.0102	.0617	.0156	.0112	.0109
Craftsmen, foremen.........	.0056	.0121	.0082	.0041	.0457	.0952	.1154	.1008
Operatives.........................	.3488	.4247	.2799	.1060	.2551	.3353	.2969	.1747
Private household workers......	.3436	.2895	.4775	.6769	.0103	.0090	.0182	.0315
Service workers..............	.1420	.1120	.1275	.1276	.2186	.1284	.1403	.2327
Farm laborers and foremen..................	.0230	.0097	.0078	.0082	.1032	.0451	.0353	.0442
Laborers............................	.0202	.0201	.0158	.0132	.2593	.2808	.2818	.2657
Proportions summed (ΣX)	.9999	1.0000	1.0000	1.0001	1.0000	1.0000	1.0000	1.0001
Integration measure (ΣX^2)............	.2668	.2844	.3250	.4871	.1980	.2227	.2055	.1743
Column total ÷ table total........	.0011	.0074	.0156	.0024	.0014	.0097	.0229	.0053

	White Females by Age				White Males by Age			
	14-19	20-29	30-54	55+	14-19	20-29	30-54	55+
Professional & technical	.0485	.1131	.1272	.1351	.0257	.1045	.1150	.0785
Farmers, farm managers	.0005	.0005	.0026	.0077	.0053	.0083	.0136	.0306
Managers, officials, and proprietors............	.0038	.0166	.0537	.0745	.0134	.0649	.1580	.1681
Clerical................................	.5231	.4912	.2658	.1392	.1727	.1138	.0777	.0642
Sales workers..................	.1136	.0535	.0775	.0774	.1290	.0832	.0687	.0599
Craftsmen, foremen	.0085	.0138	.0226	.0197	.0882	.2089	.2381	.2348
Operatives.........................	.2143	.2507	.3285	.2695	.2991	.2797	.2130	.1682
Private household workers........	.0280	.0072	.0252	.1063	.0022	.0004	.0007	.0020
Service workers..............	.0474	.0447	.0829	.1501	.0673	.0392	.0565	.1044
Farm laborers and foremen..................	.0046	.0026	.0068	.0111	.0634	.0177	.0079	.0124
Laborers............................	.0076	.0061	.0073	.0095	.1336	.0793	.0507	.0770
Proportions summed (ΣX)..............	.9999	1.0000	1.0001	1.0001	.9999	.9999	.9999	1.0001
Integration measure (ΣX^2)............	.3380	.3223	.2118	.1563	.1710	.1651	.1570	.1435
Column total ÷ table total........	.0208	.0811	.1383	.0328	.0184	.1331	.3803	.1297

the last column in the table thus represents the proportion of employed persons in the state of New Jersey who were white males 55 years of age and over as of 1950. The values in the bottom row are necessary for computing a weighted total status integration measure as described in the preceding chapter. For each state, the weighted total status integration measure was computed by multiplying the value in the next to last row of each column by the value immediately below it and summing the products. For New Jersey, the weighted total status integration measure is .1877.

The suicide rates used to test the hypotheses are set forth in Table 6, with the rate representing mean annual number of resident suicides in a state over the three-year period 1949-1951 per 100,000 residents 14 years of age and over as of 1950.[6] (Unless otherwise noted, all suicide rates presented in this report are mean annual rates per 100,-000 population.) The two status integration measures which were used in the test of the two hypotheses are also shown in Table 6.

A Test of the Hypotheses. The first hypothesis anticipates a negative relationship between the values shown in the first two columns of Table 6. The product moment coefficient of correlation (r) proved to be —.52. The second hypothesis anticipates a negative r between the values shown in the first and last column of Table 6. The coefficient proved to be —.57.

A Second Intersocietal Test of the Major Theorem. A second opportunity for testing the major theorem on political divisions of the United States is provided in reports by the Bureau of the Census in which occupation is given by age, sex, and color for certain standard metropolitan areas with a population of 250,000 or more in 1950.[7] These areas are defined as follows:

Except in New England, a standard metropolitan area is a county or group of contiguous counties which contains at least one city of 50,000 inhabitants or more. In addition to the county, or counties, containing such a city, or cities, contiguous counties are included in a standard metropolitan area if according to certain

---

[6] The suicide statistics used throughout this study to compute suicide rates for the United States or individual states by age, sex, color, or total population were drawn from the following sources: U.S. Federal Security Agency, *Vital Statistics of the United States, 1949*, Part II, Table 22, pp. 252-457; U.S. Department of Health, Education and Welfare, *Vital Statistics of the United States, 1950*, Vol. III, Table 56, pp. 246-451; U.S. Department of Health, Education and Welfare, *Vital Statistics of the United States, 1951*, Vol. II, Table 57, pp. 160-363. Population figures were drawn from *U.S. Census of Population: 1950*. Vol. II, *Characteristics of the Population*, Part 1, United States Summary, Chapter B, p. 124.

[7] *U.S. Census of Population: 1950*. Vol. II, *Characteristics of the Population*, Parts 2-50, Chapter C, Table 76.

criteria they are essentially metropolitan in character and socially and economically integrated with the central city.[8]

Table 6. TOTAL STATUS INTEGRATION MEASURES AND
WEIGHTED TOTAL STATUS INTEGRATION MEASURES, 1950,* AND
RESIDENT SUICIDE RATES, 1949-1951,† THIRTY STATES, UNITED STATES

State	Mean Annual Suicide Rate	Total Status Integration Measure	Weighted Total Status Integration Measure
California	23.0	2.89	.1576
Washington	21.3	2.81	.1538
Arizona	18.0	3.24	.1531
Indiana	17.7	3.44	.1676
Kansas	16.7	3.43	.1606
Florida	16.0	3.39	.1751
Connecticut	15.7	3.84	.1900
Ohio	15.7	3.45	.1742
New Jersey	15.3	3.83	.1877
Maryland	15.3	3.60	.1828
Missouri	15.0	3.21	.1597
Virginia	14.7	3.44	.1766
Illinois	14.3	3.25	.1689
West Virginia	14.0	4.55	.2080
Michigan	14.0	3.42	.1850
New York	13.7	3.47	.1724
Pennsylvania	13.7	3.48	.1800
Massachusetts	13.3	3.41	.1826
Kentucky	13.3	3.85	.1831
New Mexico	13.0	3.26	.1491
Texas	12.3	3.48	.1622
Georgia	12.0	3.64	.1910
Tennessee	11.3	3.51	.1806
North Carolina	11.0	3.77	.2029
Oklahoma	11.0	3.30	.1587
Arkansas	10.0	3.58	.1870
South Carolina	9.3	3.92	.2104
Alabama	9.3	3.59	.1917
Mississippi	9.0	4.04	.2314
Louisiana	9.0	3.43	.1755

* Both measures are based on the integration of occupation with age, sex, and color, 1950.
† For population 14 years of age and over.

Standard metropolitan areas are of particular importance since they constitute units of observation that differ from the individual states in two significant respects. Although their boundaries are political lines, from an ecological point of view, in comparison to the states, they more nearly approximate functional entities. The criteria employed to demarcate standard metropolitan areas are also of significance in the

[8] U.S. Census of Population: 1950. Vol. II, Characteristics of the Population, Part 1, United States Summary, Chapter B, p. vii.

sense that the units of observation so formed are much more homogeneous with respect to population size, population density, demographic composition, and economic structure than is an aggregate of states drawn from different regions of the United States.

The Bureau of the Census reports give occupation by age, sex, and color for twenty-nine standard metropolitan areas with a population of 250,000 or more in 1950. These data were treated in a manner identical to that used with the states. This means that a counterpart to Table 5 was prepared for each standard metropolitan area, and the same operations were performed on the figures in its cells. The end products are a total measure and a weighted total measure, with both expressing the degree of occupational integration as in the case of states.

Although the population figures necessary for computing suicide rates were available,[9] the task was complicated by the fact that suicides are not reported for a standard metropolitan area as a whole. Since, with the exception of those located in New England, these areas are composed of one or more counties, the number of resident suicides in a standard metropolitan area can be obtained by adding up the number of cases in its constituent counties.[10] The only difficulty encountered here, other than the labor involved, is the fact that the boundaries of the standard metropolitan areas in New England do not coincide with those employed in reports of suicide. For this reason Boston was excluded, leaving a total of 28 standard metropolitan areas.

The mean annual suicide rates for residents 15 years of age and over in 1950 are given in Table 7 along with the status integration measures, both total and weighted total.

Two hypotheses were advanced regarding the variability in the suicide rates of the standard metropolitan areas shown in Table 7: (1) *Among the standard metropolitan areas there will be an inverse relationship between suicide rates and total status integration measures,* and (2) *Among the standard metropolitan areas there will be an inverse relationship between suicide rates and weighted total status integration measures.*

In operational terms, the first hypothesis anticipates a negative coefficient of correlation between the values shown in the first two columns of Table 7. The computed *r* proved to be —.64. The second hypothesis anticipates a negative coefficient of correlation between the

---

[9] *Ibid.*, pp. 141-142.

[10] *Vital Statistics of the United States, 1949,* Part II, Table 14, pp. 526-634; *Vital Statistics of the United States, 1950,* Vol. III, Table 60, pp. 486-607; *Vital Statistics of the United States, 1951,* Vol. II, Table 59, pp. 366-443.

values shown in the first and the last column of Table 7. The coefficient in this case is —.63.

Table 7. TOTAL STATUS INTEGRATION MEASURES AND WEIGHTED TOTAL STATUS INTEGRATION MEASURES,* 1950, AND RESIDENT SUICIDE RATES, 1949-1951,† TWENTY-EIGHT STANDARD METROPOLITAN AREAS, UNITED STATES

Standard Metropolitan Areas	Mean Annual Suicide Rate	Total Status Integration Measure	Weighted Total Status Integration Measure
San Francisco-Oakland	24.3	3.14	.1775
Los Angeles	22.7	3.10	.1607
Tampa-St. Petersburg	21.7	3.62	.1788
Indianapolis	18.3	3.62	.1923
Miami	18.0	3.79	.1913
Cincinnati	16.0	3.91	.1878
Houston	16.0	4.05	.2091
Richmond	15.3	3.94	.2144
Baltimore	15.0	3.86	.1989
Washington, D.C.	14.7	4.01	.2250
Kansas City, Missouri	14.7	3.70	.1874
Jacksonville	14.3	3.87	.2180
Louisville	14.0	3.85	.1900
Cleveland	14.0	3.58	.1847
St. Louis	13.7	3.54	.1877
Chicago	13.7	3.48	.1906
Pittsburgh	13.7	3.78	.1877
New York-N.E. New Jersey	13.3	3.73	.1855
Columbus, Ohio	13.3	3.72	.1912
Nashville	12.7	3.80	.2015
Philadelphia	12.7	3.61	.1830
Norfolk-Portsmouth	12.7	3.82	.2253
Detroit	12.3	3.71	.2162
Atlanta	12.3	4.21	.2200
Dallas	10.3	4.32	.2114
Memphis	10.0	3.75	.2147
Birmingham	8.3	4.25	.2409
New Orleans	8.3	3.82	.2021

* Both measures are based on the integration of occupation with age, sex, and race.
† For population 15 years of age and over.

EXPERIMENTATION

The suicide rates used above are for populations age 14 and over and 15 and over. A more conventional measure is one that is based on the population of all ages or, in demographic terms, a crude suicide rate. For the sake of comparison, the hypotheses were tested again with crude rates computed for each state and standard metropolitan areas shown in Tables 6 and 7 by the same procedure as described above except that the total population was used as the base rather than persons age 15 and over.

The coefficients of correlation between total status integration measures and crude suicide rates are —.51 by states and —.64 by standard metropolitan areas. In the case of the weighted total status integration measures, the corresponding coefficients are —.54 and —.66. These findings cannot be construed as providing additional support for the major theorem, but they do demonstrate that an inverse relationship holds also for the more conventional type of suicide rate.

As the coefficients of correlation reported in this chapter indicate, total and weighted total status integration measures have a similar degree of relationship with suicide rates. To some extent this was surprising since the weighted measure appears more adequate. That the two measures are closely linked is shown by correlations of + .77 between them among the standard metropolitan areas and + .85 among the states.

INADEQUACIES IN THE DATA

The measures of status integration by states and standard metropolitan areas are particularly inadequate insofar as they are based on only four statuses. Ideally, they should express the degree of occupational integration for status configurations which encompass more than age, sex, and color. At a minimum, marital, parental, and religious statuses should have been included, but the data necessary for a more complete measure of status integration are not currently available, nor are they likely to be in the immediate future.

Another obvious deficiency in the measures of status integration by states and standard metropolitan areas relates to the nature of categories that were treated as statuses. With the exception of sex, all of the categories that were employed in the tables probably operate to mask status integration to a considerable degree. With reference to the categories treated as racial statuses, we find, for example, that persons of Mexican birth or ancestry are lumped with persons of northern European extraction as whites. The category of nonwhite is even more heterogeneous, with no distinction being drawn among Negroes, American Indians, and Asians. In either instance, the effects of lumping distinct racial statuses probably varies considerably from one state to the next, and this is particularly undesirable.

Some of the inadequacies in the measures cannot be attributed to the categories employed in the reports of the Bureau of the Census. Given adequate financial resources, much finer distinctions could have been drawn for occupation and age. Although the present study had to be content to work with four age categories and eleven occupational categories, future tests may be based on eleven rather than four age categories and on an almost unlimited number of occupational statuses.

Furthermore, in addition to the changes just suggested, a truly adequate measure of status integration for a state would take into consideration the variation that exists among communities within the state. This means that measures would be computed for each community in the state, and these values weighted according to the populations involved would then be summed to provide a total state measure. Though this would involve a tremendous amount of labor, as a minimum step in this direction, measures should be computed separately for the rural and urban populations, with the total state measure being the sum of these two.

One of the less apparent faults in the tests lies not in the measures of status integration but in the nature of the suicide rates. Since the integration measures were based only on employed persons, the suicide rate should have been based on that population also. Suicide in the United States is not reported for states by employment status, however, and consequently the status integration measures relate to less than 50 per cent of the population while the suicide rate involves the total population. On this basis alone, one should not expect the correlation between the two to be extremely high.

Though the coefficients of correlation reported in this chapter will be considered in a later over-all evaluation of the tests of the major theorem, it is of considerable importance that the above inadequacies in the data be noted at this time. When they are taken into consideration, the findings certainly lend some support to the theory.

CHAPTER FIVE

Suicide Differentials
by Race and Sex

IT HAS already been emphasized that a general theory must be
capable of explaining more than one form of variability in suicide
rates. In addition to accounting for spatial variability, such as differences in the suicide rates of populations demarcated along political
lines, it must also come to grips with some of the more fundamental
facts concerning differential suicide rates among populations not so
demarcated.

With the possible exception of variation by age, the most outstanding differences in suicide rates within a society are found in the comparison of race and sex. Almost every study has noted the extreme
variations that may be found by race and sex, and yet these fundamental differences have yet to be explained. What few explanations
have been offered are untested, untestable, or unrelated to explanations of variability on a societal level. For an explanation of differences in suicide by race and sex to be accepted, it must not only yield
correct predictions regarding race and sex differentials within a society but also be consistent with an explanation of differences among
societies; the explanation, in short, must be derived from a general
theory.

By the very nature of the categories, explanations of differential
amounts of suicide by race and sex tend to be biologically oriented.
Biological explanations of differences in this case are particularly objectionable because they postulate a constant to explain something

59

that is variable. We find that not only does the suicide rate for women vary considerably from one society to the next but also that the immunity they enjoy in comparison to men is relative to particular age groups and particular societies. The same may be said regarding racial differences.

In terms of the general theory presented here, variability in suicide rates by race and sex can be understood only through the realization that the determinants of behavioral differences among races and between the two sexes are predominantly social and, consistent with the theory, that the primary locus of the social determinants of behavior is in the statuses of individuals.

This chapter is concerned with the application of the major theorem to differences in suicide rates by race and sex only in the United States. The results cannot be construed to be conclusive proof that the theorem can account for differences by race and sex for all places and all times. They are important, however, in that the failure of the major theorem to account for such fundamental facts of suicide as race and sex differences in the United States would cast grave doubts on the theory.

RACE AND SEX DIFFERENCES IN THE UNITED STATES

As shown in Table 8, there are considerable differences in suicide rates by race and sex in the United States.[1] Given these rates, the major theorem would call for females in the United States to have greater status integration than males. Among the three racial groups the greatest degree of status integration should prevail among Negroes and the lowest degree among the group that includes all persons other than white or Negro (Chinese, Japanese, American Indians, and Filipinos account for practically all of the persons in this category).

---

[1] The suicide rates by race and sex reported in this chapter are based on suicide data drawn from *Vital Statistics of the United States, 1949*, Part I, Table 9, p. 152; *Vital Statistics of the United States, 1950*, Vol. III, Table 52, p. 118; *Vital Statistics of the United States, 1951*, Vol. II, Table 54, p. 86. The population figures used to compute suicide rates by race and sex were drawn from the *U.S. Census of Population: 1950*. Vol. II, *Characteristics of the Population*, Part 1, United States Summary, Table 36, p. 88.

Authors' note: The usage of the U.S. Bureau of Census is to identify and differentiate populations by "color" into two broad categories—white and nonwhite. In some instances, the nonwhite population is classified further by "race" as Negro, Indian, Japanese, Chinese, and all other. The usage followed in this book parallels that of the Census Bureau. For a discussion of the Census Bureau's usage see *U.S. Census of Population: 1950. Vol. II, Characteristics of the Population*, Part 1, United States Summary, Chapter B, p.x.

In keeping with the postulated importance of occupations, measures of occupational integration were used to test the above predictions. They were used, however, with the full realization that they are based on only one status and take into account only the employed persons for a given race or sex. Ideally, the suicide rates by race and sex should also have been for employed persons only. Since this was not possible, it was necessary to use the total suicide rate for a given race or sex with anticipation of only moderate success in prediction.

Table 8. MEAN ANNUAL SUICIDE RATES BY RACE
AND SEX, UNITED STATES, 1949-1951

Race and Sex	Suicide Rate
Race	
White	11.9
Negro	3.7
Other	14.6
Sex	
Male	17.3
Female	4.9

Detailed occupations for employed persons 14 years of age and over by sex[2] and race[3] are given in reports of the 1950 census by the Bureau of the Census. The eleven occupational groups used to measure status integration for states and standard metropolitan areas were employed. Table 9 gives measures of occupational integration for the five populations shown in Table 8.

Without exception the predictions made are correct; by race and by sex, measures of occupational integration vary inversely with the suicide rate.

A More Complex Problem in Prediction. The differences found in suicide rates by race and sex within a society are magnified when race and sex are combined to form status configurations, and this provides another opportunity for a predictive test of the theory. Sources previously cited provide data necessary for computing a suicide rate and a measure of occupational integration for six race-sex status configurations in the United States. These variables are shown in Table 10. The hypothesis tested in this case reads as follows: *There will be an inverse relationship between measures of occupational integration*

---

[2] *U.S. Census of Population: 1950.* Vol. II, *Characteristics of the Population,* Part 1, United States Summary, Table 127, pp. 273-275.
[3] *Ibid.,* pp. 276-278.

and suicide rates by race-sex status configurations. This hypothesis was tested by computing a rank-difference correlation (ρ)[4] between the ranks given in Table 10. The value of ρ proved to be —.94.

Table 9. OCCUPATIONAL INTEGRATION BY SEX AND RACE, UNITED STATES, 1950

Occupational Group	Sex Males	Females	White	Race Negro	Other
Professional and technical	.0742	.1256	.0944	.0341	.0521
Farmers and farm managers	.1046	.0075	.0757	.0937	.1247
Managers, officials, and proprietors	.1084	.0439	.0982	.0174	.0767
Clerical and kindred	.0650	.2781	.1341	.0343	.0652
Sales workers	.0648	.0862	.0771	.0121	.0361
Craftsmen and foremen	.1882	.0153	.1497	.0531	.0527
Operatives	.2029	.1956	.2022	.1914	.1380
Private household workers	.0018	.0865	.0118	.1531	.0383
Service workers	.0593	.1240	.0688	.1543	.1438
Farm laborers and foremen	.0487	.0291	.0373	.0945	.1809
Laborers	.0821	.0082	.0508	.1620	.0914
Status integration measures	.1258	.1648	.1204	.1334	.1147

Table 10. MEAN ANNUAL SUICIDE RATES, 1949-1951, AND MEASURES OF OCCUPATIONAL INTEGRATION, 1950, FOR SIX RACE-SEX STATUS CONFIGURATIONS, UNITED STATES

Race-Sex Status Configuration	Occupational Integration Measure	Rank	Suicide Rate	Rank
White male	.1295	5	18.5	2
Negro male	.1588	3	6.1	3
Other male	.1243	6	21.3	1
White female	.1828	2	5.3	5
Negro female	.2473	1	1.5	6
Other female	.1416	4	5.9	4

This relationship is particularly striking when one considers that the proportion of employed persons in each of the status configurations varies by sex. Since there are far fewer females than males employed, a more realistic comparison involves the consideration of the two sexes taken separately. Among the males there are no exceptions in Table 10 to the inverse relationship, and the same is true for the females. This indicates that as the proportions of employed persons tend to be equal, the more consistent is the inverse relationship between measures of occupational integration, based on employed persons, and suicide rates for the total population.

---

[4] The small number of categories makes ρ a more appropriate measure than r.

INTEGRATION OF OCCUPATION WITH AGE AND
VARIABILITY IN SUICIDE RATES BY SEX AND RACE

A measure of status integration should take into account as many statuses as possible, a point stressed earlier in Chapter IV. All of the integration measures by race and sex considered thus far have been based only on occupation. There remains, however, within the limits imposed by the availability of data, one additional status to be taken into account. Reports by the Bureau of the Census give, for the United States as a whole, detailed occupations by age and sex for employed persons 14 years of age and over.[5] These data are also given elsewhere for nonwhite males and nonwhite females[6] and for total males and females.[7] By subtracting the nonwhites from the totals it is possible to obtain occupation by age for white males, white females, nonwhite males, and nonwhite females. These can in turn be combined so as to give occupation by age for whites and nonwhites, disregarding distinctions by sex.

Although a measure of status integration based on occupation and age is superior to occupation alone, its value is marred by the fact that the data are reported by "color" and not by distinct races. This means that we are once again confronted with the heterogeneous category of nonwhites. However, since a measure of status integration based on occupation and age offers a great deal, the decision was made to test the major theorem on color categories even though they are most unsatisfactory. Though the use of obviously unsatisfactory categories could easily lead to a premature rejection of the major theorem, they cannot be excluded from the tests without a bias in selection.

The importance of including age lies in the possibility that it operates to mask status integration when not taken into account. The same may be said, of course, for any other family of statuses not included in the measurements but it is particularly true for age in the case of occupational integration.

Detailed occupations by sex and color are given in the reports of the Bureau of the Census for the following age categories: 14-15, 16-17, 18-19, 20-24, 25-29, 30-34, 35-44, 45-54, 55-59, 60-64, and 65 and over. All of these categories were used to compute measures of the integration of occupational status with age except the first three, which were combined into one category, 14-19.

---

[5] See above, note 2.
[6] *U.S. Census of Population: 1950.* Vol. IV, *Special Reports*, Part 1, Chapter B, *Occupational Characteristics*, Table 7, pp. 81-92.
[7] *Ibid.*, Table 6, pp. 69-80.

Table 11. INTEGRATION OF OCCUPATION WITH AGE AMONG WHITE MALES, UNITED STATES, 1950

Occupational Group	14-19	20-24	25-29	30-34	Age Group 35-44	45-54	55-59	60-64	65+
Professional and technical	.0153	.0608	.1035	.0976	.0897	.0766	.0660	.0608	.0643
Farmers and farm managers	.0291	.0538	.0718	.0840	.0983	.1145	.1368	.1544	.2248
Managers, officials, and proprietors	.0105	.0372	.0739	.1067	.1390	.1574	.1514	.1349	.1332
Clerical and kindred	.0784	.1020	.0834	.0711	.0608	.0615	.0601	.0571	.0495
Sales workers	.1254	.0765	.0804	.0734	.0652	.0621	.0570	.0573	.0611
Craftsmen and foremen	.0637	.1615	.2030	.2162	.2202	.2220	.2120	.2049	.1553
Operatives	.2153	.2897	.2454	.2302	.2065	.1704	.1566	.1455	.1016
Private household workers	.0016	.0006	.0003	.0003	.0007	.0010	.0012	.0018	.0026
Service workers	.0680	.0370	.0360	.0367	.0422	.0550	.0727	.0825	.0982
Farmer laborers and foremen	.2639	.0798	.0368	.0259	.0233	.0221	.0218	.0281	.0426
Laborers	.1287	.1005	.0654	.0578	.0542	.0573	.0645	.0727	.0669
Status integration measures	.1643	.1522	.1431	.1435	.1414	.1365	.1322	.1283	.1290

Table 11, which relates to white males, illustrates the measurement of occupational integration with age among males, females, whites, nonwhites, white males, white females, nonwhite males, and nonwhite females. The total measure of the integration of occupation with age among white males constitutes the sum of the integration values shown at the bottom of each column, which in this case is 1.27. Corresponding measures for seven additional sex and color categories in the United States as of 1950 are as follows: males, 1.25; females, 1.54; whites, 1.17; nonwhites, 1.34; white females, 1.68; nonwhite males, 1.61; nonwhite females, 2.47.

On the basis of the above measures three predictions were made in line with the major theorem:

(1) The mean annual suicide rate of males in the United States, 1949-1951, will be higher than the mean annual suicide rate of females.

(2) The mean annual suicide rate of whites in the United States, 1949-1951, will be higher than the mean annual suicide rate of non-whites.

(3) Among the four color and sex categories in the United States an inverse relationship will hold between measures of the integration of occupation with age as of 1950 and mean annual suicide rates for the years 1949-1951.

Table 12 provides the data necessary for an evaluation of the three predictions. The first two are both correct. The third was tested by computing a rank-difference correlation between the ranks shown; ρ proved to be -1.00.

Table 12. MEASURES OF THE INTEGRATION OF OCCUPATION WITH AGE, 1950, AND MEAN ANNUAL SUICIDE RATES, 1949-1951, EIGHT SEX AND COLOR CATEGORIES, UNITED STATES

Race-Sex Category	Measure of the Integration of Occupation with Age	Rank of Measure	Mean Annual Suicide Rate	Rank of Rate
Males	1.25	....	17.3	....
Females	1.54	....	4.9	....
Whites	1.17	....	11.9	....
Nonwhites	1.34	....	4.2	....
White males	1.27	4	18.5	1
White females	1.68	2	5.3	3
Nonwhite males	1.61	3	6.9	2
Nonwhite females	2.47	1	1.6	4

65

It will be noted in comparing the integration measures of the various race and sex status configurations in the United States that the differences appear to be relatively small in comparison to the magnitude of the variations in suicide rates. To appreciate the magnitude of the differences, however, one must take into account the absolute lower limit of the measure of status integration. For the integration of occupation with age, for example, as shown in Table 11, the lower limit of the total measure is .82. Thus, while the total status integration measure for the nonwhite female in Table 12 is only 1.20 higher than that of the white male, the former is 201 per cent higher than the lower limit, while the latter is only 55 per cent above the lower limit.

Notwithstanding the support provided for the major theorem by the findings, the tests are by no means conclusive even for the United States. Much remains to be done. For one thing, numerous statuses are not taken into account. Further research must attempt to take marital status into account regarding status integration by race and sex, even though marital integration and occupational integration will have to be measured separately. Other reports by the Bureau of the Census[8] offer possibilities in obtaining integration measures for racial categories less heterogeneous than "races other than white or Negro" and "nonwhites." As to the dependent variable, the most pressing need is suicide rates for employed persons.

---

[8] See, for examples: *U.S. Census of Population: 1950.* Vol. IV, *Special Reports,* Part 3, Chapter B, *Nonwhite Population by Race.*

CHAPTER SIX

Age and Suicide

V ARIABILITY by age is one of the fundamental features of sui-cide rates. Although frequently noted in other investigations of suicide, it has defied explanation even more than variability by race and sex. In comparison to race and sex, age is by far a more complex variable. In addition to having biological correlates, age has social consequences that are not as obvious as those of sex and race in many societies, particularly where explicit and formal age grading is not pronounced. In such societies, age seems only a chronological conti-nuum, with its social consequences not always evident. Though numer-ous complex methodological problems are encountered in the analysis of age as a status, the fact that its consequences may not clearly reveal themselves should not be taken to mean that they are nonexistent.

If we deny the particular social correlates of age, then the only other explanation of the remarkable patterns of variability in suicide rates is a biological one. This, as with race and sex, is immediately objectionable, because a pattern of variation found in one society may be absent in an-other. For example, mean annual suicide rates of males in Baden, 1891-1905, begin at 2.0 per 100,000 in the age group 10-14 and increase con-sistently through nine age groups to 80 years and over, where the rate stands at 140.8.[1] In contrast to this, among Italian males, 1901-1905, the mean annual suicide rates for ten age groups are as follows: 10-14, 0.5; 15-19, 7.1; 20-24, 16.6; 25-29, 13.8; 30-39, 12.6; 40-49, 16.5; 50-59, 20.8; 60-69, 22.3; 70-79, 21.0; 80 and over, 20.2.

---

[1] Data in this paragraph and the next are all from John Rice Miner, "Suicide and Its Relation to Climatic and Other Factors," *American Journal of Hygiene,* Monographic Series, No. 2 (1922), pp. 34 and 35.

Some populations show a pronounced pattern of increasing suicide with increasing age, while in others the increase is negligible or erratic. For example, among Italian females, 1901-1905, none of the seven older groups had a mean annual suicide rate higher than the rate for the 20-24 category (4.8 per 100,000), and the instances of increase in suicide rate of one age group over the preceding one do not outnumber those where the rate of a category is lower than the preceding one. However, among ten age groups of females in France, 1893-1906, there is only one exception to increasing suicide with increasing age. In the face of such evidence, it is difficult to see how there is anything biologically inherent in age that can explain variation in suicide rates. If the suicide rate increased uniformly with age in all populations, a biological explanation would warrant serious consideration, but it does not.

Variability in suicide rates by age may be adequately explained only by the social consequences of age; these must be partly the product of different types of demands and expectations placed upon individuals on the basis of age. In this sense, then, the age of a person constitutes one of his statuses. One need not argue, however, from variability in suicide rates to justify treating age as a status. It would violate the most elementary forms of social experience to maintain that patterned demands and expectations (roles) have no relationship to age. The crucial question, then, is determining the age distinctions that are recognized in a society and the nature of the roles associated with them.

We have mentioned earlier that there appears to be only limited systematic knowledge of age as a status, particularly in societies where age-grading is not pronounced, such as the United States. But even if we knew more about it, availability of data would dictate the age categories to be used in the measurement of status integration and the computation of suicide rates—that is, the choice of age categories to be treated as statuses. We have, therefore, used as many age categories as possible, for the technical reasons discussed earlier and in the hope of contributing to knowledge of age-grading in the United States.

MEASURES OF STATUS INTEGRATION AND
VARIABILITY IN SUICIDE RATES BY AGE

In populations where suicide increases with increasing age, we should expect to find decreasing measures of status integration with increasing age. This, of course, is merely another way of stating the major theorem, which calls for an inverse relationship to hold between measures of status integration and suicide rates. The purpose of this chapter is to report a series of tests of the ability of the major theorem to account for variability in suicide rates by age. Within the limitations imposed upon the study by the availability of data and resources for research, such a series of tests was conducted for nine sex and color categories in the United States. The nine hypotheses tested may be summarized in the form of a more general proposition: *For each of the nine sex and color categories in the United States, there will be an inverse relationship between measures of the integration of occupation with age and suicide rates by age.*

An example of the measurement of integration of occupation with age has already been provided in Table 11, where measures for white males are given for nine age categories.[2] For each of the sex and color categories used to test the major theorem, mean annual suicide rates for 1949-1951[3] were computed for the nine age groups shown in this table.[4]

Before reporting the results of the tests, it is again necessary to point to the shortcomings in the measures of status integration. First, the measures are based only on the integration of occupation with age, which means that several important statuses are ignored. Then, in contrast to the suicide rates, the measures of the integration of occupation with age apply not to the total population but only to employed persons. And, finally, the color categories used are unsatisfactory substitutes for specific racial categories, particularly the "nonwhite" category which includes Negroes and Asians of all types.

TESTS OF THE NINE HYPOTHESES

When the hypothesis presented above in general terms is stated with specific references to white males it reads as follows: *Among white males in the United States there will be an inverse relationship by age groups between suicide rates and measures of the integration of occupation with age.* Table 13 gives measures of the integration of occupation with age for nine age groups and illustrates the nature of the tests for the remaining eight hypotheses.

---

[2] See Chapter V, notes 2 and 3, for the sources of data used in computing measures of the integration of occupation with age for nine age categories by sex and color.

[3] See Chapter IV, note 6, for the sources of suicide data by age, sex, and color. Population figures by age, sex, and color were drawn from *U.S. Census of Population: 1950.* Vol. II, *Characteristics of Population*, Part 1, United States Summary, Table 38, p. 90.

[4] Because suicides are not reported for the age group, 14-19, the rate for 15-19 was used as the best approximation.

The hypothesis was tested by computing a rank-difference coefficient of correlation between the ranks given in Table 13. The coefficient proved to be –.97.

Table 13. MEASURES OF THE INTEGRATION OF OCCUPATION WITH AGE, 1950, AND SUICIDE RATES BY AGE, 1949-1951, WHITE MALES, UNITED STATES

Age Group	Mean Annual Suicide Rate	Rank of Suicide Rate	Measure of the Integration of Occupation with Age	Rank of Measure
14-19	3.7	9	.1643	1
20-24	9.4	8	.1522	2
25-29	11.8	7	.1431	4
30-34	14.7	6	.1435	3
35-44	22.3	5	.1414	5
45-54	32.8	4	.1365	6
55-59	41.5	3	.1322	7
60-64	47.0	2	.1283	9
65+	54.3	1	.1290	8

The hypotheses pertaining to the eight remaining sex and color categories were tested in exactly the same manner on the basis of tables corresponding to Table 13. Rather than present each of the specific hypotheses and the data used in the tests, we have summarized the findings for all nine hypotheses in Table 14. (To obtain the work tables summarized in Table 14, see page v.)

Table 14. RANK-DIFFERENCE COEFFICIENTS OF CORRELATION BETWEEN MEASURES OF THE INTEGRATION OF OCCUPATION WITH AGE, 1950, AND SUICIDE RATES BY AGE, 1949-1951, FOR NINE SEX AND COLOR CATEGORIES, UNITED STATES

Sex and Color Category	ρ
White males	–.97
White females	–.83
Nonwhite males	–.72
Nonwhite females	–.21
Males	–.95
Females	–.87
Whites	–.97
Nonwhites	–.80
Total population	–.93

It may be seen that all the computed ρ's are in the predicted direction and all are of substantial magnitude except that pertaining to nonwhite females. We have, in this test, a specific hypothesis, a clear-cut

70

case of the failure of a measure of status integration to vary inversely to a substantial degree with suicide rates. The interpretation of negative results in this case is very difficult. It is known that there are at least three defects in the measure of status integration employed: numerous statuses are not taken into account; the proportion of white and of non-white females employed is less than for white or nonwhite males; and the nonwhite categories are racially heterogeneous. Because all three defects may apply particularly to the nonwhite female, the inverse relationship is least likely to hold here; but the finding taken at face value still provides little support for the major theorem.

The results are not entirely negative, however; if we examine the variability of suicide rates by age among the nonwhite females in Table 15, either relative to the other three categories or in absolute terms, we find that endemic suicide[5] is virtually nil. This takes on particular sig-

Table 15. MEASURES OF THE INTEGRATION OF OCCUPATION WITH AGE, 1950, AND SUICIDE RATES BY AGE, 1949-1951, NONWHITE FEMALES, UNITED STATES

Age Group	Mean Annual Suicide Rate	Rank of Suicide Rate	Measure of the Integration of Occupation with Age	Rank of Measure
14-19	1.4	9	.2393	6
20-24	2.5	4.5	.1981	9
25-29	2.1	6	.2073	8
30-34	3.2	1	.2284	7
35-44	2.5	4.5	.2559	5
45-54	2.8	2	.2993	4
55-59	2.6	3	.3277	3
60-64	1.8	8	.3402	2
65+	2.0	7	.3724	1

nificance when it is linked to status integration measures by age groups among the nonwhite females. Here we find a very distinct pattern peculiar to the nonwhite female, with measures of status integration showing a uniform increase with increasing age. Under such conditions, we would not expect to find a pattern of endemic suicide, and this expectation is borne out in the suicide rates in Table 15. The failure of the hypothesis lies in the random decreases and increases in the suicide rates of the nonwhite female by age groups.

In comparison to the pattern for white males, the decreases and increases in suicide rate by age groups for nonwhite females are random

[5] Endemic suicide refers to the situation within a population in which suicide rates increase with each increase in the age of the group under consideration. That is, the longer an individual is exposed to this social structure the more likely he is to commit suicide.

and microscopic; there seems to be nothing in the patterns of social experience among nonwhite females which is inherently conducive to endemic suicide. The differences in the suicide rates of nonwhite female age groups are not uniform or large, and they may be nothing more than unstable fluctuations. This poses an interesting question insofar as status integration is concerned. Although the measures of integration are of the grossest sort, it is possible that even the most refined measures may prove to be incapable of accounting for microscopic differences in suicide rates. This would appear to be a real possibility when, as in the case just considered, the measures of status integration are high and the suicide rates being compared are very low.

As a further point regarding the evaluation of the results, some comment should be made about the independence of the tests. At first glance it might appear that the test reported on males is in no way independent of the two conducted on white males and nonwhite males considered separately. It could be argued that if an inverse relationship holds among both white males and nonwhite males, then it must also hold when the two are combined. This argument completely ignores the fact that when two or more statuses are combined into one category the resulting status integration measures cannot be deduced mathematically from the measures of the statuses taken separately. This applies not only to males in the United States but to females, whites, and the total population as well.

INCREASING VARIABILITY IN MEASURES OF STATUS INTEGRATION WITH INCREASING AGE

We have seen that, in comparison to other color-sex categories, a pattern of endemic suicide was conspicuously absent from the non-white female group; this was explained by increasing occupational integration with increasing age. In other words, the suicide rate of the nonwhite female becomes more and more unlike that of other categories with increasing age, because she alone exhibits increasing integration with increasing age. Far from being *ad hoc* in character, this explanation is linked to a more general proposition:

The amount of variability in the status integration measures of populations tends to vary directly with the amount of variability in their suicide rates. Although the limitations imposed on the study made it impossible to test this proposition on societies, we have sufficient data for its test on four populations in the United States in the form of the following hypothesis:

The differences by age groups between the lowest and highest meas-

ures of occupational integration among white males, white females, nonwhite males, and nonwhite females will vary directly with the differ- ence between the lowest and highest suicide rates. As the hypothesis indicates, the range was taken as a gauge of the amount of variability. Table 16 gives the maximum difference found in the suicide rates and the measures of occupational integration among the four populations in nine age groups.

Table 16. MAXIMUM DIFFERENCE IN MEASURES OF THE INTEGRATION OF OCCUPATION WITH AGE, 1950, AND SUICIDE RATES BY AGE GROUPS, 1949-1951, AMONG WHITE MALES, WHITE FEMALES, NONWHITE MALES AND NONWHITE FEMALES, UNITED STATES

Age Group	Maximum Difference in Measures of Integration of Occupation with Age		Maximum Difference in Mean Annual Suicide Rates	
	Difference	Rank	Difference	Rank
14-19	.1120	7	2.3	9
20-24	.1450	5	6.9	8
25-29	.0949	8	9.7	7
30-34	.0849	9	11.5	6
35-44	.1145	6	19.8	5
45-54	.1628	4	30.0	4
55-59	.1955	3	38.9	3
60-64	.2119	2	45.2	2
65+	.2434	1	52.3	1

The hypothesis was tested by computing a rank-difference correla- tion between the ranks given in Table 16. The coefficient proved to be +.80. Without exception, the variability in the suicide rates of the four populations by age groups, as measured by the range, increases with in- creasing age.

COLOR-SEX-AGE STATUS CONFIGURATIONS IN THE UNITED STATES

Although the findings reported in this chapter demonstrate the ca- pacity of the major theorem to cope with variability in suicide rates by age, the data lend themselves to other types of tests. Given measures of occupational integration and suicide rates for four color-sex status configurations (white males, white females, nonwhite males, nonwhite females) within nine age groups, the major theorem should enable one to predict the rank order of the suicide rates of the status configurations within each age group. In order to test the predictive power of the major theorem along these lines, Table 17 was prepared, showing in columns 3 and 4 the ranks of the occupational measures and suicide rates for the four color-sex status configurations within each of nine age groups.

Table 17. SUICIDE RATES, 1949-1951, AND MEASURES OF OCCUPATIONAL INTEGRATION, 1950, FOR THIRTY-SIX COLOR-SEX-AGE STATUS CONFIGURATIONS, UNITED STATES

Color-Sex-Age Status Configuration	(1) Mean Annual Suicide Rate	(2) Measure of Occupational Integration	(3) Rank of Column 1 Within Each Age Group	(4) Rank of Column 2 Within Each Age Group	(5) Rank of Column 1	(6) Rank of Column 2
WM* 14-19......	3.7	.1643	1	4	24	21
WF† 14-19......	1.7	.2230	3	3	35	11
NM‡ 14-19......	2.1	.2763	2	1	31	6
NF§ 14-19......	1.4	.2393	4	2	36	8
WM 20-24......	9.4	.1522	1	4	18	26
WF 20-24......	3.3	.2972	3	1	25	5
NM 20-24......	8.0	.1741	2	3	21	16
NF 20-24......	2.5	.1981	4	2	29.5	13
WM 25-29......	11.8	.1431	1	4	10	28
WF 25-29......	4.6	.2380	3	1	23	9
NM 25-29......	10.5	.1684	2	3	14	18.5
NF 25-29......	2.1	.2073	4	2	32	12
WM 30-34......	14.7	.1435	1	4	7	27
WF 30-34......	5.6	.1927	3	2	22	15
NM 30-34......	10.0	.1684	2	3	17	18.5
NF 30-34......	3.2	.2284	4	1	26	10
WM 35-44......	22.3	.1414	1	4	5	29
WF 35-44......	8.0	.1736	3	2	20	17
NM 35-44......	11.2	.1650	2	3	12	20
NF 35-44......	2.5	.2559	4	1	29.5	7
WM 45-54......	32.8	.1365	1	4	4	31
WF 45-54......	10.2	.1538	3	3	16	24
NM 45-54......	11.7	.1563	2	2	11	22
NF 45-54......	2.8	.2993	4	1	27	4
WM 55-59......	41.5	.1322	1	4	3	33
WF 55-59......	10.5	.1388	3	3	13	30
NM 55-59......	14.7	.1524	2	2	8	25
NF 55-59......	2.6	.3277	4	1	28	3
WM 60-64......	47.0	.1283	1	4	2	36
WF 60-64......	10.5	.1337	3	3	15	32
NM 60-64......	17.4	.1544	2	2	6	23
NF 60-64......	1.8	.3402	4	1	34	2
WM 65+......	54.3	.1290	1	4	1	35
WF 65+......	9.3	.1321	3	3	19	34
NM 65+......	12.7	.1940	2	2	9	14
NF 65+......	2.0	.3724	4	1	33	1

* WM, white male; † WF, white female; ‡ NM, nonwhite male; § NF, nonwhite female.

According to the major theorem, we should find that within each age group the ranks in columns 3 and 4 vary inversely. Figure 1 shows that this is substantially true.

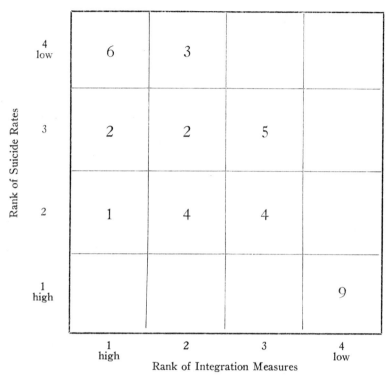

Fig. 1. RELATIONSHIP WITHIN AGE GROUPS BETWEEN RANKS OF THE SUICIDE RATES, 1949-1951, AND RANKS OF THE MEASURES OF OCCUPATIONAL INTEGRATION, 1950, FOR 36 COLOR-SEX-AGE CONFIGURATIONS IN THE UNITED STATES.

Whereas one would expect to be able to correctly predict the rank of the suicide rates on the basis of chance in 9 out of the 36 cases, knowledge of the occupational integration measure makes it possible to predict correctly in 21 of the cases. The ratio of correct predictions to that expected on the basis of chance is thus 21 to 9, or 2.3 to 1. Of the 15 errors, in only one instance is the rank predicted more than one removed from the actual rank. Or, stated differently, if there were no relationship between the ranks, at least 12 of the predicted ranks[6]

---

[6] The number in the cells two or more ranks from the diagonal would vary if all cases were distributed evenly, since 36 cases cannot be distributed uniformly in 16 cells.

would be more than one rank away from the diagonal cells, but only one deviation of such magnitude is observed.

A More Complex Test of the Major Theorem. Although measures of occupational integration have proved to have considerable predictive power regarding differences in suicide rates between and within age groups, they may be subjected to a more crucial test. When the data are brought together in one table (see Table 17), there are 36 color-sex-age status configurations, each of which has a measure of occupational integration and a suicide rate. If the major theorem is valid, there should be an inverse relationship here between the suicide rates and occupational integration measures shown in columns 1 and 2. Figure 2 reveals this to be substantially true.

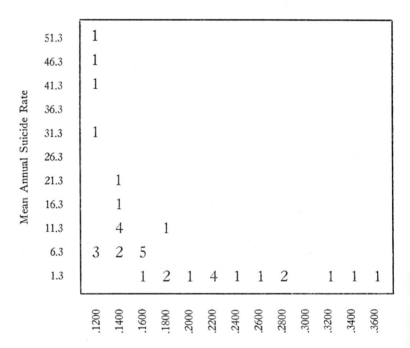

Measure of Occupational Integration

FIG. 2. RELATIONSHIP BETWEEN RANKS OF THE SUICIDE RATES, 1949-1951, AND RANKS OF THE MEASURES OF OCCUPATIONAL INTEGRATION, 1950, FOR 36 COLOR-SEX-AGE CONFIGURATIONS IN THE UNITED STATES.

Although Figures 2 makes it obvious that an inverse relationship holds between suicide rates and occupational integration measures, the strength of the relationship cannot be expressed by a product-moment coefficient of correlation because the relationship shown is clearly nonlinear.[7] Consequently, a rank-difference correlation was computed to gauge the predictive power of occupational integration measures. According to the major theorem, the ranks of suicide rates (column 5, Table 17) and the occupational integration measures (column 6, Table 17) would vary inversely. This proved true, with ρ equal to —.84. This demonstrates that measures of occupational integration have a considerable amount of predictive power in distinguishing color-sex-age status configurations with low suicide rates from those with high suicide rates.

SUMMARY

In this chapter, we have examined the relationship between age and suicide. Status integration measures were found to be associated inversely with suicide rates by age groups in different segments of the United States population. Additional tests demonstrated the ability of the major theorem to predict the rank order of the suicide rates of sex-color status configurations within age groups. In what was perhaps the most crucial test, it proved possible to correctly predict the approximate rank order of the suicide rates of 36 age-sex-color status configurations.

---

[7] This nonlinear relationship was not anticipated, and it remains one of several findings in this study that call for special attention in the subsequent development of the theory.

CHAPTER SEVEN

Differences in Suicide Rates by Color, Age, and Sex Within Individual States

OCCUPATIONS by color, sex, and age for 1950 have been reported by the Bureau of Census for 30 of the 48 states. These data, when coupled with suicide rates, make it possible to repeat in each state the tests reported for the United States as a whole in Chapter VI. Because of limited resources for research and the amount of work entailed, the tests have been repeated in only nine of the thirty states. These nine, selected to provide rough regional representation, are: California, Florida, Illinois, Massachusetts, Mississippi, New Jersey, Tennessee, Texas, and Washington.

TESTING HYPOTHESES BY INDIVIDUAL STATES

Because the tests for individual states correspond to those reported for the United States in Chapter VI,[1] we shall not repeat the formal hypothesis for each case. Because of space limitations, only a summary table of measures of the relationships is presented. (To obtain the work tables summarized in Table 18, see p. v.)

---

[1] The tests pertaining to whites, nonwhites, and the total population have not been repeated for the individual states because of the labor required to consolidate the data.

The first series of tests in each state was concerned with variability in suicide rates by age groups among males, females, white males, white females, nonwhite males, and nonwhite females. The variables employed were a suicide rate, 1948-1952,[2] and a measure of occupational integration, 1950,[3] for each age group, and they were treated identically to the United States data in Table 13. The results are reported for each of nine states in the first six columns of Table 18.

A general version of the first six hypotheses tested in each state reads as follows: *There will be an inverse relationship by age groups between suicide rates and measures of occupational integration.* In the analysis just presented, this hypothesis was tested on six different color-sex status configurations in each state with the following results:

White Males. Seven of the ρ's are negative as predicted, ranging in value from —.38 to —.98. There were two contradictory findings— +.47 for Mississippi and +.48 for Tennessee. In comparison, ρ for the United States is —.97.

White Females. The ρ's for all nine states are in the predicted direction and range from —.35 to —.90 as compared to —.83 for the United States.

Nonwhite Males. Values of ρ for six of the states were negative, ranging from —.07 to —.54. There were three cases of incorrect prediction, varying from +.18 to +.84. The United States ρ is —.72.

Nonwhite Females. Coefficients could be computed for only eight states. Six had negative signs as predicted and ranged from —.17 to —.77. The two contradictory findings are +.02 for Mississippi and +.58 for California. The value for the United States is —.21.

Males. Seven states have negative ρ's, with a range from —.23 to —.98. The two failures in prediction are +.32 for Tennessee and +.45 for Mississippi. The United States ρ is —.95.

Females. The ρ values are negative for all nine states, ranging from —.33 to —.92, as compared to —.87 for the nation.

---

[2] The number of resident suicides by color, sex, and age in each state was obtained from U. S. Department of Health, Education and Welfare, *Vital Statistics of the United States, 1948,* Vol. II; *1949,* Vol. II; *1950,* Vol. III; *1951,* Vol. II; *1952,* Vol. II. The population figures used to compute rates for each of the nine states were drawn from *U.S. Census of Population: 1950.* Vol. II, *General Characteristics,* Table 15.

[3] Occupations by color, sex, and age for each state are reported in *Census of Population: 1950.* Vol. II, Parts 5, 10, 13, 21, 24, 30, 42, 43, and 47.

Table 18. RELATIONSHIP BETWEEN MEASURES OF OCCUPATIONAL INTEGRATION, 1950, AND MEAN ANNUAL SUICIDE RATES, 1948-1952, BY COLOR-SEX-AGE STATUS CONFIGURATIONS IN SELECTED STATES, UNITED STATES

| States | v's by Nine Age Groups | | | | | | Predictions of Rank of Suicide Rate of Four Color-Sex Categories Within Each of Nine Age Groups | | | v's by 36 Color-Sex-Age Categories |
	Males	Females	White Males	White Females	Nonwhite Males	Nonwhite Females	Number Correct*	Ratio of Number Correct to Chance Expectancy†	Number of Errors of More Than One Rank	
California	−.95	−.73	−.95	−.72	+.84	+.58	17	1.9	2	−.63
Florida	−.80	−.72	−.47	−.37	−.47	−.23	23	2.6	1	−.80
Illinois	−.97	−.92	−.97	−.88	−.10	−.77	22	2.4	2	−.82
Massachusetts	−.95	−.90	−.97	−.90	−.25	−.17	12	1.3	6	−.60
Mississippi	+.45	−.33	+.47	−.35	+.27	+.02	4	0.4	12	−.15
New Jersey	−.98	−.90	−.98	−.90	−.07	−.24	22	2.4	0	−.76
Tennessee	+.32	−.57	+.48	−.38	−.54	−.17	25	2.8	7	−.63
Texas	−.23	−.70	−.38	−.62	−.32	−.17	19	2.1	1	−.73
Washington	−.88	−.52	−.88	−.52	+.18	‡	13	1.4	2	−.58

*Of a total of 36 predictions.
†One of every four predictions expected to be correct on a chance basis.
‡Insufficient number of cases.

In summary, out of 53 tests on color-sex status configurations in nine states, only 9 coefficients of rank difference correlation are not in the predicted direction.

In a second series of tests, the objective was to determine the consistency with which the rank of the suicide rate of a color-sex status configuration (white male, white female, nonwhite male, or nonwhite female) within an age group can be correctly predicted from the rank of its measure of occupational integration. For example, within the age group 25-29 in California, can the rank of the suicide rate of nonwhite males be correctly predicted from their measure of occupational integration? The predictions made in each state are like those made with reference to columns 3 and 4 of Table 17, which relate to the United States as a whole. The results of the predictions by states are shown in the "Predictions" columns of Table 18.

The ratio of correct predictions to that expected on a chance basis range from .4 to 1 in the case of Mississippi (the only state with a number of correct predictions less than that expected by chance) to 2.8 to 1 for Tennessee. In five of the nine states the ratio was more than 2 to 1. Only in a few cases of error in prediction do we find the rank predicted more than one rank removed from the actual rank. If in any test of the hypothesis there had been no relationship between the two sets of ranks, at least 12 of the cases would have been more than one rank from the diagonal cells.[4] If there had been no relationship between the ranks in all nine separate tests there would thus have been a total of at least 108 cases two ranks or more removed from the diagonal cells. In contrast, in only 33 instances is the rank predicted more than one rank removed from the actual rank.

The third and final series of state tests was concerned with an attempt to predict the rank of 36 color-sex status configurations from the rank of their measures of occupational integration, the two sets of ranks corresponding to those shown in the last two columns of Table 17. The relationships between the ranks in each state are expressed as values of ρ in the last column of Table 18.[5] The general hypothesis tested for each of the nine states reads: *There will be an inverse relationship by color-sex-age status configurations between suicide rates and measures of occupational integration.* In comparison to the ρ of —.84 for the United States, the values for the states range from —.15 for Mississippi

---

[4] See Chapter VI, note 6, regarding source of this figure.

[5] In each of the nine states, the relationship between the two variables proved to be highly curvilinear, corresponding to the relationship found in the United States as a whole. See Chapter VI, Figure 2.

to —.82 for Illinois. All values are negative as predicted. (To obtain the work tables summarized in Table 18, see p. v.)

INSTANCES OF NEGATIVE RESULTS

From both a practical and methodological point of view, negative results in the test of a theory are not entirely without value. An analysis of exceptions to the rule may lead to a further understanding of the phenomenon at hand and a reformulation of the theory so as to maximize its predictive power. One of the more serious shortcomings of the present study is the failure to adequately analyze instances of negative results. This is largely because of limited resources for research and the even more limited data.[6]

In consideration of the fact that occupational integration is only one of several dimensions of status integration that could operate to produce differences in suicide rates among age groups, it is not unexpected that cases arise in which measures of occupational integration fail to correlate inversely with suicide rates by age groups. Ideally, in every case where negative results have been obtained, measures other than that of occupational integration should be brought into play. Unfortunately, we have had to be content with the analysis of selected instances where the results of the test proved to be diametrically opposed to the major theorem. Three such cases occurred in the tests reported in this chapter. For both nonwhite males and females in California, measures of occupational integration varied directly and not inversely with suicide rates by age groups, ρ being $+.84$ for nonwhite males and $+.58$ for nonwhite females.

These negative results were not entirely unexpected since the category "nonwhite" is particularly heterogeneous in California. In addition, there remains the possibility that too many dimensions of status integration have been left uncontrolled[7] and, if all dimensions had been considered, the major theorem would have been supported.

As an exploratory step in considering additional statuses, measures of marital integration by age groups were computed for nonwhite males and females in California.[8] Measures of the degree of marital integra-

---

[6] For all practical purposes, only two dimensions of status integration other than occupational integration can be taken into account by age groups within states; these two are marital integration and labor force integration.

[7] There is no reason to believe that the effect of leaving a large number of dimensions of status integration uncontrolled is equal for whites and nonwhites.

[8] Data used to compute these measures were drawn from *U. S. Census of Population: 1950.* Vol. II, Part 5, California, Table 57, pp. 212-213.

tion within nine age groups for nonwhite males in that state are shown in Table 19. The ρ between the ranks is —.75.

Table 19. MEASURES OF MARITAL INTEGRATION, 1950, AND RANKS OF SUICIDE RATES, 1948-1952, FOR NONWHITE MALES BY AGE GROUPS, CALIFORNIA

Age Group	Rank of Suicide Rate	Measure of Marital Integration	Rank
15-19	9	.9356	1
20-24	6	.5244	7
25-29	7	.5250	6
30-34	8	.6554	2
35-44	5	.6318	3
45-54	4	.5910	4
55-59	3	.5322	5
60-64	2	.5209	8
65+	1	.4262	9

Measures of marital integration by age groups for nonwhite females in California are shown in Table 20. The ρ between the ranks is —.35.

Table 20. MEASURES OF MARITAL INTEGRATION, 1950, AND RANKS OF SUICIDE RATES, 1948-1952, FOR NONWHITE FEMALES BY AGE GROUPS, CALIFORNIA

Age Group	Rank of Suicide Rate	Measure of Marital Integration	Rank
15-19	9	.6849	2
20-24	8	.5199	6
25-29	6	.6754	3
30-34	5	.7270	1
35-44	3	.6701	4
45-54	2	.5353	5
55-59	7	.4519	8
60-64	1	.4275	9
65+	4	.4682	7

It would appear that for nonwhite males in California marital integration is of considerable importance, but this does not seem to be true for nonwhite females.

A third population which proved an outstanding exception to the rule of an inverse relationship between measures of occupational integration and suicide rates by age groups is the white males of Tennessee. Table 21 gives measures of marital integration by age groups for the population in question.

The ρ between the ranks shown in the table is $-.22$. This low correlation, when coupled with negative results for occupational integration, indicates that differences in suicide rates of white male age groups in Tennessee must be attributed to factors other than occupational and marital integration.

Table 21. MEASURES OF MARITAL INTEGRATION, 1950, AND RANKS OF SUICIDE RATES, 1948-1952, FOR WHITE MALES BY AGE GROUPS, TENNESSEE

Age Group	Rank of Suicide Rate	Measure of Marital Integration	Rank
15-19	9	.9039	1
20-24	8	.4864	9
25-29	7	.6712	7
30-34	6	.7724	4
35-44	5	.8173	2
45-54	4	.8050	3
55-59	3	.6897	6
60-64	2	.7258	5
65+	1	.5750	8

CONCLUSIONS

In evaluating the tests by states which are reported in this chapter, we find that nonwhites conform to the major theorem less than whites, which was also true for the United States as a whole for 1950. Negative results in testing nonwhites are to be expected, as we noted earlier, since it is a heterogeneous category and may mask a high degree of status integration among specific races. Also, it is possible that dimensions of status integration other than occupational may account for differences in the suicide rates of nonwhite age groups; this is confirmed by the relationship between measures of marital integration and suicide rates by nonwhite age groups in California, especially nonwhite males.

Speaking in terms of states as a whole rather than particular color-sex-age status configurations, it is obvious that Mississippi is a negative case as far as the major theorem is concerned. We think that a considerable amount of masking of status integration may have occurred in all states as a consequence of not having separate measures for the rural and urban residents within each state. In states with a small farm population, the failure to distinguish between rural and urban residents probably has negligible consequences as far as the masking of status integration is concerned. But, if masking does occur and in proportion to the size of the rural population, it would influence the results for Mississippi to a considerable degree.[9] Since it is not possible to obtain either suicide rates or occupation by age, sex, and color for the rural and urban populations separately, the effect of a failure to distinguish between the two remains unknown. This is one of several crucial questions that cannot be answered until additional data are made available.

---

[9] It could be argued that the effect of the failure to distinguish between urban and rural residents is a constant from one age group to the next; but this assumes an identical age structure for the rural and urban populations, which is not the case. Further, because of differences in the occupational structures of age groups, the failure to distinguish between rural and urban does not influence measures of occupational integration in the same way for all age groups.

CHAPTER EIGHT

Suicide
and Marital Status

OBSERVATIONS on the variability in suicide rates by marital status offer a strong temptation to indulge in *ad hoc* explanations. When it is noted that married persons in a society tend to have lower suicide rates than those who are single, widowed, or divorced, the difference is likely to be all too easily understood. Thus, it would appear to be self-evident that married persons are less lonely, better adjusted, and more accepted than the single, widowed, or divorced. There are at least three problems present in such explanations, however: The alleged differences between married and unmarried persons may prove to be fictitious; then, granting that the differences do exist, before they can become acceptable explanations they must also account for forms of variability in suicide rates other than varibality by marital status, i.e., the self-evident reasons for the differences must be derived from a general theory; and, finally, an explanation of the greater immunity to suicide of the married must also account for the fact that this immunity is variable. As we shall see, the immunity to suicide enjoyed by married persons is relative to age. As one goes up or down the age scale in a society, the immunity of married persons, either in absolute terms or relative to the other marital statuses, varies considerably, even to the point where the suicide rate of married persons in certain age groups is higher than that of one or more of the other marital statuses.

Consistent with the general theory, variability in suicide rates by marital status and an inconstant immunity to suicide provided by a particular marital status are conceived in the present study as being primarily a function of status integration.

VARIABILITY IN SUICIDE RATES BY AGE AND
INTEGRATION OF MARITAL STATUS WITH AGE

Before undertaking a formal analysis of variability in suicide rates by marital status, some attention should be given to their variability by age, which has heretofore been treated only as a function of the integration of occupation with age. Though a person's occupational status in the United States is undoubtedly a crucial one, the same may be said for marital status. Consequently, in line with the major theorem, it should be expected that differences in suicide rates by age would be linked to the integration of marital status with age as well as occupation.

Three Type 2 (between-columns) hypotheses have been tested regarding suicide rates by age and their connection to the integration of marital status with age. They may be summarized in the following proposition: *Suicide rates by age groups vary inversely with measures of the integration of marital status with age.*

Table 22. MEASURES OF THE INTEGRATION OF MARITAL STATUS WITH AGE
FOR TEN AGE GROUPS, UNITED STATES, 1950

Age Group	Single	Marital Status Married	Marital Status Widowed	Divorced	Measure of Status Integration (ΣX^2)
15-19	.8980	.0991	.0010	.0020	.8162
20-24	.4529	.5311	.0030	.0129	.4874
25-34	.1488	.8199	.0079	.0235	.6950
35-44	.0893	.8563	.0237	.0307	.7427
45-54	.0818	.8155	.0704	.0322	.6777
55-59	.0800	.7604	.1324	.0272	.6028
60-64	.0838	.6961	.1969	.0232	.5309
65-69	.0857	.6097	.2857	0189	.4611
70-74	.0870	.5119	.3864	.0147	.4191
75+	.0873	.3383	.5651	.0093	.4415

Hypothesis No. 1. The first hypothesis tested reads as follows: *In the United States, there will be an inverse relationship by age groups between suicide rates and measures of the integration of marital status with age.* Table 22 provides an illustration of the measure of the integration of marital status with age.[1]

---

[1] Population figures for marital status by age and sex used in this study have been drawn from the *U.S. Census of Population: 1950.* Vol. II, *Characteristics of the Population,* Part 1, United States Summary, Table 103, p. 181.

It should be noted that what would ordinarily be columns in a table designed to measure status integration are rows in this particular table. Consequently, the measures of marital integration for each age group are found at the end of the rows and not, as before, at the bottom of the columns.

Table 23 gives suicide rates[2] for the age groups shown in Table 22 and their corresponding measures of the integration of marital status with age. The hypothesis stated above was tested by computing a rank-difference correlation between the ranks given in Table 23. The coefficient proved to be —.79.

Table 23. MEASURES OF THE INTEGRATION OF MARITAL STATUS WITH AGE, 1950, AND SUICIDE RATES BY AGE, 1949-1951, UNITED STATES

Age Group	Mean Annual Suicide Rate	Rank of Suicide Rate	Measure of the Integration of Marital Status with Age	Rank of Measure
15-19	2.6	10	.8162	1
20-24	6.2	9	.4874	7
25-34	8.8	8	.6950	3
35-44	14.2	7	.7427	2
45-54	20.2	6	.6777	4
55-59	24.8	5	.6028	5
60-64	27.5	4	.5309	6
65-69	28.2	3	.4611	8
70-74	28.6	2	.4191	10
75+	29.9	1	.4415	9

Hypothesis No. 2. The second hypothesis considered reads as follows: *For males in the United States, there will be an inverse relationship by age groups between measures of the integration of marital status with age and suicide rates.* Table 24 gives measures of the integration of marital status with age and suicide rates for ten age groups. The value of ρ for the two sets of values in the table proved to be —.59.

Hypothesis No. 3. The third hypothesis tested reads as follows: *For females in the United States, there will be an inverse relationship by age groups between measures of the integration of marital status with age and suicide rates.* Table 25 gives measures of the integration of marital status with age and suicide rates for ten age groups. Here, ρ proved to be —.66.

---

[2] The suicide rates used in this chapter are for the years 1949-1951. For the source of the data used in their computation, see Chapter VI, note 3.

Table 24. MEASURES OF THE INTEGRATION OF MARITAL STATUS WITH AGE, 1950, AND SUICIDE RATES BY AGE, 1949-1951, FOR MALES, UNITED STATES

Age Group	Mean Annual Suicide Rate	Rank of Suicide Rate	Measure of the Integration of Marital Status with Age	Rank of Measure
15-19	3.5	10	.9361	1
20-24	9.3	9	.5086	9
25-34	13.0	8	.6610	5
35-44	21.1	7	.7668	2
45-54	30.8	6	.7434	3
55-59	39.5	5	.7017	4
60-64	45.0	4	.6461	6
65-69	47.7	3	.5782	7
70-74	50.4	2	.5122	8
75+	56.8	1	.4291	10

Possibilities for Future Research. For the most part the present study has been restricted to a consideration of occupational integration; consequently, a great deal of research remains to be done regarding the influence of marital integration on variability in suicide rates. Available data pertaining to marital status have by no means been exhausted, and future investigations will find it possible to repeat virtually every test in the present study that involved occupational integration by sub-

Table 25. MEASURES OF THE INTEGRATION OF MARITAL STATUS WITH AGE, 1950, AND SUICIDE RATES BY AGE, 1949-1951, FOR FEMALES, UNITED STATES

Age Group	Mean Annual Suicide Rate	Rank of Suicide Rate	Measure of the Integration of Marital Status with Age	Rank of Measure
15-19	1.6	10	.7151	3
20-24	3.2	9	.5350	6
25-34	4.8	8	.7311	1
35-44	7.5	7	.7203	2
45-54	9.5	4	.6218	4
55-59	10.0	1	.5262	7
60-64	9.9	3	.4566	8
65-69	9.9	2	.4153	10
70-74	8.6	5	.4263	9
75+	7.7	6	.5510	5

stituting marital integration. However, while a series of tests of the major theorem in terms of marital integration would be a first step, future research should seek to combine measures of marital and occupational integration. Under ideal conditions, any table used to measure integration would include both occupational and marital statuses. Since the nature of the data now available precludes their treatment on this

89

level, the most appropriate alternative lies in separate measures of marital and occupational integration for each population. The combination of separate measures will not be as simple as might appear, because the proportion of the population influenced by the two measures must be taken into account as well as the fact that the two have different minimal values. Regardless of the amount of labor involved, however, the combination of the two measures may well prove to be of singular importance, since they vary independently of each other in certain cases.

PROBLEMS IN PREDICTION

It has been noted previously[3] that the major theorem generates predictions concerning suicide rates for the individual cells in a status integration table. Heretofore, the report has been focused only on the integration of a status configuration with a family of statuses and with total status integration. This is because of the limitations imposed on the study by the absence of data on suicide rates for status configurations that include occupational statuses in the United States.

With the publication by the National Office of Vital Statistics of data pertaining to suicide by marital status in the United States, 1949-1951,[4] there is a most fortunate opportunity for a Type 1 test of the major theorem. The figures in each cell of Table 26 represent the proportion of persons of a given age with a given marital status. In terms of the theory, the proportions constitute measures of status integration. The major theorem calls for an inverse relationship to hold between measures of status integration and suicide rates by marital statuses within each age group. Thus, for example, within the age group, 65-69, in Table 22, the major theorem calls for married persons to have the lowest suicide rate; the widowed, the next to the lowest; the single, next to the highest; and the divorced, the highest. With reports of suicide by age and marital status, it is possible to compare the suicide rates for the four marital statuses within the age group, 65-69, and evaluate the accuracy of the predictions that follow from the major theorem. Stated in terms of a formal hypothesis, the predictions read: *Within each age group in the United States, there will be an inverse relationship between measures of the integration of marital status with age and suicide rates by marital status.*

Table 26 gives suicide rates and measures of the integration of mari-

---

[3] See Chapter III, p. 39.
[4] U. S. Department of Health, Education and Welfare "Mortality from Selected Causes by Marital Status, United States, 1949-1951," *Vital Statistics—Special Reports,* Vol. 39 (1956), pp. 370-371, and 426-427.

Table 26. MEASURES OF THE INTEGRATION OF MARITAL STATUS WITH AGE, 1950, AND MEAN ANNUAL SUICIDE RATES, 1949-1951, BY MARITAL STATUS AND AGE, UNITED STATES

Age Group	Single				Married				Widowed				Divorced			
	MSI*	Rank of MSI	SR†	Rank of SR	MSI	Rank of MSI	SR	Rank of SR	MSI	Rank of MSI	SR	Rank of SR	MSI	Rank of MSI	SR	Rank of SR
15-19	.898	1	2.4	4	.099	2	3.4	2	.001	4	3.2	3	.002	3	12.6	1
20-24	.453	2	7.6	3	.531	1	4.5	4	.003	4	24.3	1	.013	3	16.7	2
25-34	.149	2	16.0	3	.820	1	6.7	4	.008	4	22.8	2	.024	3	29.6	1
35-44	.089	2	23.1	2	.856	1	12.0	4	.024	4	20.1	3	.031	3	43.6	1
45-54	.082	2	30.4	2	.816	1	17.3	4	.070	3	23.7	3	.032	4	54.2	1
55-59	.080	3	42.4	2	.760	1	21.8	4	.132	2	23.4	3	.027	4	54.1	1
60-64	.084	3	43.9	2	.696	1	24.0	4	.197	2	24.7	3	.023	4	72.2	1
65-69	.086	3	45.7	2	.610	1	24.7	4	.286	2	25.1	3	.019	4	67.9	1
70-74	.087	3	46.1	2	.512	1	25.6	3	.386	2	25.1	4	.015	4	80.0	1
75+	.087	3	39.2	2	.338	2	28.5	3	.565	1	27.0	4	.009	4	90.5	1

* Measure of status integration.
† Suicide rate.

tal status with age for four marital statuses within ten age groups in the United States. In analyzing Table 26 and similar tables which follow, it should be noted that suicide rates and measures of status integration are to be read within rows and not within columns. For purposes of presentation, what would ordinarily be the columns in a table designed to measure status integration are rows in Table 26.

Rather than compute a rank-difference correlation between the ranks within each of the ten age groups in Table 26, the hypothesis just stated has been evaluated in terms of the number of correct predictions that follow from it. According to the hypothesis, one should expect to find in Table 26 that within each of the age groups the ranks of the measures of the integration of marital status with age and the ranks of the suicide rates are inverted. Thus, any cell with a rank of four for the measure of the integration of marital status with age should have a rank of one for its suicide rate and vice versa. Figure 3 is a scatter dia-

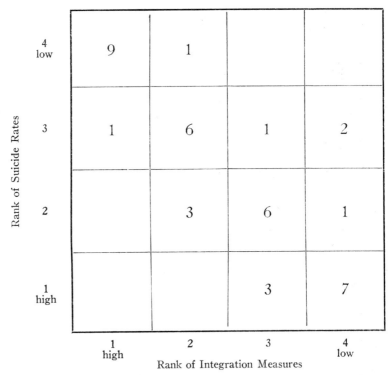

FIG. 3. RELATIONSHIP WITHIN AGE GROUPS BETWEEN RANKS OF THE SUICIDE RATES, 1949-1951, AND RANKS OF THE MEASURES OF MARITAL STATUS WITH AGE, 1950, FOR 40 AGE-MARITAL STATUS CONFIGURATIONS IN THE UNITED STATES.

gram showing the relationship between the ranks for the forty cells (status configurations) in Table 26.

The pattern anticipated by the hypothesis is definitely present in this figure. Within an age group, the marital status with a low suicide rate has a high measure of status integration. On the basis of chance, one would expect thirty errors in forty predictions of the rank of the suicide rate of a marital status within an age group; Figure 3 shows only 12 errors made in 40 predictions. That is, the ratio of correct predictions to that expected on the basis of chance is 28 to 10, or 2.8 to 1. It is also of interest to note that, of the 12 errors in prediction, in only two cases is the predicted rank more than one rank removed from the actual rank.

The importance of the type of test reported above lies not only in demonstrating the applicability of the major theorem to statuses other than occupation but also in the evidence it brings to bear on a serious question regarding the theory as a whole. In testing the major theorem on an intersocietal level, the independent variable is a measure of total status integration. In purely empirical terms, this measure is indicative of the degree to which persons in a society do or do not conform to a pattern in their occupancy of statuses. Now it could be argued that a low measure of total status integration for a society is merely indicative of the fact that the exercise of individual choice in the society is particularly prevalent. If this prevalence is accompanied, as Fromm maintains,[5] by a growing sense of isolation and moral aloneness, then a society with a low measure might have a high suicide rate without the status configurations with the lowest degree of status integration necessarily having the highest suicide rates within the society. Given this possibility, within-columns tests of the major theorem (using a Type 1 measure of status integration) are of considerable importance; for, when successful, they demonstrate that it is the infrequently occupied status configurations which are characterized by high suicide rates.

The results of the within-column test reported above are also of significance in that they bring evidence to bear against what might be a fundamental objection to the theory of status integration. It could be argued that while all incompatible status configurations may be infrequently occupied, not all infrequently occupied status configurations are the incompatible ones. This is tantamount to holding that a low measure of status integration may be a necessary condition for reflecting incompatible statuses, but not a sufficient one. In terms of the theory,

---

[5] Erich Fromm, *Escape from Freedom* (New York, 1941), pp. 24-39.

Table 27. MEASURES OF THE INTEGRATION OF MARITAL STATUS WITH AGE, 1950, AND MEAN ANNUAL SUICIDE RATES, 1949-1951, FOR MALES BY MARITAL STATUS AND AGE, UNITED STATES

Age Group	Single				Married				Widowed				Divorced			
	MSI*	Rank of MSI	SR†	Rank of SR	MSI	Rank of MSI	SR	Rank of SR	MSI	Rank of MSI	SR	Rank of SR	MSI	Rank of MSI	SR	Rank of SR
15-19	.967	1	3.4	3	.031	2	6.6	2	.001	3	0.0	4	.001	4	13.6	1
20-24	.591	1	10.2	3	.399	2	7.1	4	.002	4	66.2	1	.009	3	28.2	2
25-34	.187	2	22.7	3	.791	1	9.5	4	.003	4	65.9	1	.019	3	50.7	2
35-44	.096	2	37.1	3	.870	1	17.2	4	.009	4	59.7	2	.025	3	80.8	1
45-54	.085	2	49.7	3	.857	1	25.6	4	.028	4	64.4	2	.030	3	94.5	1
55-59	.083	2	71.6	2	.831	1	32.7	4	.059	3	63.3	3	.027	4	90.7	1
60-64	.086	3	76.4	2	.793	1	36.2	4	.096	2	64.7	3	.025	4	111.1	1
65-69	.087	3	82.1	2	.740	1	36.8	4	.150	2	65.8	3	.023	4	104.9	1
70-74	.083	3	89.1	2	.675	1	37.3	4	.222	2	66.9	3	.019	4	117.4	1
75+	.078	3	87.2	2	.524	1	38.6	4	.385	2	71.3	3	.013	4	134.8	1

* Measure of status integration.
† Suicide rate.

94

this would mean that all status configurations with a high suicide rate would tend to have a low degree of status integration (be infrequently occupied) but status configurations with a low degree of status integration may have either high, medium, or low suicide rates. As an inspection of Table 26 will show, this is definitely not the case. Within age groups, it is found that not only do the status configurations with high suicide rates tend to have low measures of status integration but also that status configurations with a low degree of status integration tend to have high suicide rates. In short, in this particular case, a low degree of status integration appears to be both a necessary and sufficient condition for a high suicide rate.

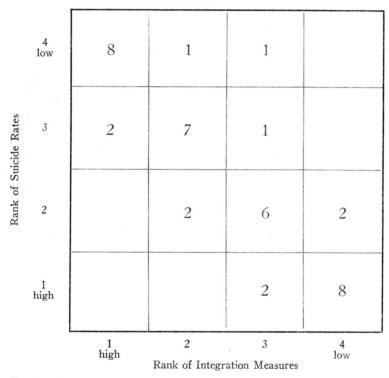

FIG. 4. RELATIONSHIP WITHIN AGE GROUPS BETWEEN RANKS OF THE SUICIDE RATES, 1949, 1951, AND RANKS OF THE MEASURES OF THE INTEGRATION OF MARITAL STATUS WITH AGE, 1950, FOR 40 AGE-MARITAL STATUS CONFIGURATIONS AMONG MALES IN THE UNITED STATES.

A Second Problem in Prediction. A second hypothesis regarding the relationship between suicide rates and measures of marital integration

Table 28. MEASURES OF THE INTEGRATION OF MARITAL STATUS WITH AGE, 1950, AND MEAN ANNUAL SUICIDE RATES, 1949-1951, FOR FEMALES BY MARITAL STATUS AND AGE, UNITED STATES

Age Group	Single				Married				Widowed				Divorced			
	MSI*	Rank of MSI	SR†	Rank of SR	MSI	Rank of MSI	SR	Rank of SR	MSI	Rank of MSI	SR	Rank of SR	MSI	Rank of MSI	SR	Rank of SR
15-19	.829	1	1.3	4	.167	2	2.8	3	.001	4	6.3	2	.003	3	12.3	1
20-24	.323	2	3.2	3	.656	1	3.0	4	.004	4	9.2	2	.017	3	10.6	1
25-34	.113	2	5.6	3	.847	1	4.2	4	.012	4	12.3	2	.028	3	15.8	1
35-44	.083	2	7.7	3	.843	1	6.8	4	.038	3	10.9	2	.036	4	18.2	1
45-54	.078	3	9.9	3	.776	1	8.4	4	.111	2	13.5	2	.035	4	20.7	1
55-59	.077	3	11.6	3	.691	1	8.8	4	.205	2	12.1	2	.027	4	17.2	1
60-64	.082	3	10.1	3	.601	1	8.1	4	.297	2	12.1	2	.021	4	26.5	1
65-69	.084	3	10.7	3	.489	1	7.9	4	.411	2	11.5	2	.015	4	18.2	1
70-74	.090	3	10.7	2	.366	2	6.1	4	.533	1	9.5	3	.011	4	22.1	1
75+	.095	3	6.8	3	.187	2	5.4	4	.712	1	8.2	2	.006	4	15.1	1

* Measure of status integration.
† Suicide rate.

Rank of Suicide Rates	Rank of Integration Measures: 1 high	2	3	4 low
4 low	8	2		
3	1	4	5	
2	1	4	2	3
1 high			3	7

FIG. 5. RELATIONSHIP WITHIN AGE GROUPS BETWEEN RANKS OF THE SUICIDE RATES, 1949-1951, AND RANKS OF THE MEASURES OF THE INTEGRATION OF MARITAL STATUS WITH AGE, 1950, FOR 40 AGE-MARITAL STATUS CONFIGURATIONS AMONG FEMALES IN THE UNITED STATES.

within age groups reads as follows: *Within each age group of the male population in the United States there will be an inverse relationship between measures of status integration and suicide rates by marital statuses.* Table 27 provides the data required for a test of the hypothesis.

As with Table 26, the hypothesis calls for an inverse relationship to hold between the ranks of the suicide rates and the ranks of the measures of integration for the four marital statuses within each age group. Figure 4 shows the relationship that holds between the ranks.

On the basis of chance, one would expect correct predictions of the rank of the suicide rate in only 10 out of 40 cases. We find instead that correct predictions can be made in 29 out of 40 cases. Whereas one would expect 30 errors on the basis of chance, only 11 errors are found. The ratio of the number of correct predictions to that expected by chance is thus 29 to 10, or 2.9 to 1. In only one out of the 11 cases of error in prediction do we find a rank more than one removed from that anticipated.

A Third Problem in Prediction. A third hypothesis regarding the relationship between suicide rates and measures of marital integration within age groups reads as follows: *Within each age group of the female population of the United States there will be an inverse relationship between measures of integration and suicide rates by marital statuses.*

The hypothesis constitutes a prediction that there will be an inverse relationship between the ranks shown for each of the ten age groups in Table 28. Figure 5 graphically represents the degree with which correct predictions can be made.

Although the anticipated pattern of an inverse relationship between measures of the integration of marital status with age and suicide rates is definitely present among females in the United States, the number of errors made in predicting the rank of one from the rank of the other is considerably more than is the case for males. Whereas ten predictions would be expected to be correct on the basis of chance, 21 correct predictions can be made, a ratio of 2.1 to 1. Although the number of errors in prediction is only 11 less than would be expected on the basis of chance (19 as compared to 30), in only one case out of the 19 errors does one find a rank more than one removed from that predicted.

Durkheim's Problem. Durkheim was one of the first persons to make an exhaustive analysis of the relative immunity of the married to suicide. In his analysis of the ratio of the suicide rates of unmarried persons to the suicide rates of married persons, Durkheim noted that the ratios, which he called "coefficients of preservation," vary considerably with age and sex. The variability was of such extent that Durkheim was led to believe that being married plays only a minor part in providing immunity to suicide. "The immunity of married persons in general is thus due, wholly for one sex and largely for the other, to the influence not of conjugal society but of family society" (page 189). Though we agree with Durkheim that the presence or absence of children is an important factor (since they determine one of a person's statuses), the variability in the immunity of married persons to suicide relative to the unmarried is, in terms of the present theory, not only understandable but expected for reasons above and beyond the presence or absence of children. In contrast to Durkheim, the present theory holds that there is nothing inherent in any status that will provide invariable immunity to suicide; it is always a matter of the context of a status. This being the case, one would expect that the immunity of married persons is relative. The present study has concentrated on variation by age in the immunity of married persons to suicide relative to other marital statuses.

Table 29. RATIO OF SUICIDE RATES OF WIDOWED PERSONS TO MARRIED PERSONS, 1949-1951, AND RATIO OF MEASURES OF INTEGRATION WITH AGE FOR STATUS OF MARRIED TO STATUS OF WIDOWED BY AGE GROUPS, 1950, UNITED STATES

Age Group	Ratio of Suicide Rate of Widowed to Married	Rank	Ratio of Integration Measure of Married to Widowed	Rank
15-19	.97	9	99.1	3
20-24	5.40	1	177.0	1
25-34	3.40	2	103.8	2
35-44	1.67	3	36.1	4
45-54	1.37	4	11.6	5
55-59	1.07	5	5.7	6
60-64	1.03	6	3.5	7
65-69	1.01	7	2.1	8
70-74	.98	8	1.3	9
75+	.95	10	.6	10

The first column in Table 29 illustrates the problem to which Durkheim devoted much attention. The ratios of the suicide rates of widowed persons to married persons as shown there leave little doubt that the comparative immunity of married persons to suicide is relative to age. In terms of the present theory, variation by age in these ratios should be linked to variation in the ratios of the measure of integration with age for the married status to the widowed status. The latter variable is shown in the next to the last column of Table 29. The hypothesis reads as follows: *There will be a direct relationship by age groups between the ratio of the suicide rate of widowed persons to married persons and the ratio of the measure of integration with age for the status of married to the status of widowed.* This hypothesis was tested by computing a rank-difference correlation between the ranks given in Table 29. The value of ρ is $+.75$.

Following the procedure described above, eight additional hypotheses were tested regarding variation by age groups in the immunity of married persons to suicide relative to the other three marital statuses. Since each of the eight was tested in the same way as the one stated above, only coefficients of correlation need be shown; however, each of the tests can be replicated on the basis of the data given in Tables 26-28. (To obtain the work tables summarized in Table 30, see p. v.) Table

30 shows the results of the tests, including the one already reported. In a total of nine tests, the relationship was without exception in the direction anticipated by the hypotheses.

Table 30. RELATIONSHIP BETWEEN THE RATIO OF THE SUICIDE RATE OF UNMARRIED TO MARRIED, 1949-1951, AND THE RATIO OF THE STATUS INTEGRATION MEASURE OF MARRIED TO UNMARRIED, 1959, BY AGE GROUPS, UNITED STATES

	Both Sexes			Males			Females		
	Single to Married	Widowed to Married	Divorced to Married	Single to Married	Widowed to Married	Divorced to Married	Single to Married	Widowed to Married	Divorced to Married
ρ	+.53	+.75	+.65	+.05	+.65	+.60	+.03	+.73	+.62

The Question of Selectivity. In accord with their urge to explain all behavior in psychological terms, opponents of a sociological theory of differences in suicide rates dismiss the empirical regularities which support the theory by appealing to the concept of selectivity. They argue that a given sociological condition does not generate a high suicide rate—if a sociological condition is associated with a high suicide rate, it is because the condition attracts persons who are (for one reason or another) predisposed to suicide. A proponent of the selectivity notion[6] would have no difficulty explaining the regularities revealed in the analysis of Tables 26-28. He would argue that suicide-prone people are either unsuited for marriage and remain single[7] or fail in marriage and become divorced, and therefore suicide rates are higher for the unmarried.

What the advocate of the selectivity notion must ignore, however, is that considerable differences are found within age groups among the suicide rates of the single, widowed, and divorced, and these differences are in line with differences in measures of status integration. The notion that the married have low suicide rates because marriage attracts the "healthy" persons in a society can be questioned on the grounds that the suicide rate of the married, as witness the findings, varies tremendously from one age group to the next. Perhaps the most devastating evidence against the selectivity notion, however, is the findings reported

---

[6] It can hardly be called a theory, since its advocates are apparently unable to formulate a general proposition as to what conditions do or do not attract the suicide-prone. The advocates of selectivity appear to be able to make their argument only after the fact of a high suicide rate for a given sociological condition is established.

[7] It may be claimed, of course, that the widowed are unsuited for marriage and find it difficult to remarry.

in this section of the chapter. On the basis of the data reported in Tables 26-28 it can be shown that the ratio of the suicide rate of the single, widowed, or divorced to the married varies considerably by age groups. In the face of change in the immunity of the married by age groups, it is difficult if not impossible to see how the married are healthy, as a result of selectivity, in one age group but not in another. This becomes even more evident when one considers that the suicide rate of the married more nearly approximates that of the other marital statuses in the older age groups,[8] and in some of the older age groups may actually be slightly higher than that of the widowed (see Table 29).[9] Whereas the selectivity notion presents the married as the more "healthy" segments of a population, they actually have a suicide rate that may be higher in certain cases than that of one of the "unhealthy" segments of the population.

In passing, it should also be mentioned that selectivity does not explain differences in suicide rates by race and sex; ascribed race and sex statuses do not attract individuals, "unhealthy" or otherwise.

RESULTS OF TESTS OF THE MAJOR THEOREM
ON MARITAL STATUS

In evaluating the above tests of the major theorem on marital status, one must remember that all of the tests have ignored a large number of statuses. In the face of the results reported in earlier chapters, the tests should have at least included occupational status. Since the nature of available data precludes such control, we can only speculate as to the consequences of leaving occupational statuses uncontrolled. Although the effect of decreasing occupational integration with increasing age has probably been controlled to some extent by comparing the suicide rates of marital statuses within the same age group, there are no assurances that the integration of occupation with age decreases uniformly for each of the four marital statuses.

When a family of statuses is ignored in a test of the major theorem, the implicit assumption is that the influence of that family remains constant insofar as the persons occupying the status configurations are concerned. In some cases there is no way of knowing the extent to which the assumption is justified. In other cases, however, there is consider-

---

[8] It should also be noted that, consistent with the theory, it is at this point (among the older age groups) that measures of status integration for the married more nearly approximate those of the other marital status.

[9] Again, it should be noted that it is the widowed who have status integration measures in the older age groups that are as high if not higher than the married.

able evidence that it is not justified. One such instance happens to be found in a particular marital status. In comparing the measures of the integration of the four marital statuses with age it is obvious that the influence of one ignored family of statuses is variable for only three of the four marital statuses. This family relates to parental status and remains constant only for single persons.[10] Though it cannot be assumed that the influence of parental status among the married, widowed, and divorced is brought under control simply because it is variable for all three, it is obvious that its being ignored creates a more systematic bias when one is comparing single persons to married persons than is true when one is comparing the divorced or widowed to the married.

The factor of parental status is not, however, the only variable that operates to create a systematic bias peculiar to single persons. It was noted earlier[11] that a definitive test of the major theorem would include a comparison of the suicide rates of persons who have occupied different status configurations for the same length of time. When the factor of time is ignored, it is assumed that the persons in the status configurations being compared have occupied them for approximately the same number of months or years. But it is clearly obvious that this assumption is not justified in the comparison within age groups of single persons to married, widowed, or divorced persons. Whereas the single person has been single all of his life, the length of time that persons have been married, widowed, or divorced bears no necessary relationship to their age. As far as the single persons are concerned, there is a systematic bias operating to give them the highest average length of occupancy within each age group.

There is some evidence in the results of the tests reported above that the factor of time in the occupancy of statuses may well be of considerable importance. In three tests,[12] regarding the connection by age between measures of marital integration status and suicide rates, it may be seen that the age group, 20-24, is an outstanding exception to the rule of an inverse relationship between the two variables. While the 20-24 group has a low measure of marital integration, its suicide rate is also low. However, on the basis of age alone it is obvious that persons in this age group have been exposed to a low degree of marital integration, for only a comparatively short period of time. In line with the previously advanced belief that the consequences of a lack of status

---

[10] This is ignoring the relatively few cases of parenthood among single persons, where, it must be admitted, parenthood may be a markedly important status when it does occur.

[11] See p. 46.

[12] See pp. 87-89.

integration are not instantaneous, it is then not surprising to find that the age group, 20-24, has a suicide rate not commensurate with its measure of marital integration.

In view of the fact that a systematic bias probably operates as a consequence of ignoring parental status and the factor of time, it is not altogether unexpected to find that both of the two cases of clear-cut negative results in the tests of the major theorem in this chapter[13] involve a comparison of the suicide rates of single persons to married persons. The fact that a corresponding test involving single persons of both sexes yielded somewhat more positive results does, of course, complicate the matter. Even here, however, the coefficient of correlation is lower than any of those found in tests involving other marital statuses.

The inference should not be drawn from the foregoing comments that the failure of the tests involving a comparison of single persons to married persons is to be dismissed as irrelevant. Taken at face value, the tests must be recognized as constituting negative evidence as far as the theory is concerned.

In pointing to the inadequacies of the data employed in the tests, it should be remembered that while the inability to take parental status and the factor of time in the occupancy of statuses into account applies particularly to single persons, it also gives us an inferior test for the other marital statuses. Even for the married, widowed, and divorced, it is unreasonable to expect anything approaching perfect results as long as parental status and the factor of time remain uncontrolled.

The possibilities for refined tests of the major theorem are severely limited, at least in the United States. Even if it were possible, through the use of available data, to take more statuses into account in the measurement of marital integration, suicide rates can only be computed for marital status by age, sex, and color. Future research will be able to go beyond the present study by testing the hypotheses for whites and nonwhites separately, but other possibilities of a more fruitful nature are virtually nil with the available data. We mentioned earlier that the one exception is the combination of measures of occupational and marital integration by age groups.

---

[13] See Table 30.

CHAPTER NINE

Replication of Tests on 1940 Data for the United States

IN THE PRECEDING chapters, the results of a series of tests of hypotheses derived from the major theorem were presented. These tests, which made use of various measures of status integration, related to the United States as of 1950, and the results provide strong support for the theory. This cannot be taken to mean, however, that the major theorem will hold for all places and all times. As part of an attempt to establish the universality of the relationship between status integration and suicide rates, another series of tests was conducted for the United States—for the year 1940. The tests were made, within the limits imposed by the availablity of data and resources for research, replications of those conducted on the basis of 1950 statistics.

OCCUPATIONAL INTEGRATION AND SUICIDE RATES

Suicide Rates by Race and Sex. One of the crucial tests for a theory of variability in suicide rates is the prediction of differences in suicide rates among race-sex configurations.[1] With this in mind, 1940 measures of occupational integration and mean annual suicide rates,[2] 1939-

---

[1] See pp. 60-61.

[2] Data used to compute suicide rates were drawn from: *Vital Statistics of the United States, 1939,* Table 10; *Vital Statistics of the United States, 1940,* Table 11;

1941, were computed for six race-sex status configurations. These are shown in Table 31. The measures of status integration in this table are similar to those used in the 1950 test,[3] which also involved six race-sex configurations.[4]

Table 31. MEASURES OF OCCUPATIONAL INTEGRATION, 1940, AND MEAN ANNUAL SUICIDE RATES, 1939-1941, FOR SIX RACE-SEX CONFIGURATIONS, UNITED STATES

Occupational Category	Race-Sex					
	White Male	White Female	Negro Male	Negro Female	Other Male	Other Female
Professional and semi-professional	.0592	.1485	.0222	.0430	.0242	.0478
Farmers and farm managers	.1413	.0110	.2588	.0302	.2026	.0552
Proprietors, managers, and officials	.1067	.0436	.0155	.0071	.0876	.0416
Clerical, sales, and kindred	.1398	.3318	.0244	.0136	.0567	.1192
Craftsmen, foremen, and kindred	.1568	.0110	.0541	.0016	.0319	.0069
Operatives and kindred	.1896	.2057	.1535	.0628	.0986	.2487
Domestic service workers	.0019	.1108	.0357	.5993	.0377	.1695
Protective service workers	.0215	.0004	.0067	.0001	.0086	.0002
Service workers	.0375	.1159	.1445	.1042	.1390	.1186
Farm laborers and foremen	.0701	.0122	.0245	.1296	.2340	.1842
Laborers, except farm and mine	.0759	.0090	.2601	.0085	.0791	.0082
Measure of Occupational Integration, ΣX^2	.1275	.2025	.1852	.3938	.1451	.1600
Rank of ΣX^2	6	2	3	1	5	4
Rank of Suicide Rate	2	4	5	6	1	3
Suicide Rate	22.6	7.1	5.8	1.8	25.6	7.5

Vital Statistics of the United States, 1941, Table 8. The population figures used to compute suicide rates by age, sex, and color were drawn from: *U.S. Census of Population: 1950.* Vol. II, *Characteristics of the Population,* Part 1, United States Summary, Table 39, 93-94.

[3] See Table 10, p 62.

[4] A comparison of Table 9, p. 62, with Table 31, above, will reveal that the 1940 and 1950 measures are not based on identical occupational categories. The data used in computing the 1940 measures of occupational integration measures for the six race-sex status configurations were drawn from *Sixteenth Census of the United States: 1940, Population,* Vol. III, *The Labor Force,* Part 1, United States Summary, Table 62, 88-90.

In the 1950 test, the hypothesis was as follows: *There will be an inverse relationship between measures of occupational integration and suicide rates by race-sex configurations.* To test this same hypothesis on the 1940 data, ρ was computed for the suicide rates and occupational integration measures shown in Table 31. The value of ρ is —.89, a figure somewhat smaller than the —.94 obtained for the 1950 data.

Occupational Integration and Suicide Rates by Age Groups. Consistent with the 1950 series of tests,[5] the relationship between 1940 suicide rates and measures of occupational integration by age groups is examined in this section. The method employed in computing measures of occupational integration[6] within age groups was identical with the method employed in the treatment of the 1950 data.

Because this section reports a replication of previous tests, the hypotheses need not be stated in formal terms; this general proposition was applied to each of the nine status configurations: *There will be an inverse relationship by age groups between measures of occupational integration and suicide rates for sex and sex-color status configurations.* The values of ρ, based on nine tests, are presented in Table 32. (To obtain the work tables summarized in Table 32, see page v.)

Table 32. CORRELATIONS BETWEEN MEASURES OF OCCUPATIONAL INTEGRATION, 1940, AND SUICIDE RATES, 1939-1941, BY AGE GROUPS, FOR SEX AND SEX-COLOR STATUS CONFIGURATIONS, UNITED STATES

Status Configuration	ρ
White Males	—.09
White Females	—.78
Nonwhite Males	—.24
Nonwhite Females	+.01*
Males	+.01*
Females	—.92
Whites	—.74
Nonwhites	—.33
United States	—.43

* Not in predicted direction.

Of the nine ρ's computed, only three are of any appreciable magnitude. Though it may be said that some support for the major theorem

---

[5] See pp. 68-72.

[6] The eleven occupational categories used in computing 1940 measures of occupational integration are shown in Table 31. Data pertaining to occupation by age, sex, and color in the United States as of 1940 were drawn from *Sixteenth Census of the United States: 1940, Population,* Vol. III, *The Labor Force,* Occupational Characteristics, Table 1, 11-21.

is provided with seven out of nine in the predicted direction, any comparison of these results with those obtained for 1950 makes it clear the theory performed much more adequately in 1950; for that year, all the values are in the predicted direction and only one is below —.72.

Although the results presented in this section cannot be regarded as a complete failure on the part of the theory, they do point up the value of replicating tests of theories in time and pose some important questions which will be discussed at the end of this chapter.

Measures of Occupational Integration and Suicide Rates by Sex and Color Within Age Groups. For the year 1950, it has been shown[7] that measures of occupational integration can be used to predict differences between the suicide rates of four color-sex status configurations within nine age groups. We now turn to an identical test for 1940.

	1 high	2	3	4 low
4 low	10	1		
3	1	8	2	
2		2	7	2
1 high			2	9

Rank of Suicide Rates (vertical axis)

Rank of Integration Measures (horizontal axis)

FIG. 6. RELATIONSHIP WITHIN AGE GROUPS BETWEEN RANKS OF THE SUICIDE RATES, 1939-1941, AND RANKS OF THE OCCUPATIONAL INTEGRATION MEASURES, 1940, FOR 44 COLOR-SEX-AGE STATUS CONFIGURATIONS IN THE UNITED STATES.

[7] See pp. 73-76.

Table 33. MEAN ANNUAL SUICIDE RATES, 1939-1941, AND MEASURES OF
OCCUPATIONAL INTEGRATION, 1940, FOR FORTY-FOUR
COLOR-SEX-AGE STATUS CONFIGURATIONS, UNITED STATES

Color-Sex-Age Status Configuration	(1) Suicide Rate	(2) Measure of Occupational Integration	(3) Rank of Column 1 Within Each Age Group	(4) Rank of Column 2 Within Each Age Group	(5) Rank of Column 1	(6) Rank of Column 2
WM* 14-19......	4.5	.2290	1	3	31	17
WF† 14-19......	3.0	.2217	2	4	36	18
NM‡ 14-19......	2.2	.4388	3	1	42	1
NF§ 14-19......	1.8	.3958	4	2	43	4
WM 20-24......	12.6	.1522	1	4	17	33
WF 20-24......	5.0	.2510	3	2	30	14
NM 20-24......	7.7	.1997	2	3	28	21
NF 20-24......	3.9	.3884	4	1	32	8
WM 25-29......	17.5	.1436	1	4	9	38
WF 25-29......	7.1	.2441	3	2	29	15
NM 25-29......	10.5	.1652	2	3	25	27
NF 25-29......	2.8	.3902	4	1	37	6
WM 30-34......	21.4	.1385	1	4	8	40.5
WF 30-34......	9.2	.2363	3	2	27	16
NM 30-34......	10.8	.1606	2	3	21	28
NF 30-34......	3.5	.3876	4	1	33.5	9
WM 35-39......	26.7	.1361	1	4	7	44
WF 35-39......	10.5	.2138	2	2	24	19
NM 35-39......	10.0	.1594	3	3	26	30
NF 35-39......	2.5	.4008	4	1	38	2
WM 40-44......	31.0	.1367	1	4	6	43
WF 40-44......	11.4	.1891	3	2	20	23
NM 40-44......	12.2	.1567	2	3	18	31
NF 40-44......	2.3	.3966	4	1	41	3
WM 45-49......	37.7	.1376	1	4	5	42
WF 45-49......	13.5	.1665	3	2	14	26
NM 45-49......	13.5	.1605	2	3	13	29
NF 45-49......	3.5	.3921	4	1	33.5	5
WM 50-54......	45.6	.1385	1	4	4	40.5
WF 50-54......	13.8	.1551	2	3	11	32
NM 50-54......	13.6	.1767	3	2	12	25
NF 50-54......	3.0	.3891	4	1	35	7
WM 55-59......	53.6	.1404	1	4	3	39
WF 55-59......	13.3	.1479	2	3	15	36
NM 55-59......	11.7	.1970	3	2	19	22
NF 55-59......	2.4	.3680	4	1	39	11
WM 60-64......	57.8	.1458	1	4	2	37
WF 60-64......	12.9	.1504	3	3	16	35
NM 60-64......	14.1	.2128	2	2	10	20
NF 60-64......	1.4	.3832	4	1	44	10
WM 65+	60.4	.1793	1	3	1	24
WF 65+	10.8	.1512	2	4	22	34
NM 65+	10.6	.3017	3	2	23	13
NF 65+	2.3	.3558	4	1	40	12

* WM, white male; † WF, white female; ‡ NM, nonwhite male; § NF, nonwhite female.

Table 33 sets forth the 1940 occupational integration measures and suicide rates of 44 color-sex-age status configurations. The ranks of the suicide rates and the occupational integration measures of the color-sex-age status configurations within eleven age groups are given in columns 3 and 4 of Table 33. Within each age group, the major theorem calls for the rank of the suicide rate of a status configuration to vary inversely with the rank of its occupational integration measure. For example, a rank of 1 in column 3 should be associated with a rank of 4 in column 4. Figure 6 shows the extent to which the anticipated pattern holds true.

Eleven correct predictions of the rank of the suicide rate of a color-sex-age status configuration could be expected on the basis of chance; 34 of 44 are correct in Figure 6. The ratio of correct predictions to the number expected on the basis of chance is thus 34 to 11 or 3.09 to 1. None of the ranks incorrectly predicted is more than one rank removed from the actual rank. The results of this test are better than those for 1950.

A More Complex Test of the Major Theorem. Consistent with the 1950 tests,[8] we now turn to a crucial test of the major theorem for the year 1940. Given the data in Table 33, we can attempt to predict the differences between the suicide rates of 44 status configurations.[9]

To evaluate the predictive power of the major theorem the measure of occupational integration and the suicide rate of each of the 44 color-sex-age status configurations were assigned a rank as shown in columns 5 and 6 of Table 33, with the expectation that the ranks in column 5 would vary inversely with those in column 6. A rank-difference correlation between the two proved to be —.87. This compares to a ρ of —.84 for the 1950 data. Considering their simplicity, measures of occupational integration have a remarkable predictive power in this case.[10]

MARITAL INTEGRATION AND SUICIDE

In Chapter VIII, we saw that in 1949-1951 suicide rates by age and

---

[8] See pp. 76-77.

[9] Here the question is correctly predicting differences, not within age groups, but between all status configurations regardless of age.

[10] If the suicide rates and measures of occupational integration shown in columns 1 and 2 of Table 33 are plotted on a scatter diagram, it will be seen that the relationship between the two is nonlinear and very much like the relationship which proved to hold between the two in 1950 (see pp. 76-77). Because of the nonlinear relationship, a rank-difference correlation was used to express the predictive power of measures of occupational integration.

marital status conformed to the major theorem to a high degree. Let us now turn to an almost identical series of tests for the year 1940.

Suicide and Marital Integration with Age. In the tables to follow, suicide rates are given for ten age groups in the United States as of 1940,[11] along with measures of the degree of marital integration[12] within each of the age groups.[13] The data in Table 34 pertain to the total population of the United States. The major theorem predicts an inverse relationship between the two variables shown in this table, a prediction that was borne out by a ρ of —.62. The corresponding ρ for 1950 was —.79.

Table 34. MEASURES OF THE INTEGRATION OF MARITAL STATUS WITH AGE, 1940, AND SUICIDE RATES BY AGE, 1939-1941, UNITED STATES

Age Group	Mean Annual Suicide Rate	Rank	Measure of the Integration of Marital Status with Age	Rank
15-19	1.2	10	.873	1
20-24	3.0	9	.511	6
25-34	4.5	8	.595	4
35-44	6.5	7	.686	2
45-54	9.2	6	.649	3
55-59	11.3	2	.575	5
60-64	11.6	1	.510	7
65-69	11.0	5	.448	8
70-74	11.1	3	.413	10
75+	11.1	4	.447	9

Table 35 is identical to the previous table except that it is concerned only with males. The value of ρ here is —.56, a figure almost identical with the —.59 obtained for 1950.

The data for females are shown in Table 36. The value of ρ is —.48, somewhat smaller than the —.66 value obtained in the earlier test with 1950 data.

A Problem in Prediction. Consistent with the 1950 tests, the major theorem was tested as to its power to predict differences in the 1940

---

[11] All of the data in this chapter which pertain to suicide by age and marital status in the United States as of 1940 were drawn from *Vital Statistics—Special Reports, 1945,* Vol. XXIII, No. 7, Table 1, pp. 150-151, and Table 2, pp. 162-63.

[12] Measures of marital integration in this chapter are based on data drawn from *Sixteenth Census of the United States: 1940, Population,* Vol. IV, Characteristics by Age, Part 1, U. S. Summary, Table 4.

[13] See pp. 87-88 for an illustration of the measurement of the degree of marital integration within an age group.

suicide rates of marital statuses within age groups. In Table 37, suicide rates and measures of integration are given for the four marital statuses within ten age groups.

Tablie 35. MEASURES OF THE INTEGRATION OF MARITAL STATUS WITH AGE, 1940, AND SUICIDE RATES BY AGE, 1939-1941, FOR MALES, UNITED STATES

Age Group	Mean Annual Suicide Rate	Rank	Measure of the Integration of Marital Status with Age	Rank
15-19	1.4	10	.967	1
20-24	4.3	9	.596	6
25-34	6.4	8	.568	7
35-44	9.4	7	.699	3
45-54	13.9	6	.700	2
55-59	18.1	4	.656	4
60-64	19.0	2	.612	5
65-69	17.9	5	.554	8
70-74	18.7	3	.488	9
75+	20.6	1	.419	10

Table 36. MEASURES OF THE INTEGRATION OF MARITAL STATUS WITH AGE, 1940, AND SUICIDE RATES BY ARE, 1939-1941, FOR FEMALES, UNITED STATES

Age Group	Mean Annual Suicide Rate	Rank	Measure of the Integration of Marital Status with Age	Rank
15-19	0.9	10	.790	1
20-24	1.6	9	.486	7
25-34	2.7	8	.631	3
35-44	3.5	6	.671	2
45-54	4.4	1	.603	4
55-59	4.1	3	.510	6
60-64	4.1	4	.443	8
65-69	4.2	2	.411	10
70-74	3.7	5	.435	9
75+	2.8	7	.571	5

One should expect on the basis of the major theorem that the rank of the suicide rate of a marital status within an age group varies inversely with the rank of its measure of integration. Figure 7 shows that this is substantially true; one may predict the rank of the suicide rate of a marital status within an age group with a considerable degree of success. Correct predictions can be made in 24 cases, and the ratio of this number to that expected on the basis of chance is 2.4 to 1. Of the 16 errors in prediction, in only one case is the actual rank more than one rank removed from that predicted.

Suicide rates and measures of status integration are shown for males

Table 37. MEASURES OF THE INTEGRATION OF MARITAL STATUS WITH AGE, 1940, AND MEAN ANNUAL SUICIDE RATES, 1939-1941, BY MARITAL STATUS AND AGE, UNITED STATES

Age Group	Single				Married				Widowed				Divorced			
	M.S.I.*	Rank	S.R.†	Rank	M.S.I.	Rank	S.R.	Rank	M.S.I.	Rank	S.R.	Rank	M.S.I.	Rank	S.R.	Rank
—20‡	.932	1	0.3	3	.066	2	1.8	2	.001	3.5	0.0	4	.001	3.5	6.7	1
20-24	.595	1	3.2	3	.396	2	2.2	4	.004	4	8.9	2	.006	3	11.4	1
25-34	.237	2	6.6	3	.734	1	3.4	4	.012	4	8.9	2	.016	3	15.1	1
35-44	.122	4	9.1	2	.818	1	5.4	4	.038	2	8.4	3	.023	3	20.4	1
45-54	.099	2	12.0	2	.795	1	8.0	4	.085	3	10.6	3	.021	4	24.6	1
55-59	.098	3	16.2	2	.737	1	9.7	4	.147	2	11.6	3	.018	4	27.7	1
60-64	.099	3	17.4	2	.675	1	10.1	4	.211	2	10.5	3	.015	4	27.9	1
65-69	.098	3	15.9	2	.592	1	9.5	4	.297	2	10.4	3	.013	4	31.2	1
70-74	.097	3	15.1	2	.495	1	10.0	4	.398	2	10.2	3	.010	4	41.2	1
75+	.090	3	14.4	2	.330	2	10.1	4	.574	1	10.4	3	.006	4	45.0	1

* M.S.I., measure of status integration; † S.R., suicide rate; ‡ measures of integration shown in this row are based on the population 15-19 and the suicide rates are based on the population under 20.

Rank of Suicide Rates	Rank of Integration Measures: 1 high	2	3	4 low
4 low	7	2		1
3	3	6	1	
2		2	5	3
1 high			3	7

FIG. 7. RELATIONSHIP WITHIN AGE GROUPS BETWEEN RANKS OF THE MEASURES OF THE INTEGRATION OF MARITAL STATUS WITH AGE, 1940, AND RANKS OF SUICIDE RATES, 1939-1941, FOR 40 AGE-MARITAL STATUS CONFIGURATIONS IN THE UNITED STATES.

by marital status and age in Table 38. In line with the major theorem the rank of the suicide rate of a marital status within an age group varies inversely with the rank of its measure of integration. Figure 8 reveals that predictions can be made with a considerable degree of success.

Correct predictions of the rank of the suicide rate of a marital status within an age group can be made from the rank of its measure of integration in 32 cases. The ratio of this number to that expected on the basis of chance is 3.2 to 1. Of the eight errors in prediction, in four cases the rank predicted is more than one rank removed from that predicted.

To complete this report of a series of tests, suicide rates and status integration measures for females by marital status and age are presented in Table 39.

Table 38. MEASURES OF THE INTEGRATION OF MARITAL STATUS WITH AGE, 1940, AND MEAN ANNUAL SUICIDE RATES, 1939-1941, BY MARITAL STATUS AND AGE, FOR MALES, UNITED STATES

Age Group	Single				Widowed				Married				Divorced			
	M.S.I.*	Rank	S.R.†	Rank	M.S.I.	Rank	S.R.	Rank	M.S.I.	Rank	S.R.	Rank	M.S.I.	Rank	S.R.	Rank
−20‡	.983	1	0.4	2	.017	2	3.8	1	.000	3.5	0.0	3.5	.000	3.5	0.0	3.5
20-24	.722	1	4.3	3	.274	2	3.8	4	.001	4	27.8	1	.003	3	20.8	2
25-34	.287	2	8.8	3	.697	1	4.7	4	.005	4	28.3	1	.011	3	27.1	2
35-44	.140	2	12.7	3	.824	1	7.7	4	.017	4	19.5	2	.019	3	32.9	1
45-54	.111	2	17.0	3	.828	1	11.7	4	.041	3	25.6	2	.020	4	38.6	1
55-59	.108	2	24.8	3	.799	1	14.6	4	.074	3	29.3	2	.019	4	46.5	1
60-64	.105	3	28.3	2	.767	1	15.2	4	.111	2	24.8	3	.017	4	43.6	1
65-69	.103	3	26.8	2	.719	1	13.3	4	.162	2	26.1	3	.016	4	40.5	1
70-74	.099	3	25.1	2	.649	1	13.9	4	.238	2	25.0	3	.014	4	54.9	1
75+	.091	3	29.1	2	.502	1	13.3	4	.398	2	25.5	3	.009	4	61.7	1

* M.S.I., measure of status integration; † S.R., suicide rate; ‡ measures of integration shown in this row are based on the population 15-19 and the suicide rates are based on the population under 20.

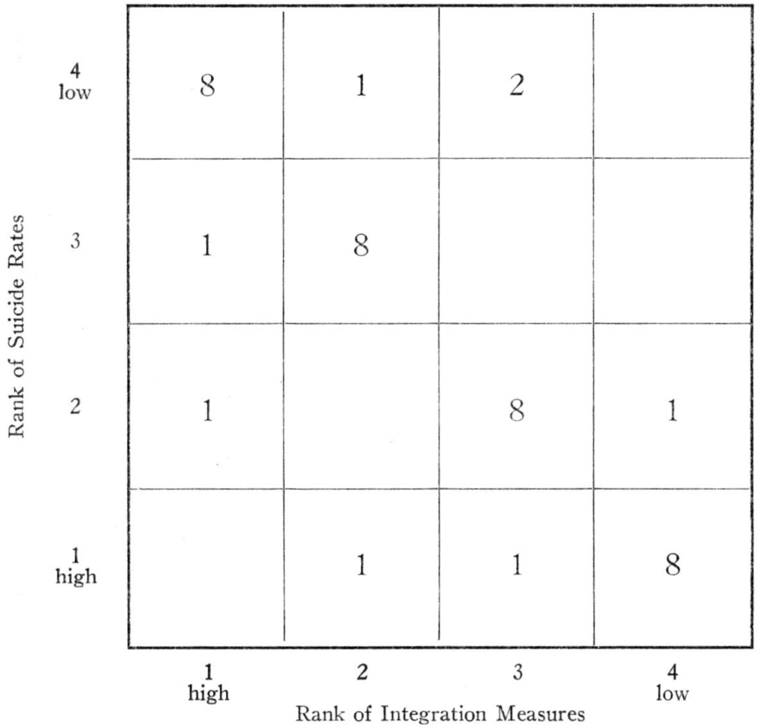

Rank of Suicide Rates	Rank of Integration Measures →			
	1 high	2	3	4 low
4 low	8	1	2	
3	1	8		
2	1		8	1
1 high		1	1	8

FIG. 8. RELATIONSHIP WITHIN AGE GROUPS BETWEEN RANKS OF THE MEASURES OF THE INTEGRATION OF MARITAL STATUS WITH AGE, 1940, AND RANKS OF SUICIDE RATES, 1939-1941, FOR 40 AGE-MARITAL STATUS CONFIGURATIONS AMONG MALES IN THE UNITED STATES.

The expected pattern is shown in Figure 9. The ratio of the number of correct predictions that can be made to the number expected on the basis of chance is 20 to 10 or 2.0 to 1. Of the 20 cases of error in prediction, only three of the observed ranks are more than one rank removed from that predicted.

The findings reported in this chapter leave little doubt that the major theorem holds for the United States in 1940 as well as 1950.

An Additional Series of Replications. Chapter VIII reports a series of tests of the proposition that, by age groups, the ratio of the integration measure of the status of married to that of another marital status varies directly with the ratio of the suicide rate of the other marital status to the rate of the married status. Nine specific hypotheses were tested on the basis of 1950 data, and each of the tests were repeated

Table 39. MEASURES OF THE INTEGRATION OF MARITAL STATUS WITH AGE, 1940, AND MEAN ANNUAL SUICIDE RATES, 1939-1941, BY MARITAL STATUS AND AGE, FOR FEMALES, UNITED STATES

Age Group	Single				Married				Widowed				Divorced			
	M.S.I.*	Rank	S.R.†	Rank	M.S.I.	Rank	S.R.	Rank	M.S.I.	Rank	S.R.	Rank	M.S.I.	Rank	S.R.	Rank
−20‡	.881	1	0.2	3	.116	2	1.4	2	.001	4	0.0	4	.002	3	7.4	1
20-24	.472	2	1.6	3	.513	1	1.4	4	.006	4	4.1	2	.009	3	8.4	1
25-34	.189	2	3.2	3	.771	1	2.3	4	.019	4	3.3	2	.021	3	8.8	1
35-44	.104	2	4.3	3	.810	1	3.0	4	.059	3	5.1	2	.027	4	11.6	1
45-54	.087	3	5.2	3	.760	1	3.7	4	.131	2	5.7	2	.022	4	11.3	1
55-59	.087	3	4.7	3	.672	1	3.6	4	.224	2	5.4	2	.017	4	6.1	1
60-64	.093	3	4.8	3	.580	1	3.2	4	.313	2	5.3	2	.014	4	7.4	1
65-69	.094	3	4.1	3	.465	1	3.7	4	.431	2	4.5	2	.010	4	17.0	1
70-74	.095	3	4.9	2	.343	2	2.8	4	.555	1	4.0	3	.007	4	15.4	1
75+	.090	3	1.8	4	.178	2	2.0	3	.729	1	3.0	2	.004	4	6.7	1

* M.S.I., measure of status integration; † S.R., suicide rate; ‡ measures of integration shown in this row are based on the population 15-19 and the suicide rates are based on the population under 20.

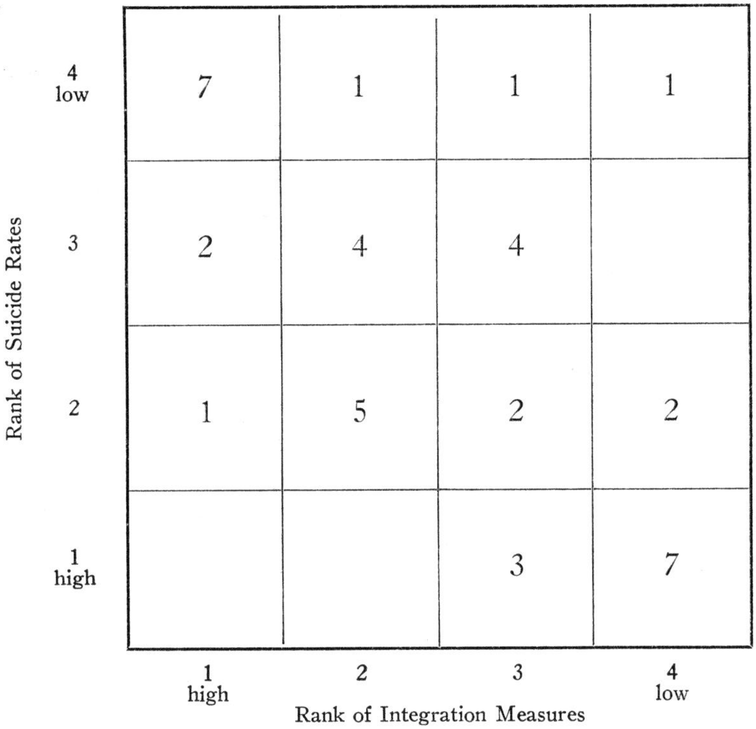

Fig. 9. RELATIONSHIP WITHIN AGE GROUPS BETWEEN RANKS OF THE MEASURES OF THE INTEGRATION OF MARITAL STATUS WITH AGE, 1940, AND RANKS OF SUICIDE RATES, 1939-1941, FOR 40 AGE-MARITAL STATUS CONFIGURATIONS AMONG FEMALES IN THE UNITED STATES.

for 1940. The results of the latter are reported in Table 40, which corresponds to Table 30 for the year 1950. (To obtain the work tables summarized in Table 40, see page v.)

Table 40. RELATIONSHIP BETWEEN THE RATIO OF THE SUICIDE RATE OF UNMARRIED TO MARRIED, 1939-1941, AND THE RATIO OF THE STATUS INTEGRATION MEASURES OF MARRIED TO UNMARRIED, 1940, BY AGE GROUPS, UNITED STATES

	Both Sexes			Males			Females		
	Single to Married	Widowed to Married	Divorced to Married	Single to Married	Widowed to Married	Divorced to Married	Single to Married	Widowed to Married	Divorced to Married
ρ	+.44	+.97	+.68	+.20	+.88	+.65	+.55	+.45	+.65

In general, it may be seen that all of the ρ's are in the predicted direction, as is true for the 1950 tests. Furthermore, the results of the two series of tests tend to be quite similar. The ρ's computed for the 1940 data are somewhat higher than those computed for the 1950 data except in two cases: single and married persons, and widowed and married females.

DISCUSSION

In general, the results of replications reported in this chapter have shown that the major theorem is supported by the 1940 data, as it is by the 1950 data. The results for the two different periods are actually quite similar. One possible exception is the series of nine 1940 tests on pages 106 and 107, which pertains to various sex, color, and sex-color status configurations in the United States. In this series of tests, the major theorem received strong support in only three instances. Moreover, the values of ρ computed for the 1940 data sometimes differed markedly from corresponding 1950 values. For example, for males, ρ was $+.01$ in 1940 and $-.95$ in 1950, while for nonwhites the corresponding values were $-.33$ and $-.80$.

The findings reported here pose important theoretical questions. Why, for example, should the theory make such a relatively poor showing in particular tests for 1940? It might be that occupational integration at that particular time was a less important aspect of total status integration than other components, such as marital integration. It seems quite possible that over long periods of time such variations in the relative importance of particular statuses might occur. However, if this were a valid assumption in this particular instance, all of the 1940 tests utilizing measures of occupational integration should have made a poor showing relative to 1950. That this is not the case may be ascertained easily by a detailed comparison of the results of the 1940 and 1950 tests.

The replication of tests presented here shows marked congruity between the 1940 and 1950 results but at the same time reveals sufficient discrepancies to emphasize the need for continued and more elaborate replications.

PART THREE

Tests for Other Countries

CHAPTER TEN

Predicting Differences in the Suicide Rates of Countries

SOCIOLOGICAL theory has been plagued by two major problems: Much of what passes for theory in the field is in the form of vaguely stated ideas and, as such, cannot be subjected to an empirical test; secondly, the validity of the few testable theories in sociology remains in question primarily because of the limited amount of evidence that has been brought to bear on them in a systematic way. One of the reasons for the second problem is that most theories stand or fall on tests conducted only within one country. There has always been and will continue to be a pressing need for cross-cultural or international tests. In recognition of the importance of testing the major theorem of the present study on populations outside of the United States, a considerable amount of time was expended searching for data which are international in scope.

A TEST USING A MEASURE OF LABOR FORCE INTEGRATION WITH SEX

An effort to test the major theorem on a cross-societal level meets with several problems. Data necessary for even simple measures of status integration are not available for a large number of countries;[1]

---

[1] For the most part, these are non-European countries; consequently, the major theorem cannot be tested on a completely random sample of all countries.

and further, where such data do exist, they are rarely comparable.[2]

A search of publications pertaining to national censuses has revealed that the only comparable data relevant to status integration in a large number of countries are labor force statistics. A large number of politically autonomous nations report the numbers of persons economically active and not economically active ("in the labor force" and "not in the labor force") by age[3] and sex. However, not all of these countries could be included, since, in a few cases, suicide rates for approximately the same period of years were not available. The reverse also proved to be true; some of the countries with suicide statistics did not report labor force status by age and sex for a corresponding period of time.

Measures of the integration of labor force status with sex were computed for the 32 nations utilized in the test. The computations for two countries—Austria and Guatemala—are presented in Table 41 as examples.

Table 41. THE INTEGRATION OF LABOR FORCE STATUS WITH SEX IN AUSTRIA, 1951, AND GUATEMALA, 1950, FOR PERSONS FIFTEEN YEARS OF AGE AND OVER*

| Labor Force Status | Austria | | Guatemala | |
	Males	Females	Males	Females
Economically active (in labor force)	$X=.838$	.438	.949	.139
	$N=2,054,432$	1,304,206	762,488	112,006
Not economically active (not in labor force)	$X=.162$	.562	.051	.861
	$N=397,076$	1,674,816	40,800	695,957
$\Sigma X=$	1.000	1.000	1.000	1.000
$\Sigma X^2=$	.728	.508	.903	.761
$\Sigma\Sigma X^2=$	1.236		1.664	

* For the sources of data for Austria and Guatemala and the other 30 countries see note for Table 42.

From the viewpoint of prediction, a measure of the integration of labor force status with sex expresses the degree to which knowledge of a person's sex enables one to correctly predict the labor force status of the person. For such a table as Table 41 the maximum magnitude of the measure is 2.000 (ΣX^2 of males plus ΣX^2 of females) and the

[2] As an example of this, while several countries report data pertaining to the division of labor by age and/or sex, some countries use specific occupations in their reports and others use only broad industrial categories.

[3] Several countries could not be included in the sample because their labor force statistics did not take age into account. Age as a status must be taken into account when measuring the integration of labor force status with sex because if left uncontrolled it tends to mask status integration.

minimum possible magnitude is 1.000, with the former indicating that all of the persons in the population of the same sex have the same labor force status.

Questions and Problems Pertaining to the Data. Before presenting measures of the integration of labor status with sex and suicide rates for the 32 countries, it is wise to consider some of the problems posed in the use of labor force statistics and suicide data on an international basis.

In an earlier section, attention was given to the general problem of reliability and comparability of suicide statistics. These problems become increasingly important as the investigator turns to the analysis of data for different countries and dissimilar cultures. Since some writers hold that the problems involved in international analysis make comparisons impractical if not meaningless, some comments on the nature of the data used in the tests are in order.

In the first place, it is undoubtedly true that the vital statistics of individual countries have improved with the development of modern recording procedures and record-keeping equipment. Further improvement has resulted from the greater adherence of all nations to the International Classification of Death. Also, for the rates presented below we have had the benefit of a publication of the World Health Organization that provides the best possible suicide data for those countries that have maintained satisfactory records over a considerable period of years.[4] For these countries, a rate was computed by averaging the annual rates for five years centering around 1950. However, in order to have some of the less well-developed and non-European countries represented, it was necessary to draw on sources other than the World Health publication. In some instances, this meant compiling suicide data for individual years from several different sources. Occasionally, as is true for Mexico and Guatemala, it was necessary to use a broken series of years in computing a rate. The least stable rates are those for Bolivia, Greece, El Salvador, and Hungary; for these countries, data for a single year were used.[5] Consequently, in evaluating these international suicide rates, it must be recognized that there is a wide variation in the quality of the data among the 32 countries. On the other hand, in virtually all cases there are supplementary data,

---

[4] World Health Organization, "Mortality from Suicide," *Epidemiological and Vital Statistics Reports*, Vol. IX, No. 4 (1956).

[5] In addition, these tend to be the countries in which the year for which a suicide rate could be computed differs from the year for which the labor force data were available. See Table 42.

Table 42. MEAN ANNUAL SUICIDE RATES AND MEASURES OF THE INTEGRATION OF LABOR FORCE STATUS WITH SEX FOR THIRTY-TWO COUNTRIES, *circa* 1950

Country	Year of Suicide Rates*	Suicide Rate	Year of Economically Active Data	Lower Age of Economically Active	Measure of the Integration of Labor Force Status with Sex
Mexico	1952, 1954†	1.0	1950	12	1.553
Guatemala	1948-49, 1952‡	1.5	1950	15	1.664
Bolivia	1947§	2.5	1950	15	1.363
Ireland	1949-53	2.5	1951	14	1.340
Costa Rica	1950-52‖	2.6	1950	15	1.623
Greece	1955**	3.6	1951	15	1.493
El Salvador	1950††	4.1	1950	15	1.605
Chile	1950-51	4.4	1952	15	1.394
Venezuela	1950-52‡‡	4.7	1950	15	1.521
Yugoslavia	1950-54§§	5.0	1953	15	1.335
Ceylon	1944-47	5.9	1946	15	1.382
Netherlands	1946-48	7.0	1947	14	1.355
Norway	1945-47	7.2	1946	15	1.375
Canada	1949-53	7.4	1951	14	1.347
Israel	1947-49‖‖	8.6	1948	15	1.361
Union of South Africa	1944-48	8.8	1946	15	1.390
Australia	1946-48	9.7	1947	15	1.404
Portugal	1948-51	10.1	1950	15	1.442
New Zealand	1944-46	10.3	1945	14	1.338
England and Wales	1949-53	10.4	1951	15	1.335
U.S.A.	1948-52	10.9	1950	14	1.255
France	1945-47	12.4	1946	14	1.255
Belgium	1946-48	14.7	1947	15	1.317
Sweden	1948-52	15.6	1950	15	1.336
Cuba	1948-49***	16.4	1953	14	1.544
Finland	1948-52	16.4	1950	14	1.284
Japan	1948-52	17.9	1950	14	1.224
West Germany	1948-52	17.9	1950	15	1.251
Hungary	1955†††	20.6	1949	15	1.373
Switzerland	1948-52	22.4	1950	15	1.353
Austria	1949-53	23.4	1951	15	1.236
Denmark	1948-52	23.9	1950	15	1.295

* Except where otherwise indicated, rates are based on data from World Health Organization, *Epidemiological & Vital Statistics Reports,* Vol. IX, No. 4 (1956), pp. 250-253.
† *Demographic Yearbook,* 1955, p. 714; 1956, p. 699.
‡ *Ibid.,* 1954, pp. 560-61, 573.
§ *Ibid.,* 1952, p. 335.
‖ Ministerio de Economia y Hacienda, *Anuario Estadistico, 1951-52* (San Jose), p. 23.
** *Demographic Yearbook,* 1955, p. 81.
†† *Epidemiological and Vital Statistics Report,* (1953), p. 171.
‡‡ Ministerio de Sanidad y Assistencia Social, *Anuario de Epidemiology y Estadistica Vital* (Caracas), 1950, Vol. II, p. 622; 1951, Vol. II, p. 720; 1952, Vol. II, p. 718.
§§ Federativna Naradna Republika Jugoslavija, *Savezni Zavod Za Statistiku, Statiskički Godišnjak F.N.R.J.,* 1955 (Beograd, 1955), p. 76.
‖‖ *Demographic Yearbook,* 1952, p. 337.
*** Direccion General de Estadistica, *Anuario Estadistica de Cuba, 1952* (Havana), p. 72.
††† *Demographic Yearbook,* 1956, p. 707.

frequently data for earlier years, which indicate that the suicide rates are not subject to a high degree of fluctuation from one year to the next.

The data on age-sex composition of the labor force provided for 77 geographic areas by the 1957 *Demographic Yearbook* are the best available. In this publication, the population defined as economically active "includes, unless otherwise specified, all persons stated to be employed or seeking to be employed in a productive capacity in some sector of the economy."[6] Certain limitations of these data are recognized and described in detail in *Application of International Standards to Census Data on the Economically Active Population.*[7] This report, as summarized in the *Demographic Yearbook* for 1957, lists the following limitations of the data:

(1) Adoption of the "gainful worker" approach in enumerating the economically active population by some countries and the "labor force" approach by others; (2) different treatment of certain groups, such as unpaid family workers, retired persons, the armed forces, inmates of institutions, etc.; (3) use of different age limits in enumerating the economically active; and (4) variations in the formulation of census questions which have produced significant variations in the results.[8]

Furthermore, not only may the dates of census vary but also identical census dates may connote different seasonal structures of the working population.[9]

It must be admitted that to some extent the data presented in this section are affected by the factors just described. However, those countries, such as Egypt, with obviously incommensurable data have been omitted. The remaining 32 countries are included as having labor force data generally comparable as to content and having sufficient reliability for testing purposes.

Testing the Hypothesis. The hypothesis derived from the major theorem reads as follows: *Among countries, an inverse relationship will hold between suicide rates and measures of the integration of labor force status with sex.* This hypothesis anticipates that a negative coefficient of correlation will hold between the sets of values shown in columns 2 and 5 of Table 42.

It should be mentioned, before proceeding to an analysis of the test of the above hypothesis, that only a moderately high correlation may be expected to hold, primarily because a measure that takes into account only sex and labor force statuses ignores several other dimensions of

---

[6] United Nations, *Demographic Yearbook* (1957), p. 37.

[7] United Nations, (New York, 1951).

[8] *Demographic Yearbook* (1957), p. 35.

[9] *Ibid.,* p. 37.

status integration. Such a measure may, in addition, operate to mask the actual prevalence of sex-labor force integration because marital status and parental status are ignored. Under ideal conditions, the measure would express the degree of integration between labor force status and all other occupied status configurations in a society.

When the hypothesis stated above was tested, a product-moment correlation (r) of $-.59$ proved to hold between the values shown in columns 2 and 5 of Table 42, indicating that those countries with a high measure of integration of labor force with sex tend to be the countries with low suicide rates and vice versa.

Table 43. COUNTRIES ABOVE AND BELOW THE MEDIAN* WITH RESPECT TO SUICIDE RATES AND MEASURES OF THE INTEGRATION OF LABOR FORCE STATUS WITH SEX, *circa* 1950

High Suicide Rate	Denmark Austria Switzerland Japan W. Germany Finland Sweden Belgium France United States England and Wales New Zealand	Hungary Cuba Portugal Australia
Median		
Low Suicide Rate	Netherlands Canada Yugoslavia Ireland	Israel South Africa Norway Ceylon Chile Venezuela Greece El Salvador Costa Rica Bolivia Guatemala Mexico
	Low Integration of Labor Force Status with Sex	Median High Integration of Labor Force Status with Sex

* Median suicide rate is 9.2; median integration measure is 1.358.

Table 43 shows that eight out of the 32 countries are exceptions to the rule of high integration measures and low suicide rates or low integration measures and high suicide rates. Of these eight, Cuba is the only country that violates the rule to an appreciable degree (see Table 42). Canada, Yugoslavia, The Netherlands, and Ireland are all only slightly below the median for the measures of the integration of labor force status with sex. Hungary's measure of the integration of labor force status with sex is only slightly above the median. The two remaining exceptions, Australia and Portugal, have suicide rates within two points (2.0) of being below the median suicide rate.

COMPONENT AND COMPOSITE MEASURES OF STATUS INTEGRATION

In Chapters IV through IX, it was shown that within the United States, measures of occupational integration and marital integration tend to vary inversely with suicide rates, sometimes to a high degree. These results would lead one to expect that measures of occupational integration or marital integration can be used to distinguish countries with high suicide rates from countries with low suicide rates. Such an expectation ignores, however, the possibility that a simple measure of only one dimension of status integration may work very well within a country, but not among countries. Within a particular country consequences of ignoring several dimensions of status integration may have negligible consequences because the other dimensions are more or less a constant from one division of the country's population to the next. When the level of an analysis is shifted to an international level, however, the chances are increased that there is considerable variation among the countries with respect to a large number of dimensions of status integration. In short, one cannot assume that status integration is a unitary phenomenon, meaning that all of the dimensions of status integration vary directly with each other. It may well be that within a universe of countries the different dimensions of status integration vary either independently or inversely with each other. In either case, an attempt to distinguish countries with high and low suicide rates on the basis of a simple measure of only one dimension of status integration would meet with only moderate success. Thus, in working with countries, as opposed to intranational comparisons, there is a far greater need for measures that represent a combination of several different dimensions of status integration.

With the above methodological considerations in mind, an attempt was made to compute measures of as many dimensions of status integration in as many countries as possible, with the goal being that of combining each of the individual measures into one composite variable. The attempt met with numerous difficulties. It is difficult enough to obtain comparable measures of even one dimension of status integration for a large number of countries, much less measures of several dimensions. An exhaustive search ended with the computation of measures of occupational, marital, and labor force integration for thirteen countries.

Table 44. MEAN ANNUAL SUICIDE RATES AND TOTAL OCCUPATIONAL INTEGRATION MEASURES FOR AUTONOMOUS COUNTRIES, *circa* 1950

Country	Suicide Rate*	Rank	Occupational Integration Measure†	Rank
Guatemala	1.5	13	.8373	1
Venezuela	4.7	12	.4834	7
Spain	5.9	11	.5933	3
Canada	7.4	10	.4340	9
Israel	8.6	9	.4341	8
New Zealand	9.2	8	.4226	11
United Kingdom	10.4	7	.3591	13
U.S.A.	10.9	6	.4196	12
Sweden	15.6	5	.4850	6
Finland	16.4	4	.5817	4
Japan	17.9	3	.6661	2
Austria	23.4	2	.5126	5
Denmark	23.9	1	.4331	10

* For source of suicide rates see Table 42.
† *Demographic Yearbook, 1956,* Table 13, pp. 388-418.

The First Component Measure: Occupational Integration. In Chapter IX, it was demonstrated that in the case of the United States a measure of integration of occupation with age and sex had a great deal of power in predicting differences in suicide rates. As a test of the generality of the theory, it is important that further investigation be carried out on this measure in a wide variety of conditions. The first test to be considered was concerned with measures of occupational integration for autonomous countries and their relationship to suicide rates.

In an international test it would be highly desirable to include either all countries or a random sample of them, but in neither case did this prove possible. The *Demographic Yearbook* for 1956 gives occupation by sex for a large number of countries, but only thirteen of them have strictly comparable data. These cases cannot be treated as a random sample, but they do constitute a wide representation of nations with differing religious, political, and other social characteristics. The thirteen countries are listed in Table 44 along with their suicide rates and occupational integration measures. The integration measures do not include age,[10] but they do take into account sex, since each is the sum of two component measures—one relating to the degree of occupational integration among males and the other to the degree of occupational integration among females.

When the ranks shown in Table 44 were correlated, ρ proved to be —.12. The direction of the relationship supports the major theorem, but the value of ρ is very low compared to those for the United States. We have in this test one instance of a particular dimension of status integration not working nearly as well at an international level as it does for an intranational test.

The Second Component Measure: Marital Integration. An additional test of the predictive power of the major theorem among autonomous countries is based on the integration of marital status with sex. Thirteen autonomous countries with their suicide rates and measures of marital integration are presented in Table 45.[11] It would have been possible to obtain measures of marital integration for more countries than are shown in this table, but this series of tests called for each country to have both measures of occupational and marital integration.

To test the major theorem, a rank-difference correlation was computed between the measure of marital integration with sex and the suicide rate. The coefficient proved to have a value of —.25. This value is small but in the predicted direction.

A Third Component Measure and a Composite Measure. In an earlier section, measures of the integration of labor force status with sex were computed for autonomous nations.[12] Here it was found that the correlation between measures of labor force integration and suicide rates by countries was —.59. Since measures of the integration of labor

---

[10] The measures of integration of occupation with sex were computed exactly as those reported on pp. 61-62, except that the following occupational classification was used: professional, technical, and related workers; managerial, administrative, clerical, and related workers; sales workers; farmers, fishermen, hunters, lumbermen, and related workers; workers in mine, quarry, and related occupations; workers in operating transport occupations; craftsmen, production process workers, and laborers not elsewhere classified; service workers; armed forces; and not classifiable elsewhere. See *Demographic Yearbook* (1956), p. 388.

[11] The measures of marital integration with age are computed by the same procedure as those shown in Table 22, p. 87. The marital statuses used are: single, married, widowed, and divorced. For Guatemala and Venezuela "married" and "consensually married" were combined. Where "separated" was given separately, it was combined with "divorced," since these two categories were combined for Japan. Source: *Demographic Yearbook* (1955), pp. 380-435.

[12] See Table 42. The measures of labor force integration pertain to England and Wales rather than to the United Kingdom.

force status with sex are available for the thirteen countries now being considered,[13] a composite measure for each country can be computed by summing the individual measures of occupational, marital, and labor force integration; this composite measure thus embraces three different dimensions of status integration. The value of the composite measure for each of the thirteen countries is shown in Table 46.

When the ranks shown were correlated, ρ proved to be $-.79$.[14] The suggestion that a comprehensive measure of status integration is needed when testing the major theorem on an international level receives considerable support from this correlation.

Table 45. MEAN ANNUAL SUICIDE RATES AND TOTAL MEASURES OF MARITAL INTEGRATION FOR AUTONOMOUS COUNTRIES, *circa*, 1950

Country	Suicide Rate*	Rank	Marital Integration Measure†	Rank
Guatemala	1.5	13	.9694	6
Venezuela	4.7	12	.9090	8
Spain	5.9	11	.8463‡	13
Canada	7.4	10	1.0039	3
Israel	8.6	9	1.0317	1
New Zealand	9.2	8	.9888	5
United Kingdom	10.4	7	1.0005§	4
U.S.A.	10.9	6	1.0043	2
Sweden	15.6	5	.8816	12
Finland	16.4	4	.8916	10
Japan	17.9	3	.8996	9
Austria	23.4	2	.8840	11
Denmark	23.9	1	.9266	7

* For source of suicide rates see Table 42.
† *Demographic Yearbook, 1955*, pp. 380-435.
‡ Data for 1940, *Demographic Yearbook, 1949-50*, pp. 203-204.
§ Data for England and Wales.

Inadequacy of Separate Measures. It was suggested in the introduction that a low relationship by countries between a measure involving only one dimension of status integration and suicide rates could conceivably result not only from the inadequacy of simple integration measures, but also from the fact that they may be working against each other. That this is true may be demonstrated by computing rank-

---

[13] Spain was omitted from the earlier test involving labor force integration because no minimum age was specified for Spain's gainfully employed. Although this presents problems of comparability, Spain has been included in the present test in order to have as many countries as possible.

[14] The countries that lower the correlations are predominantly English-speaking countries (Canada, U.S.A., United Kingdom, and New Zealand). Had age been taken into account in the measures of status integration, the correlation would probably have been higher.

difference correlations between the three measures of status integration described above. The relationship between the measures of occupational and marital integration turns out to be highly negative ($\rho =$ $-.63$). On the other hand, the measure of labor force integration with sex has very little relationship with either of these measures: $+.09$ with marital integration and $+.15$ with occupational integration.[15] The measure of labor force integration thus is free from the restrictions of a counteracting measure of integration, and, even though an extremely simple measure, has a moderately high correlation with the suicide rate ($-.59$). With the other two measures, it has been demonstrated that a high measure of occupational integration tends to be accompanied by a low degree of marital integration. Consequently, neither marital integration nor occupational integration nor the combination of the two can have even a moderately high relationship with the suicide rate ($\rho = -.25$, $-.12$, and $-.29$, respectively).

Table 46. MEAN ANNUAL SUICIDE RATES AND COMPOSITE MEASURES OF
STATUS INTEGRATION BASED ON MEASURES OF OCCUPATIONAL, MARITAL,
AND LABOR FORCE INTEGRATION BY COUNTRIES, *circa* 1950

Country	Suicide Rate	Rank	Composite Measure	Rank
Guatemala	1.5	13	3.4707	1
Venezuela	4.7	12	2.9134	2
Spain	5.9	11	2.7926	4
Canada	7.4	10	2.7849	6
Israel	8.6	9	2.8268	3
New Zealand	9.2	8	2.7494	8
United Kingdom	10.4	7	2.6946	10
U.S.A.	10.9	6	2.6789	11
Sweden	15.6	5	2.7026	9
Finland	16.4	4	2.7573	7
Japan	17.9	3	2.7897	5
Austria	23.4	2	2.6326	13
Denmark	23.9	1	2.6547	12

Additional Implications. It should be pointed out that the data presented in the preceding tables have other important implications. It is clear, for example, that Catholic countries tend to have lower suicide rates than Protestant countries. On the other hand, Austria, which was 89.5 per cent Catholic in 1951,[16] has a suicide rate only slightly lower than the country with the highest rate. Though it may be possible to explain this apparently anomalous situation in terms of subtle

---

[15] In these three correlations, we have proof that the different dimensions of status integration need not necessarily vary directly with each other, with the implication being that any one measure cannot be used with any degree of certainty as a reliable gauge of the measure of total status integration.

[16] *Demographic Yearbook* (1956), p. 277.

theological differences, it is obvious that the theory of status integration does not fail to predict this finding accurately. Examination of the composite measures resulting from the combination of all three available integration measures (column 5, Table 46) shows that three of the predominantly Catholic countries rank very high on the measure compared to the remaining ten countries: Guatemala, 1; Venezuela, 2; and Spain, 4. These high ranks for integration are consistent with the low rank on suicide, 13, 12, and 11, respectively. On the other hand, Austria has the lowest composite measure (2.6326) of all the thirteen countries, a rank which predicts very satisfactorily its high suicide rate.

An equally interesting problem that has long intrigued investigators is the marked differences in the suicide rates of Norway, Sweden, and Denmark.[17] These differences cannot be explained in terms of an obvious cultural difference such as religion, since the three are somewhat homogeneous in this respect. It was anticipated that the theory of status integration would make it possible to predict the rank of the suicide rates of these three countries relative to each other, and the data show this to be the case. In Table 42, it may be seen that the measures of the integration of labor force status with sex for the three are: Norway, 1.375; Sweden, 1.336; and Denmark, 1.295. Consistent with the major theorem, the corresponding suicide rates are 7.2, 15.6, and 23.9. Because of the absence of comparable data, Norway could not be included in subsequent tables; however, as shown in Table 46, which relates to a composite measure of status integration, the differences in the suicide rates of Denmark and Sweden are in line with the theorem.

It must be noted that the positive results do not extend to Finland, a country generally regarded as being somewhat different in cultural terms from Norway, Denmark, and Sweden. When the four are considered together the measures of labor force integration in Table 42 do not correctly predict the ranks of the suicide rates of Denmark and Finland (ρ for the four is —.80), and the composite measures in Table 46 fail to correctly distinguish Sweden and Finland. It thus appears likely that an important aspect of status integration in Finland is not taken into account by the measures; however, the theory accounts for differences among Norway, Denmark, and Sweden better than any other known to us at this writing.

[17] Veli Verkko, *Homicides and Suicides in Finland and Their Dependence on National Character* (Copenhagen, 1951).

CHAPTER ELEVEN

Tests Within Selected Countries

JUST AS a general theory must be tested on an international level, so must it be examined for its ability to account for differences in suicide rates within distinctly different societies. While a theory which holds within a Protestant, white, capitalistic country need not be labelled worthless because it fails in other types, it is obviously desirable that the theory be general enough to make correct intranational predictions regardless of political, economic, racial, or religious characteristics. The ultimate goal would be to carry out rigorous tests in every conceivable type of society, but circumstances make this impossible. Only in a few countries do we find data of the type necessary for tests of the major theorem. The writers have found it possible, however, to obtain sufficient data to carry out a small number of intranational tests. While the tests do not provide proof that the theory of status integration is valid in all societies, they do show that the theory has more than a minimum predictive power even when inadequate statistics are used.

VARIABILITY IN SUICIDE RATES BY AGE IN ENGLAND AND WALES

We have seen that one of the more pressing needs in examining the relationship by age groups between measures of occupational integration and suicide rates is for suicide data relating to employed persons. While such data are not available in the United States, they do exist for England and Wales in the form of statistics on suicide by nine age groups for occupied persons over the three-year period 1930-1932.[1] Corresponding population figures are also provided for the year 1931, giving for nine age groups the total number of occupied persons and the number of occupied persons in five occupational classes. These data are reported for occupied males, single occupied females, and married females with an occupied spouse. Suicide rates by age groups were computed for the three categories.

Notice that the category "occupied persons" embraces not only the actively employed but also the out-of-work and retired;[2] "Occupied suicides" includes suicides among the same populations. Although it would be better to work with suicide and population data for the actively employed alone, it is fortunate that the categories used here do correspond.

The five occupational classes used in reporting occupation by age are described as follows:

> So far as is possible from the material available Class I purports to represent the professional and well-to-do section of the population, Class III, Skilled artisan and analogous workers and Class V, Labourers and other unskilled callings, while Classes II and IV are intermediates comprising occupations of mixed types, or types not readily assignable to the classes on either side.[3]

While organized into a hierarchy and depicted as social classes, the categories are nevertheless occupational groups, and measures of the integration of occupation with age were computed on that basis.

There are two points to be considered prior to a statement of the hypotheses tested on data for England and Wales. First, in the case of the married female with an occupied spouse, we are dealing with a type of status configuration that has not previously been considered. In computing measures of the integration of occupation with age for this status configuration, the assumption is made that the occupational status of a married man also constitutes a status for his wife. And, second, in terms of an evaluation of the major theorem, the importance of the tests of the hypotheses lies not only in the fact of a greater comparability between suicide rates and the measures of the integration of occupation with age but also in the fact that they constitute tests of the major theorem outside of the United States.[4]

---

[1] *The Registrar-General's Decennial Supplement: England and Wales, 1931,* Part IIa, Occupational Mortality (London, 1938), pp. 216-306.

[2] *Ibid.,* p. 189.

[3] *Loc. cit.*

[4] The data for England and Wales have not been exhausted by the present study. Given the time and resources for research, it will eventually be possible

The first hypothesis advanced regarding variability in suicide rates by age in England and Wales reads as follows: *Among occupied males there will be an inverse relationship by age groups between measures of integration of occupation with age and suicide rates.* Table 47 gives measures of the integration of occupation with age and suicide rates for nine age groups.

Table 47. MEASURES OF THE INTEGRATION OF OCCUPATION WITH AGE, 1931, AND SUICIDE RATES BY AGE, 1930-1932, FOR OCCUPIED MALES, ENGLAND AND WALES

Age Group	Mean Annual Suicide Rate	Rank of Suicide Rate	Measure of the Integration of Occupation with Age	Rank of Measure
16-19	4.0	9	.3835	2
20-24	9.7	8	.3889	1
25-34	13.3	7	.3450	3
35-44	22.0	6	.3187	4
45-54	39.3	5	.2962	5
55-64	54.7	3	.2783	8
65-69	58.0	1	.2746	9
70-74	55.0	2	.2803	7
75+	51.7	4	.2858	6

The hypothesis was tested by computing a rank-difference correlation between the ranks given in the table. A high degree of relationship is indicated by a ρ of —.97.

The second hypothesis advanced regarding variability in suicide rates by age in England and Wales reads as follows: *Among occupied single females there will be an inverse relationship by age groups between measures of the integration of occupation with age and suicide rates.* Table 48 gives measures of the integration of occupation with age and suicide rates for nine age groups. In this case, ρ proved to be —.58.

The third hypothesis considered reads as follows: *Among married females with an occupied spouse there will be an inverse relationship by age groups between measures of the integration of occupation with age and suicide rates.* Table 49 gives measures of the integration of occupation with age and suicide rates for nine age groups. The value of ρ is —.80.

Though England and Wales share many societal and cultural characteristics with the United States, it would be an error to treat them as identical societies; the differences are too great for an explanation

through the use of the England and Wales data to test the major theorem by within-columns predictions of suicide rates. This should entail an analysis in terms of more refined occupational groups and the inclusion of marital status.

of the similarity of findings on the basis of a common culture. Admittedly, it will be necessary to test the theory of status integration in countries less similar to the United States before a claim for a truly general theory is warranted.

Table 48. MEASURES OF THE INTEGRATION OF OCCUPATION WITH AGE, 1931, AND SUICIDE RATES BY AGE, 1930-1932, FOR OCCUPIED SINGLE FEMALES, ENGLAND AND WALES

Age Group	Mean Annual Suicide Rate	Rank of Suicide Rate	Measure of the Integration of Occupation with Age	Rank of Measure
16-19	3.0	9	.6006	2
20-24	4.7	8	.6207	1
25-34	8.3	6	.5971	3
35-44	12.3	5	.5408	4
45-54	17.7	1	.4913	5
55-64	17.0	2	.4683	6
65-69	15.3	3	.4648	8
70-74	14.0	4	.4590	9
75+	6.0	7	.4659	7

TESTS OF THE MAJOR THEOREM IN BELGIUM

As a part of an effort to evaluate the major theorem under as many different conditions as possible, a series of tests has been made for Belgium. The Belgian data were selected not because they are ideal for the purpose, but because they offer, despite many shortcomings, an opportunity to test a series of different propositions.

Table 49. MEASURES OF THE INTEGRATION OF OCCUPATION WITH AGE, 1931, AND SUICIDE RATES BY AGE, 1930-1932, FOR MARRIED FEMALES WITH AN OCCUPIED SPOUSE, ENGLAND AND WALES

Age Group	Mean Annual Suicide Rate	Rank of Suicide Rate	Measure of the Integration of Occupation with Age	Rank of Measure
16-19	3.3	9	.3514	2
20-24	3.7	8	.3565	1
25-34	6.3	7	.3408	3
35-44	8.7	5	.3185	4
45-54	12.7	2	.3004	5
55-64	14.7	1	.2883	8
65-69	12.3	3.5	.2881	9
70-74	12.3	3.5	.2905	7
75+	6.7	6	.2978	6

Parental Status Integration by Province. The data for Belgium make possible several Type 2 (between-columns) tests. It will be recalled that the proposition in this case is that a negative relationship holds between the ΣX^2 values for the columns and the suicide rates of the populations in the columns.

Previous investigators have asserted that parental status bears an important relationship to suicide.[5] Since data are available for Belgium for families with no living children, it is possible to compute a simple parental status measure for each of the nine Belgian provinces, as shown in Table 50. This measure pertains to active parents only (i.e., those with one or more living children). The ΣX^2 values for each row (column 3) are the integration measures used in the test. These measures are extremely simple since they ignore marital, age, sex, and other important statuses.

Table 50. MEASURES OF PARENTAL STATUS INTEGRATION, 1947, AND MEAN ANNUAL SUICIDE RATES, 1946-1948, BY PROVINCES, BELGIUM

Province	Proportion Active Parent*	Proportion not Active Parent	ΣX^2	Rank	Suicide Rate†	Rank
Anvers	.753	.247	.628	6	12.7	4
Brabant	.688	.312	.571	8.5	19.2	1
Flandre Occidentale	.788	.212	.666	3	12.0	6.5
Flandre Orientale	.780	.220	.657	4	12.2	5
Hainaut	.712	.288	.590	7	18.3	2
Liège	.688	.312	.571	8.5	16.7	3
Limbourg	.846	.154	.739	1	7.2	9
Luxembourg	.796	.204	.675	2	7.3	8
Namur	.756	.244	.631	5	12.0	6.5

* Institut National de Statistique, *Recensement General de La Population, de L'Industrie et du Commerce au 31 décembre* (Bruxelles, 1951), Tome VII, Tableau 29, p. 30.
† Number of suicides, 1946-1948, and population, 1947, obtained from following source: Institut National de Statistique, *Annuaire Statistique de La Belgique et du Congo Belge* (Bruxelles, 1950), Tome LXX, pp. 29, 87.

The between-columns test in this case is actually "between-rows" because of the construction of the table. The hypothesis, however, remains the same, that an inverse relation by provinces holds between the integration measure and the suicide rate. When the rank-difference correlation was computed, ρ proved to be $-.92$. In spite of the failure of the integration measure to encompass several important statuses, it provides a good basis for predicting differences in suicide rate by provinces. This finding points up a major weakness of previous tests. In spite of its demonstrated importance, parental status could not be included in any of the measures of status integration.

[5] Durkheim, pp. 197-202.

Industry and Sex Integration by Province. A test similar to that above may be made with measures of industry and sex integration. Eight industrial categories were used in the 1947 census: *agriculture, sylviculture, pêche; industries extractives; industries manufacturières; bâtiment et construction; transport et communications; commerce, banques, assurances; hôtellerie, services personnels, divertissements et sports; services publiques et autres services d'intérêt général; activitiés mal désignées; sans activité (chômage).* Obviously, these are broad categories, and thus are poorly suited to the development of status integration measures.[6] Nevertheless, an industrial and sex integration measure was computed for each of the nine provinces by first calculating the proportion of the economically active population by sex falling into each of the eight industrial categories. The sum of these proportions squared (ΣX^2) represents for each province the measure of industry and sex integration. These measures are shown in column 1 of Table 51.

Table 51. INDUSTRY INTEGRATION MEASURES, 1947, AND SUICIDE RATES, 1946-1948, BY PROVINCES, BELGIUM

Province	Industry Integration Measure*	Rank	Mean Annual Suicide Rate†	Rank
Anvers	.4249	5	12.7	4
Brabant	.4222	6	19.2	1
Flandre Occidentale	.5103	2	12.0	6.5
Flandre Orientale	.5674	1	12.2	5
Hainaut	.4765	3	18.3	2
Liège	.4646	4	16.7	3
Limbourg	.3798	8	7.2	9
Luxembourg	.4108	7	7.3	8
Namur	.3729	9	12.0	6.5

* *Recensement Général de La Population, de L'Industrie et du Commerce au 31 décembre,* Tome VIII, p. 61.
† Number of suicides, 1946-1948, and population, 1947, obtained from following source: *Annuaire Statistique de La Belgique et du Congo Belge,* Tome LXX (1950), pp. 29, 87.

The hypothesis is: *An inverse relationship will hold by provinces between the measure of industry and sex integration and the rate of suicide.* In this case the value of ρ is $+.40$; it is a finding which does not support the hypothesis, but one which merits further consideration.

With only two or three exceptions, the industrial distribution by provinces is dominated by the proportion of the population in the manufacturing industries, a category comprising a great number of spe-

---

[6] Under ideal conditions, the measure should be based on specific occupations or, at a minimum, homogeneous occupational groups. The Belgium data fall far short of this.

cific occupational statuses. Thus, the high integration score here, far from indicating that a large proportion of the population occupies the same occupational status, probably should indicate a diversity of specific occupational statuses. The extent to which the industrial category (Table 51) influences the occupational integration measure is revealed by a ρ of $+.93$ between the two variables.

This situation is made even clearer if we examine the relationship by provinces between the proportion of the population employed in industry and the suicide rates.

Table 52. PROPORTION OF THE ECONOMICALLY ACTIVE POPULATION EMPLOYED IN MANUFACTURING INDUSTRY AND IN AGRICULTURE, FORESTRY, AND FISHING, 1947, AND SUICIDE RATES, 1946-1948, BY PROVINCES, BELGIUM

Province	Proportion in Manufacturing Industry*	Rank	Proportion in Agriculture, Forestry, and Fishing*	Rank	Mean Annual Suicide Rate† 1946-48	Rank
Anvers	.3805	5	.1014	6	12.7	4
Brabant	.3470	6	.0893	8	19.2	1
Flandre Occidentale	.4190	2	.1558	4	12.0	6.5
Flandre Orientale	.4462	1	.1479	5	12.2	5
Hainaut	.3864	4	.0822	9	18.3	2
Liège	.4075	3	.0969	7	16.7	3
Limbourg	.2104	9	.2145	2	7.2	9
Namur	.2956	7	.1693	3	12.0	6.5

* *Recensement Général de La Population, de L'Industrie et du Commerce au 31 décembre,* Tome VIII, p. 61.

† Number of suicides, 1946-48, and population, 1947, obtained from following source: *Annuaire Statistique de La Belgique et du Congo Belge,* Tome LXX (1950), pp. 29, 87.

Using the data presented in Table 52, a rank-difference correlation was computed between the ranks in column 2 and those in column 6. The value of ρ is $+.45$. In contrast, the ρ between the per cent employed in agriculture and forestry and the suicide rates by provinces is $-.95$. These two values are consistent with the preceding discussion of the heterogenous nature of the manufacturing compared to the agricultural category. In most cases, "agriculture" denotes "farmer," a relatively specific occupational status. The failure of the theory to correctly predict the direction of the relationship between the measure of industry and sex integration and the suicide rate in Belgium appears to result from attempting to develop an integration measure using impossibly broad industrial categories, with the predominant one, manufacturing industry, being a mixture of highly specialized occupational statuses having little in common except the industrial designation. In addition, of course, the integration measure was an extremely simple one that ignored such basic statuses as age, marital status, and parental status.

Industrial Integration by Province. In addition to the between-columns test already reported that used industry and sex integration measures, it is possible to make a within-columns type of test for each of the Belgian provinces. The data for making these tests are not ideal, since, as is often the case, the industrial categories used in presenting the suicide data are not identical to those used in presenting the census data. Indeed, in order to find industrial categories that could be matched even roughly with the 1946-1948 suicide categories it was necessary to use census data for 1930. The industrial categories for which 1947 suicide data were provided are: *agricole, commerciale, industrielle, intellectuelle ou libérale, inconnues et autres.* The census industry categories for 1930 were: *agriculture et forêts; pêche; industrie; commerce; professions libérales; fonctions publiques; services de la maison, des biens, et des personnes; professions non determ.* Although the two classifications differ considerably, it was possible to compute suicide rates for four broad industrial categories: agriculture,[7] commerce, industrial, and professional. All other categories were omitted.

These tests differ from those last reported in that within each province the proportion of the economically active population in a specified industrial status is related to the suicide rate of the population occupying that status rather than the suicide rate of the total population. The tests made are thus Type 1 tests, in which the proportion of the population occupying a given cell is treated as a measure of status integration. Once again the theory leads to the prediction of an inverse correlation between the individual cell proportions and the suicide rate of the population in that cell. Since the necessary data are available for each of the Belgian provinces, it is possible to make nine separate tests.

Before considering these nine tests, it is important to re-examine the several factors operating against the possibility of correct predictions. The industry categories used for census purposes and for the tabulation of suicide cases are both excessively broad and only roughly comparable. The 1946-1948 suicide rates for the four industrial categories are computed on the basis of the 1930 population figures. The 1946-1948 suicide rates thus computed are to be related to status integration measures for 1930. Finally, the status integration measures themselves are extremely simple, ignoring nearly all major statuses, including parental, marital, religious, age, and sex.

---

[7] *Agriculture et forêts* was combined with *pêche.*

Table 53. MEASURES OF INDUSTRY INTEGRATION, 1930, AND MEAN ANNUAL SUICIDE RATES, 1946-1948, BY PROVINCES, BELGIUM

Industry Category	M.S.I.*	Rank of M.S.I.	S.R.†	Rank of S.R.
Anvers				
Agriculture	.1453	3	27.0	3
Commercial	.1593	2	29.0	2
Industrial	.5451	1	18.6	4
Professional	.0361	4	10.5	1
Brabant				
Agriculture	.1309	3	35.2	3
Commercial	.2021	2	43.0	2
Industrial	.4817	1	28.0	4
Professional	.0491	4	120.9	1
Flandre Occidentale				
Agriculture	.2268	2	35.0	3
Commercial	.1394	3	36.3	2
Industrial	.5156	4	16.1	4
Professional	.0340	1	90.6	1
Flandre Orientale				
Agriculture	.2190	2	25.4	3
Commercial	.1137	3	29.2	2
Industrial	.5642	1	15.0	4
Professional	.0319	4	31.6	1
Hainaut				
Agriculture	.1030	3	43.9	2
Commercial	.1231	2	25.6	4
Industrial	.6638	1	30.0	3
Professional	.0317	4	122.9	1
Liège				
Agriculture	.1165	3	27.9	2
Commercial	.1375	2	34.7	3
Industrial	.6058	4	26.6	4
Professional	.0341	1	116.8	1
Limbourg				
Agriculture	.3604	2	23.7	3
Commercial	.0894	3	47.8	2
Industrial	.4241	1	20.7	4
Professional	.0341	4	52.8	1
Luxembourg				
Agriculture	.4044	1	12.7	3
Commercial	.0899	3	45.0	2
Industrial	.3545	2	11.4	4
Professional	.0349	4	63.1	1
Namur				
Agriculture	.2027	2	40.2	3
Commercial	.1149	3	45.3	2
Industrial	.5100	4	16.9	4
Professional	.0471	1	67.2	1

* M.S.I., Measure of status integration. Does not add to 1.000 because some categories omitted.
Source: *Annuaire Statistique de la Belgique et du Congo Belge*, p. 52.
† S.R., Suicide rate. Source: *Annuaire Statistique de la Belgique et du Congo Belge*, Tome LXX (1950), p. 87; Tome LXXI (1951), p. 92.

Presented in Table 53 are integration measures and suicide rates for the four individual industrial categories in each of the nine provinces. Examination reveals that in each province a negative relationship holds between the two variables (for example, without exception, the professional category ranks 4 on integration and 1 on suicide, while with only one exception, the corresponding ranks of the industry category are 1 and 4). The ρ values for the provinces are as follows:

Anvers	— .80	Liege	−1.00
Brabant	— .80	Limbourg	−1.00
Flandre Occidentale	−1.00	Luxembourg	— .80
Flandre Orientale	−1.00	Namur	−1.00
Hainaut	— .80		

In five of the nine provinces the rank-order of the integration measure invariably correctly predicted the rank-order of the suicide rate of the industrial categories. The over-all pattern of the nine ρ's may be construed as strong support for the major theorem. Furthermore, this degree of success, using an M.S.I. for 1930 and suicide rates for 1946-1948, indicates that status integration may remain quite stable over a considerable period of time.

Table 54. PROPORTION OF THE ECONOMICALLY ACTIVE POPULATION IN THE INDUSTRIAL CATEGORY, 1930, AND MEAN ANNUAL SUICIDE RATES OF PERSONS IN THE INDUSTRIAL CATEGORY, 1946-1948, BY PROVINCES, BELGIUM

Province	Proportion in Industrial Category*	Rank	Suicide Rate of Persons in Industrial Category†	Rank
Anvers	.5451	4	18.6	5
Brabant	.4817	7	28.0	2
Flandre Occidentale	.5156	5	16.1	7
Flandre Orientale	.5642	3	15.0	8
Hainaut	.6638	1	30.0	1
Liège	.6058	2	26.6	3
Limbourg	.4241	8	20.7	4
Luxembourg	.3545	9	11.4	9
Namur	.5100	6	16.9	6

* *Recensement Général de La Population, de L'Industrie et du Commerce au 31 décembre*, 1947, Tome VIII, p. 61.
† Source: *Annuaire Statistique de la Belgique et du Congo Belge*, Tome LXX (1950), p. 87; Tome LXX I(1951), p. 92.

Industrial Integration Measures. It will be recalled that the theory of status integration leads to the expectation that the suicide rate of any given status will vary inversely with the proportion of the population that occupies that status. That is, given two populations, *A*, in which a very small proportion are barbers and *B*, in which a larger proportion are barbers, it is predicted that the suicide rate of barbers in *A* will be higher than that of barbers in *B*. This is an unusual type of test, in that it involves a comparison of cells in different columns. In this section, four such tests are reported. The first test deals with the relationship between the proportion of the economically active population in the category "industrial" and the suicide rate in this category by provinces. The test was made on the basis of the data presented in Table 54.

The nature of the industrial category and its unsatisfactory character as a status category have already been discussed, and so it is not surprising that the present test also fails to support the theory. The value of ρ is $+.40$.

The second test is identical to the first except that it deals with the proportion of the population in the professional category and its relationship to the suicide rate of that category. Data are shown in Table 55.

Table 55. PROPORTION OF THE ECONOMICALLY ACTIVE POPULATION IN PROFESSIONS, 1930, AND MEAN ANNUAL SUICIDE RATES OF PERSONS IN THE PROFESSIONS, 1946-1948, BY PROVINCES, BELGIUM

State	Proportion in Professional Category*	Rank	Suicide Rate of Professional Category†	Rank
Anvers	.0361	3	43.8	8
Brabant	.0491	1	120.9	2
Flandre Occidentale	.0340	7	90.6	4
Flandre Orientale	.0319	8	31.6	9
Hainaut	.0317	9	122.9	1
Liège	.0341	5.5	116.8	3
Limbourg	.0341	5.5	52.8	7
Luxembourg	.0349	4	63.1	6
Namur	.0471	2	67.2	5

* *Recensement Général de La Population, de L'Industrie et du Commerce au 31 décembre*, 1947, Tome VIII, p. 61.

† Source: *Annuaire Statistique de la Belgique et du Congo Belge*, Tome LXX (1950), p. 87; Tome LXX I(1951), p. 92.

Although the professional category is much less heterogeneous than the industrial category, this test also failed to support the major theorem; in this case, ρ equals $-.01$.

The third test deals with the proportion of the population in the commerce category. The data are given in Table 56.

This table reveals that, in general, the smaller the proportion of persons in the commercial category, the higher the suicide rate. The computed ρ equals $-.45$.

The final test in the series deals with the relationship between the proportion of the population in the agricultural category and the suicide rate in this category. Table 57 presents the data necessary to conduct the test.

Table 56. PROPORTION OF THE ECONOMICALLY ACTIVE POPULATION IN COMMERCE, 1930, AND MEAN ANNUAL SUICIDE RATES OF PERSONS IN COMMERCE, 1946-1948, BY PROVINCES, BELGIUM

State	Proportion in Commerce*	Rank	Suicide Rate of Commerce Category†	Rank
Anvers	.1593	2	29.0	8
Brabant	.2021	1	43.0	4
Flandre Occidentale	.1394	3	36.3	5
Flandre Orientale	.1137	7	29.2	7
Hainaut	.1231	5	25.6	9
Liège	.1375	4	34.7	6
Limbourg	.0894	9	47.8	1
Luxembourg	.0899	8	45.0	3
Namur	.1149	6	45.3	2

* *Recensement Général de La Population, de L'Industrie et du Commerce au 31 décembre,* 1947, Tome VIII, p. 61.

† Source: *Annuaire Statistique de la Belgique et du Congo Belge,* Tome LXX (1950), p. 87; Tome LXX I(1951), p. 92.

Table 57. PROPORTION OF THE ECONOMICALLY ACTIVE POPULATION IN AGRICULTURE, 1930, AND MEAN ANNUAL SUICIDE RATES OF PERSONS IN AGRICULTURE, 1946-1948, BY PROVINCES, BELGIUM

State	Proportion in Agriculture*	Rank	Suicide Rate of Persons in Agriculture†	Rank
Anvers	.1453	6	27.0	6
Brabant	.1309	7	35.2	3
Flandre Occidentale	.2325	3	35.0	4
Flandre Orientale	.2191	4	25.4	7
Hainaut	.1030	9	43.9	1
Liège	.1165	8	27.9	5
Limbourg	.3604	2	23.7	8
Luxembourg	.4044	1	12.7	9
Namur	.2027	5	40.2	2

* *Recensement Général de La Population, de L'Industrie et du Commerce au 31 décembre,* 1947, Tome VIII, p. 61.

† Source: *Annuaire Statistique de la Belgique et du Congo Belge,* Tome LXX (1950), p. 87; Tome LXX I(1951), p. 92.

The prediction is verified in this instance; to a moderately impressive degree, the suicide rate of persons in agriculture varies inversely by provinces with the proportion of the population in the category. The value of ρ is —.73. The fact that the persons in this category probably occupy the specific occupational status "farmer" undoubtedly explains the greater success of this test.

The failure to achieve consistently favorable results in these four tests may be due in part to the broad, heterogeneous nature of the industrial categories. The discrepancy in dates may also be an important factor. It remains to be seen how successful the theory would be in making predictions of this type when clearly defined, specific status categories and comparable dates are used. The results obtained for the agricultural category give reason to pursue this type of analysis further in future research.

Marital Integration. Data on the number of suicides by marital status are available for Belgium, but only for the total population and not by sex. Since the marital status of the total population was ascertained in the Belgian census of 1947, it was possible to compute the proportion of the total population occupying each of the marital statuses for that year. These individual proportions were then related to the suicide rates by marital status for 1946-1948 in the form of a within-column test of the major theorem. The data used are presented in Table 58.

Table 58. MARITAL INTEGRATION, 1947, AND MEAN ANNUAL SUICIDE RATES BY MARITAL STATUS, 1946-1948, FOR THE TOTAL POPULATION, BELGIUM

Marital Status	Marital Integration No.*	Proportion	Rank	Suicide Rate†	Rank
Single	3,592,587	.4221	2	7.8	4
Married	4,238,493	.4979	1	15.7	3
Widowed	610,904	.0718	3	43.8	2
Divorced and not applicable	70,211	.0082	4	45.6	1

* *Annuaire Statistique de la Belgique et du Congo Belge,* Tome LXX (1950), pp. 44-45.
† *Ibid.,* p. 87 and Tome LXXI (1951), p. 81.

The major theorem leads to the prediction that the proportion of the population occupying a particular marital status will be inversely related to the suicide rate of that marital status. The fact that such a measure of integration ignores age, sex, religion, and other important statuses makes it unlikely that a particularly high predictive power will be shown. The computed ρ of —.80 supports the major theorem.

TESTS WITH ITALIAN DATA

Nineteenth-century Italy would undoubtedly be accepted as having a society distinctly different in many respects from that of twentieth-century United States. Outstanding differences would include religion, racial composition, type of government, and industry structure. For this reason, several tests have been made with nineteenth-century Italian data.

Occupational Integration and Suicide. In the earlier sections devoted to the explication of the theory, the crucial assumption was made that the actual behavior of persons moving in and out of statuses is indicative of the degree of compatibility among the statuses.[8] Two or more statuses rarely occupied simultaneously by the same persons are regarded as being incompatible. The theory further holds that those persons who are in rarely occupied status configurations will have a high suicide rate. For example, a particular occupation may rarely be occupied by persons in certain marital, sex, or racial statuses,[9] and the theory predicts that persons who do occupy such configurations will have a high suicide rate. We have repeatedly stressed that any attempt to test the relationship should take into account all major statuses —age, sex, marital, religious, and racial. However, it is possible to make a less exacting test without knowledge of the total status configurations involved.

If, for example, data on the occupational distribution of a population by sex were known, a simple Type 1 test could be made. According to the theory, the occupations held by the largest proportion of males would be characterized by the lowest suicide rate, while those held by a very small proportion would have the highest rates. Only the integration of sex and occupation is being considered in this case; all other statuses are being ignored. While such a Type 1 test could be made, the results could hardly be expected to be impressive, since so many major statuses are entirely ignored. However, Morselli[10] has presented a table of data which is more than ordinarily adequate for such a test.

Religion and race are not included in Morselli's table, but in nineteenth-century Italy they are probably relatively constant for all occupations. Marital status, parental status, and age are the only crucial statuses not taken into account. Table 59 is adapted from Morselli's original.

Examination of this table reveals that three tests can be made—one for males, one for females, and one for the total population. On the

---

[8] See pp. 25-26.

[9] The means by which this takes place are outlined on p. 25.

[10] Henry Morselli, *Suicide: An Essay on Comparative Moral Statistics* (New York, 1942).

Table 59. OCCUPATION BY PROPORTION PER THOUSAND OF THE POPULATION AND SUICIDE RATES BY OCCUPATION AND SEX, ITALY, 1866-1876*

Occupation	Males Proportion†	Males Rank	Males Suicide Rate	Males Rank	Females Proportion†	Females Rank	Females Suicide Rate	Females Rank	Total Proportion†	Total Rank	Total Suicide Rate	Total Rank
Letters and science‡	1.0	17	61.8	1	...	...	...	...	0.5	17	61.8	1
Vagrant professions‡	1.4	16	26.1	6	0.3	12	25.3	2	0.9	16	25.9	4
Instruction, education‡	1.8	15	35.5	3	2.1	9	2.0	10	2.0	12.5	17.5	7
Jurisprudence‡	1.9	14	21.8	7	...	...	...	...	1.0	15	21.8	6
Fine Arts‡	2.8	13	9.1	12	0.2	13	10.0	3	1.5	14	9.4	11
Medical profession‡	3.2	12	20.1	8	0.9	10	2.8	7	2.0	12.5	16.3	8
Religion	8.8	11	5.4	14	2.2	8	0.6	13	5.6	10	4.5	14
Public administration	9.9	10	32.4	4	...	...	...	...	5.2	11	32.4	3
Defender of country	10.8	9	40.4	2	...	...	...	...	5.4	9	40.4	2
Commerce	12.4	8	27.7	5	2.4	7	8.7	4	7.5	8	24.6	5
Domestic servant	12.5	7	11.7	11	22.3	5	4.1	6	17.7	6	6.8	12
Transport	19.5	6	15.3	10	0.6	11	(43.3)§	1	10.1	7	15.5	9
Property, movable and unmovable	30.6	5	17.3	9	26.5	4	4.4	5	28.5	5	11.4	10
Industrial supernumeraries	34.5	4	3.6	15	13.9	6	1.6	11	24.2	4	3.1	15
Industrial production	143.2	3	8.0	13	101.9	3	2.3	8	122.7	3	5.7	13
Dependents, and without fixed professions; unknown professions	282.3	2	2.2	17	597.9	1	0.6	12	439.2	1	0.8	17
Production of raw materials	423.2	1	2.7	16	227.8	2	2.2	9	326.0	2	2.5	16

* Adapted from Morselli, Table XXXV, p. 244.
† Proportion per 1,000 of the specified population.
‡ Data for 1868-1876.
§ Small number of cases.

basis of the major theorem, an inverse relationship was anticipated between the proportion of the population in a particular occupational category (in this case the number per 1,000 population) and the suicide rate of that category.[11] Rank-difference correlations were computed for each of the three panels of the table with these resulting values for ρ: males, $-.70$; females, $-.55$; and total population, $-.74$. In each case, the result clearly supports the major theorem.

The results are impressive considering the apparent inadequacy of the data, but it must be emphasized that the test situation is more favorable than it appears. For example, a larger number of specific occupations are presented in the table than is usually the practice and consequently there is less masking of occupational statuses.[12] Furthermore, as stated above, religion and probably race are constant for all occupations, so that these two statuses can be ignored as of little consequence for practical purposes. It is doubtful that a test as simple as this one would be adequate in a situation where religion and race, to mention only two statuses, are not constants.

Status Integration and Suicide Rates Among Compartimenti. While the remarkably low suicide rate of Italy in comparison to other European countries has long been recognized, the differences among the suicide rates of Italian *compartimenti* has received less attention. It is in the differences of the suicide rates of these Italian political subdivisions that the standard *ad hoc* explanation of Italy's low suicide rate can be questioned. As shown in Table 60, the differences among Italian *compartimenti* with respect to the proportion of Catholics is truly microscopic in comparison to the difference in their suicide rates. (This table, and those that follow, show eleven *compartimenti* for which both suicide rates and other measures were available.)

It is clear, however, that in comparison to international differences there was little variation in the suicide rates of the political subdivisions of Italy over the years 1864-1876. Consequently, the explanation of such variation in terms of the prevalence of Catholicism receives support by the small absolute differences in the suicide rates of Italian *compartimenti*. This in turn suggests that differences in the proportion of Catholics from one *compartimenti* to the next can account for observed differences in the suicide rate. An inspection of Table 60 reveals that this is substantially true, with the ρ between column 2 and column 4 being $-.50$.

---

[11] Conversion of the data given by Morselli to proportions would have no effect on the ranks and thus no affects on the value of ρ.

[12] Compare with the data for Belgium, p. 136 ff.

There are two points to be considered in the inverse relationship between the proportion of Catholics and the suicide rates of Italian *compartimenti*. For one thing, there is reason to anticipate that such a relationship would hold on the basis of status integration. That is, if a measure of religious integration were computed for the Italian *compartimenti*, the proportion of Catholics would be its principal component, and the two should vary directly. This suggestion was checked by

Table 60. MEAN ANNUAL SUICIDE RATES, 1864-1876, AND PROPORTION CATHOLIC, 1871, BY *compartimenti*, ITALY

Compartimenti	Proportion of Population Catholic*	Rank	Suicide Rate†	Rank
Piemonte	.9896	10	3.56	6
Liguria	.9969	2	4.74	2
Lombardia	.9953	6	4.04	5
Veneto	.9965	3	3.21	8
Emilia	.9928	8	6.30	1
Umbria	.9960	4	3.07	9
Marche	.9947	7	3.46	7
Toscana	.9906	9	4.06	4
Roma	.9846	11	4.18	3
Sicilia	.9957	5	1.85	10
Sardegna	.9992	1	1.34	11

* Source: *Annuario Statistico Italiano,* 1878, p. 44.
† Source: Morselli, p. 41.

computing such a measure on the basis of the proportion of the population in four religious statuses—*Cattolica, Evangelica, Israeliticia,* and *Altre.*[13] The resulting measures of religious integration (ΣX^2 of the four proportions) for each of 11 Italian *compartimenti* are shown in Table 61 along with the proportions of Catholics.

As suggested above, the inverse relationship between the proportion of Catholics and the suicide rates of Italian *compartimenti* is in reality not consistent with the theory of status integration, since the proportion of Catholics bears a perfect direct relationship with a measure of religious integration. All other things being equal, the theory of status integration would anticipate that differences in the suicide rates of populations vary inversely with measures of religious integration or a component measure—the proportion of the population in the largest religious category.[14]

---

[13] *Annuario Statistico Italiano,* 1878 (Rome) p. 44.

[14] The point here is that the low suicide rates of Italy or its provinces may not be the result of the content of Catholicism but rather of the religious homogeneity which creates a high degree of status integration. True, Scandinavian countries have high suicide rates and a religious homogeneity comparable to Italy's, but their other dimensions of status integration—marital, occupational, parental—are

A second point to be considered in the relationship between the proportion of Catholics and the suicide rates in Italian *compartimenti* is the amount of variability in the suicide rates that is left unexplained. To return to the original argument, it would appear that the proportion of Catholics was too constant among the *compartimenti* to adequately account for all of the variability in their suicide rates. This in turn suggests that some other important dimension of status integration was operating in Italy.

Table 61. MEASURE OF RELIGIOUS INTEGRATION AND THE PROPORTION CATHOLIC, BY *compartimenti*, ITALY, 1871

Compartimenti	Proportion Catholic	Rank	Measure of Religious Integration	Rank
Piemonte	.9896	10	.9794	10
Liguria	.9969	2	.9938	2
Lombardia	.9953	6	.9906	6
Veneto	.9965	3	.9930	3
Emilia	.9928	8	.9857	8
Umbria	.9960	4	.9920	4
Marche	.9947	7	.9894	7
Toscana	.9906	9	.9813	9
Roma	.9846	11	.9695	11
Sicilia	.9957	5	.9914	5
Sardegna	.9992	1	.9984	1

Table 62. MEASURES OF MARITAL INTEGRATION, BY *compartimenti*, ITALY, 1871

Compartimenti	Measure of Marital Integration
Piemonte	.4755
Liguria	.4755
Lombardia	.4638
Veneto	.4594
Emilia	.4594
Umbria	.4742
Marche	.4742
Toscana	.4742
Roma	.4742
Sicilia	.4742
Sardegna	.4686

Acting on this suggestion, the writers found data suited for crude measures of marital and occupational integration. Marital integration among the Italian *compartimenti* (as measured by the proportions of single, married, and widowed) [15] proved to be even more constant (see

not comparable. Also notice (Tables 41-46) that predominantly Catholic Austria has a suicide rate over twice as high as that of Great Britain, a predominantly Protestant country.

[15] *Annuario Statistico Italiano,* p. 39.

Table 62) than was religious integration and hence of questionable significance.

The remarkable constancy found in the degree of marital and religious integration among Italian *compartimenti* is not matched in the case of occupational integration. Measures of the latter are in this case based on the proportion in the following seventeen *gruppi di professioni: proprietà mobiliare e immobiliare, personale di servizio, difesa del paese, amministrazione pubblica, lettere e scienze, professioni girovaght, personale di servizio fisso, produzione delle materie prime, produzione industriale, commercio, trasporti, culto, giurisprudenza, professioni sanitario, istruzione ed educazione, belle arti;* and *personale a carico altrui e senza professione.*[16]

Table 63. MEAN ANNUAL SUICIDE RATES, 1864-1876, AND MEASURES OF OCCUPATIONAL INTEGRATION, 1871, BY *compartimenti,* ITALY

Compartimenti	Measure of Occupational Integration	Rank	Suicide Rate	Rank
Piemonte	.3424	3	3.56	6
Liguria	.3020	10	4.74	2
Lombardia	.3110	9	4.04	5
Veneto	.3456	2	3.21	8
Emilia	.3138	8	6.30	1
Umbria	.3410	4	3.07	9
Marche	.3259	6	3.46	7
Toscana	.3173	7	4.06	4
Roma	.2906	11	4.18	3
Sicilia	.3280	5	1.85	10
Sardegna	.4358	1	1.34	11

According to the major theorem, we should expect an inverse relationship to hold between suicide rates and measures of occupational integration by Italian *compartimenti*. As an inspection of Table 63 will reveal, this is substantially the case, with ρ being —.81.

Although the two cannot be construed as evidence for opposing theories, it is interesting to note that measures of occupational integration have far more predictive power than does the proportion of Catholics. The same is true for the predictive power of occupational integration in comparison to that of marital integration. The differences in the predictive power may well be because, of the three dimensions of status integration, only occupational integration varies to any significant degree among the *compartimenti*.

Ideally, a measure of status integration should incorporate all of the dimensions of status integration in a population. Since it is not

[16] *Ibid.,* pp. 40-43.

possible to prepare comprehensive measures[17] for the Italian *compartimenti* the next best alternative is to combine the separate ones for religious, marital, and occupational integration. One method for combining independent measures has been discussed previously.[18] An alternative method consists of expressing each measure as a deviation from the absolute minimum value. For example, for each of the *compartimenti* the minimum value for religious integration is .2500, for marital integration it is .3300, and for occupational integration it is .0588. When each of the three measures for a *compartimento* is expressed as the per cent that it is above the minimum value, the three can be summed to form a composite measure of status integration. The results of the above operations are shown in Table 64.

Table 64. MEASURES OF RELIGIOUS, MARITAL AND OCCUPATIONAL INTEGRATION EXPRESSED AS THE PER CENT ABOVE THE MINIMUM POSSIBLE VALUE, BY *compartimenti*, ITALY, 1871

Compartimenti	Religious Integration	Marital Integration	Occupational Integration	Sum of Measures	Rank
Piemonte	292	43	482	817	4
Liguria	298	43	414	755	10
Lombardia	296	39	429	764	9
Veneto	297	38	488	823	2
Emilia	294	38	434	766	8
Umbria	297	42	480	819	3
Marche	296	42	454	792	6
Toscana	293	42	439	774	7
Roma	288	42	394	724	11
Sicilia	297	42	458	797	5
Sardegna	299	41	641	981	1

When the ranks of the composite measures of status integration were correlated with the ranks of the suicide rates, ρ proved to be —.84. While this coefficient is not substantially higher than for occupational integration alone, it is of significance that when religious and marital integration are taken into account they improve the relationship, even if only slightly, rather than weaken it.

In recognition of the fact that there are several ways of combining independent measures of status integration,[19] the major theorem has

---

[17] Such as Table 1, p. 37.

[18] See pp. 127-130.

[19] The method of combining independent measures of status integration which will provide the most predictive power and at the same time be the most logically defensible has yet to be established.

been subjected to another test by using a method of combining measures different from that used in Table 64. Any integration measure of a population may be expressed as a per cent of the minimum value or as the absolute difference between the two, but neither of these two methods changes the magnitude of the difference between any two measures since they both involve dividing by or subtracting a constant from each measure. In view of the fact that two or more independent measures of status integration (that is, a measure of marital integration and a measure of occupational integration) are the product of identical mathematical operations, they can be combined without modification. For the Italian data this involves nothing more than adding the measures of religious, marital, and occupational integration for each of the *compartimenti*. The resulting composite measures are shown in Table 65.

Table 65. RANK OF SUICIDE RATES, 1864-1876, AND COMPOSITE MEASURES OF STATUS INTEGRATION, CONSISTING OF THE SUM OF THE MEASURES FOR RELIGIOUS, MARITAL, AND OCCUPATIONAL INTEGRATION, 1871, BY *compartimenti*, ITALY

Compartimenti	Composite Measure of Status Integration	Rank	Rank of Suicide Rate
Piemonte	1.7973	4	6
Liguria	1.7713	8	2
Lombardia	1.7654	9	5
Veneto	1.7980	3	8
Emilia	1.7590	10	1
Umbria	1.8072	2	9
Marche	1.7895	6	7
Toscana	1.7728	7	4
Roma	1.7343	11	3
Sicilia	1.7936	5	10
Sardegna	1.9028	1	11

A rank-difference correlation between the ranks proved to be —.86. It would appear from this that the straight addition of independent measures of status integration is more simple than the method used in Table 64 and yields substantially the same results. However, the method explored earlier may prove to be of value when measures of the same dimension of status integration are based on a different number of statuses. Thus, for example, a measure of occupational integration based on six occupational statuses is not comparable to one based on ten occupational statuses, but the expression of the two as a per cent of the minimum value makes them comparable.

One is justified in expecting the maximum in predictive power only when the status integration measures are refined and all-inclusive, meaning that all the major statuses are taken into account. Considering the extent to which measures used in this section do not meet this criterion, the findings support the theory to a remarkable degree.

STATUS INTEGRATION MEASURES AND SUICIDE RATES BY DISTRICTS IN WEST BENGAL

To test the major theorem in still another society, data were compiled for the computation of suicide rates and two measures of status integration for districts in West Bengal, a region with cultural traditions that are historically quite different from those of Christian-European societies. As shown in Table 66, data on suicides were available for all of the 15 districts in Bengal except Cooch Behar.[20]

Table 66. MEAN ANNUAL SUICIDE RATES BY SEX FOR DISTRICTS, WEST BENGAL, 1941-1950*

District	Male Suicides			Female Suicides			Total Suicides		
	Number	Rate	Rank	Number	Rate	Rank	Number	Rate	Rank
Burdwan.......	41	4.1	8	41	4.6	6	82	4.3	7
Birbhum........	23	4.4	7	20	3.8	9	43	4.1	8
Bankura........	35	5.4	5	32	5.0	5	67	5.2	5.5
Midnapur......	46	2.8	10	44	2.8	11	90	2.8	10.5
Hooghly........	58	7.9	3	67	10.5	1	125	9.1	1
Howrah.........	69	8.3	2	62	9.4	2	131	8.8	2
Twenty-four Parganas...	136	7.0	4	140	8.8	3	276	7.8	3
Calcutta.........	43	3.0	9	29	4.4	7	72	3.4	9
Nadia.............	24	2.5	11.5	26	3.1	10	50	2.8	10.5
Murshidabad	42	5.1	6	43	5.3	4	85	5.2	5.5
Malda............	15	2.4	13	14	2.3	12	29	2.4	12
West Dinajpur...	12	1.2	14	10	1.1	14	22	1.1	14
Jalpaiguri......	15	2.5	11.5	9	1.8	13	24	2.2	13
Darjeeling.....	18	9.0	1	7	4.0	8	25	6.6	4
West Bengal.	552	4.1	....	539	4.7	....	1091	4.4	....

* Rates and ranks based on data from *Census of India, 1951,* Vol. VI: Part 1B, *Vital Statistics in West Bengal, 1941-50,* p. 37.

These data are far from satisfactory. In the first place, figures for an entire decade reveal a very small number of cases in some districts. Second, although it was originally planned to base the decade rates on the estimated mid-decade populations, changes in district boundary

[20] *Census of India,* 1951, Vol. VI: Part 1B, "Vital Statistics, West Bengal, 1941-50" (Calcutta), pp. 37, 43.

lines during the last years of the decade made this procedure impractical. Consequently, the rates shown are based on the 1941 census population rather than a mid-decade estimate. Of course, various distortions result from differential rates of population growth over the decade, so that the suicide rates can only be regarded as crude approximations.

Measures of Integration. Two measures of status integration were computed for each of the 14 districts. One of them, a measure of marital-sex-age integration, is identical to the one described in earlier sections with the exception of two slight variations. Only three categories of marital status were provided: single, married, and a combined category—widowed and divorced.[21] The age categories were from 15 to 74 in ten-year intervals, and 75 and over.

The second measure is of some interest since it combines a rather comprehensive set of statuses somewhat different from those previously used. In addition to the same sex and age categories described above, this measure includes two residential categories, rural and urban, and an eight-category occupational classification.[22] This includes four occupations in the agricultural class, (each including dependents): cultivators of land wholly or mainly owned, cultivators of land wholly or mainly unowned, cultivating laborers, and noncultivating owners of land and agricultural rent receivers; and four in the nonagricultural class: production other than cultivation, commerce, transport, and other services and miscellaneous services.

The worksheet for computing this last integration measure involved eight occupational categories in the rows of the table, while there were seven age categories, each of which was subdivided into the two residential categories, in the table columns. One such table was constructed for males and one for females. Each of the tables contains 112 cells and the figures in each individual cell relate to the integration of occupational statuses with age, sex, and place of residence (rural or urban). For each district total unweighted and total weighted measures were computed. In addition, measures were also computed for males and females separately in each district. The total weighted integration measures are presented in Table 67.

Testing the Theorem. As in previous tests, the theory of status integration calls for an inverse relationship between the integration

---

[21] *Census of India,* 1951, Vol. VI: "West Bengal, Sikkim, and Chandernagore," Part 2, Tables, pp. 335-348.

[22] *Census of India,* 1951, Vol. VI: Part 2, pp. 298-299.

measures and the suicide rates. For West Bengal, it was recognized that there were at least two factors operating against the possibility of a high degree of relationship: the suicide rates are subject to the distortion described above, and the measures of marital and occupational integration are based on 1951 census data but the suicide rates are computed on a 1941 population base.

Table 67. TOTAL WEIGHTED MARITAL INTEGRATION MEASURES AND TOTAL WEIGHTED OCCUPATIONAL INTEGRATION MEASURES FOR DISTRICTS, WEST BENGAL, 1951

District	Marital Integration Measure	Rank	Occupational Integration Measure	Rank
Burdwan	1.3481	8	.4653	13
Birbhum	1.3536	7	.5900	7
Bankura	1.3077	10	.7039	3
Midnapur	1.3649	4	.7247	2
Hooghly	1.3079	9	.5269	12
Howrah	1.3572	6	.4492	14
Twenty-four Parganas	1.3607	5	.5412	10
Calcutta	1.1218	14	.5671	8
Nadia	1.2571	13	.6376	5
Murshidabad	1.3747	3	.5344	11
Malda	1.4159	1	.5426	9
West Dinajpur	1.3879	2	.7546	1
Jalpaiguri	1.3030	11	.6024	6
Darjeeling	1.2714	12	.6603	4

When a rank-difference coefficient of correlation was computed, between the total suicide rate and the total weighted measure of marital integration, ρ proved to be $-.14$. The corresponding value for the total weighted occupational integration measures is $-.58$. In each case the relationship is in the direction predicted by the theory. The greater magnitude of ρ in the latter case may result from the fact that the occupational measure is considerably more comprehensive than the marital status measure.[23]

Comparing Two Integration Measures. The weighted measure of the integration of occupational statuses with age, sex, and residence is more highly correlated with the suicide rate than is the weighted measure of the integration of marital status with age and sex. This finding draws attention to a methodological question discussed in an earlier section—of the various possible measures of integration, which one should be used in tests? In this connection, the findings in the case

[23] Of methodological interest here is the fact that the ρ's involving weighted measures ($-.14$ and $-.58$) are in both cases larger than the corresponding values involving unweighted measures ($-.12$ and $-.35$).

of the districts of West Bengal provide support for the idea that where alternative measures of integration are used, the most comprehensive, weighted measures should provide the best results.

Since, at the present time, any measure of status integration will be of limited comprehensiveness, there remains a basic methodological question: where two separate measures of status integration are available for a single population, is it possible to construct a more useful measure through some combination of the two? This question has been dealt with earlier in this chapter, but some further exploration is possible for the West Bengal districts.

There are two possible expectations regarding the nature of status integration within a society. One is that status integration is a general attribute and that separate measures of it should prove to be closely related. The other possibility is that status integration is not unidimensional, in which case a society might have a high degree of marital integration but a low degree of occupational integration.

In the case of the two measures of status integration for the 14 districts of West Bengal, the computation of a rank-difference correlation between the two yields a value of —.09. Although a single test necessarily has limited value in providing an answer to a theoretical problem, it will be recalled that previous tests also revealed an absence of a high positive correlation between different measures of status integration.

When the values of the two weighted measures (marital integration and occupational integration) are simply added and the resulting sums re-ranked, ρ between these ranks and the ranks of suicide is —.45.[24] Where the ranks rather than the values of the two measures are added in order to avoid the heavier weighting of the marital status measure, the corresponding ρ is —.43. Both of these values are less than the —.58 obtained when the single measure of integration of occupation with age, sex, and residence was used. Thus the combination of two measures of integration does not provide greater predictive power in this particular case.

CONCLUSION

Several tests have been discussed in this chapter which use data from countries other than the United States, and results are not without contradictions. In two instances, the observed relationship turned out to be in an opposite direction from that predicted. In both of these cases, however, it seems likely that the nature of the data used in the

---

[24] See Table 67 for the values and ranks treated in this section.

tests was partly responsible for the negative results. Of some 28 tests (not all of which are independent of each other), all but two were in the predicted direction and 19 of the ρ's were .70 or over. On this basis, even when due consideration is given to the limited number of countries involved and the crudeness of the tests, it must be conceded that the theory of status configuration seems to be remarkably free from the culture-boundness which characterizes so many sociological theories.

CHAPTER TWELVE

Suicide in
New Zealand

A LL THE TESTS of the major theorem reported in previous chapters were based on published statistics on suicide. Since these seldom report data for more than age, sex, and race—rarely for marital, occupational, and religious statuses—only very limited types of tests were possible. Consequently, it was thought desirable to obtain data from original records to compute suicide rates for status configurations not usually covered in published reports.

Original records of individual cases of suicide in New Zealand over the six-year period, 1946-1951, were obtained and statistics compiled from them.[1] Unfortunately, however, New Zealand census reports do not analyze the characteristics of the population in sufficient detail, so that, though the number of suicides in all major status configurations could be determined, measures of status integration and suicide rates could be computed for only a few of them. The New Zealand records therefore had limited value as a means for testing the major theorem, but some important tests were still possible.[2]

[1] The work on original New Zealand records reported in this chapter was made possible by a grant to Jack P. Gibbs under the Fulbright Act of 1946.

[2] The full exploitation of the New Zealand material has yet to be accomplished; but see Austin L. Porterfield and Jack P. Gibbs, "Occupational Prestige and Social Mobility of Suicides in New Zealand," *American Journal of Sociology*, LXVI (September, 1960), 147-152.

COMPILATION OF DATA

The first step in the compilation of the New Zealand data was the identification of individual cases of suicide through the inspection of *all* reports by a coroner of a death during the six-year period. Analysis of these records revealed 955 certain or probable suicides[3] and 247 possible ones.[4]

With individual suicides identified, the next step was the gathering of information on the victims' major statuses. Death certificates and birth certificates provided data on age, sex, marital status, number of children, occupation, and other characteristics, such as length of residence in New Zealand and places of residence and birth. These data served as the basis for a series of tests of the major theorem.

---

[3] In arriving at a decision as to the cause of death, the investigator found it impossible to abide by the verdict of the coroner, which was often too indefinite to serve as a useful criterion. In a few cases, the verdict was indefinite even when the deceased left a suicide note. This cannot be taken to mean that annual suicide rates for New Zealand, as given in official publications, are unreliable. Our number of definite suicides in New Zealand, 1946-1951, is 955; official publications (*New Zealand Official Yearbook, 1951-52*, p. 100, and *New Zealand Official Yearbook, 1954*, p. 96) give the number of suicides over the period as 1,000. Since every case where the coroner's verdict was "suicide" or words to that effect was included in the 955 cases, it would appear that medical statisticians in New Zealand are not governed by the coroner's verdict in assigning causes of death for statistical purposes. It is of interest to note that the mean annual suicide rate in New Zealand over the period, 1946-1951, is 9 per 100,000 population (including Maoris) when reckoned by numbers of suicides reported in official publications, a rate identical to that which is obtained when our count is used.

[4] In these cases of possible suicide, the behavior of the individual prior to his death (previous attempts of suicide, expressions of a wish to die, threats of suicide, etc.) led the investigator to suspect suicide, but the absence of a suicide note or the mode of death (being struck by a train, an overdose of drugs, and drowning accounted for the majority of these cases) left a possibility that the death was accidental. In consideration of the fact that the reliability of suicide rates remains a crucial question, these possible cases of suicide were not ignored in the course of the investigation. The demographic characteristics of each of these possible suicide cases were recorded from the death register with a view toward comparing them with the 955 cases of definite suicide; unfortunately, however, because of limited resources for research, an analysis of these possible cases of suicide could not be incorporated in the present study. We hope eventually to undertake such an analysis.

It should be noted that the 955 cases of definite suicide probably represent the minimum number of suicides in New Zealand, and this number plus the 247 cases of possible suicide probably represents the maximum number of suicides (1,202). Thus, the true mean annual suicide rate for New Zealand over the years 1946-1951, was probably between 9 and 11 per 100,000, and the rank of New Zealand's suicide rate among other countries is substantially the same whether the maximum or the minimum rate is used.

VARIABILITY IN SUICIDE RATES BY AGE

We have seen that in the United States during 1949-1951, differences in suicide rates by age groups were somewhat closely related to the degree of occupational integration within the age groups. Although occupational categories different from those in the United States are used, the New Zealand census of 1951[5] makes it possible to compute measures of occupational integration within eleven groups. These occupational integration measures were computed exactly as shown in Table 11, except that the New Zealand measures are based on eleven age groups and eleven occupational categories rather than nine age groups and eleven occupational categories. The eleven occupational categories employed in the New Zealand census reports are: (1) professional, technical, and related workers; (2) managers, administrators, and officials; (3) clerical, office, and related workers; (4) salesmen, and related workers; (5) farmers, fishermen, hunters, lumbermen, and related workers; (6) workers in mine, quarry, and related occupations; (7) workers in operating transport occupations; (8) craftsmen, production process workers, and workers in related occupations; (9) manual workers and laborers not elsewhere included; (10) service and related workers; (11) armed forces.[6]

In Table 68, measures of the degree of occupational integration within age groups and suicide rates for the age groups are given for non-Maori males in New Zealand.

Table 68. MEASURES OF OCCUPATIONAL INTEGRATION, 1951, AND MEAN ANNUAL SUICIDE RATES, 1946-1951, FOR NON-MAORI MALES BY AGE GROUPS, NEW ZEALAND

Age Group	Suicide Rate	Rank	Measure of Occupational Integration	Rank
16-19	6.1	11	.2014	1
20-24	10.7	9	.1778	3
25-29	8.8	10	.1747	4
30-34	14.1	6	.1704	5
35-39	11.7	8	.1656	7
40-44	13.5	7	.1635	8
45-49	23.2	4	.1576	10
50-54	22.9	5	.1515	11
55-59	25.9	3	.1595	9
60-64	26.4	2	.1678	6
65+	35.1	1	.2008	2

[5] *New Zealand Population Census, 1951*, Vol. IV: "Industries, Occupations and Incomes" (Wellington), Table 11, p. 83.

[6] For a description of these categories, see *New Zealand Census, ibid.*, pp. 8-9.

A ρ of —.36 between the ranks shown in this table supports the major theorem (that the suicide rate of a group tends to vary inversely with the degree of occupational integration within the age group), but the relationship is not a substantial one. This low correlation suggests that dimensions of status integration other than occupational are of importance in producing differences in suicide rates among age groups in New Zealand. To test this suggestion the measures of marital integration[7] and labor force integration[8] by age groups shown in Table 69 were computed.

Table 69. MEASURES OF MARITAL INTEGRATION, 1945-1951, LABOR FORCE INTEGRATION, 1951, AND MEAN ANNUAL SUICIDE RATES, 1946-1951, FOR NON-MAORI MALES, BY AGE GROUPS, NEW ZEALAND

Age Group	Measure of Marital Integration	Rank	Measure of Labor Force Integration	Rank	Suicide Rate	Rank
16-19	.9865	1	.7022	9	6.1	11
20-24	.6633	7	.9210	6	10.7	9
25-29	.5168	10	.9558	3	8.8	10
30-34	.6571	8	.9577	1	14.1	6
35-39	.7131	4	.9562	2	11.7	8
40-44	.7384	2	.9518	4	13.5	7
45-49	.7283	3	.9418	5	23.2	4
50-54	.7035	5	.8840	7	22.9	5
55-59	.6781	6	.7686	8	25.9	3
60-64	.6322	9	.5385	11	26.4	2
65+	.4792	11	.6100	10	35.1	1

The rank-difference correlation between the ranks of the measures of marital integration and the ranks of the suicide rates by age groups as shown in Table 69 proved to be —.40. A corresponding ρ for measures of labor force integration and suicide rates proved to be —.47.

The correlations reported above are in the direction anticipated by the major theorem but, as in the case of occupational integration, they

---

[7] Measures of the degree of marital integration within age groups in New Zealand have been computed according to the method illustrated in Table 22. The measure within each group is based on the proportions "never married," "married," "legally separated," "widowed," and "divorced." The proportions in each of the five marital statuses were derived by combining the population figures of the 1945 census (Vol. IV, Table 20, p. 40) with the 1951 census (Vol. II, Table 11, p. 83.

[8] The method employed in computing measures of labor force integration has been explained elsewhere. The proportions in this measure for New Zealand are based on the number of persons in each age group "engaged in an occupation" and the number "not engaged in an occupation." These numbers were derived from *Population Census, 1951*, Vol. IV: "Industries, Occupations and Incomes," Table 11, p. 83

are not particularly high. Considering that as many dimensions of status integration should be taken into account as possible, a composite measure was computed for each of the age groups. This composite measure represents the sum of the individual values of occupational, marital, and labor force integration and is shown in Table 70.

Table 70. THE SUM OF MEASURES OF OCCUPATIONAL, MARITAL, AND LABOR FORCE INTEGRATION AND MEAN ANNUAL SUICIDE RATES, BY AGE GROUPS, FOR NON-MAORI MALES, NEW ZEALAND

Age Group	Sum of Integration Measures	Rank	Suicide Rate	Rank
16-19	1.8901	1	6.1	11
20-24	1.7621	6	10.7	9
25-29	1.6473	8	8.8	10
30-34	1.7852	5	14.1	6
35-39	1.8349	3	11.7	8
40-44	1.8537	2	13.5	7
45-49	1.8277	4	23.2	4
50-54	1.7390	7	22.9	5
55-59	1.6062	9	25.9	3
60-64	1.3385	10	26.4	2
65+	1.2900	11	35.1	1

The ρ between the ranks shown in Table 70 is $-.67$, which clearly indicates that as more and more dimensions of status integration are taken into account, the differences in the suicide rates by age groups among males become more and more predictable.

All of the tests reported above concerning variability in suicide rates by age among non-Maori males in New Zealand have been repeated for the non-Maori females. Since the measures of integration and the sources of the data employed are identical for males and females, it is only necessary to give a comprehensive table for the females and the results of the tests.

As the rank-difference correlations in the bottom row of Table 71 show, measures of labor force integration vary directly with the non-Maori female suicide rates by age groups (ρ equals $+.89$) and not inversely as anticipated by the major theorem. Since the three remaining correlations are all somewhat low, it would appear that a considerable amount of the differences in the suicide rates of non-Maori females by age groups must be attributed either to factors independent of status integration or to dimensions of status integration not taken into account in the tests reported above.

Table 71. MEASURES OF STATUS INTEGRATION, 1945-1951, AND MEAN ANNUAL SUICIDE RATES, 1946-1951, BY AGE GROUPS, FOR NON-MAORI FEMALES, NEW ZEALAND

Age Group	(1) Measure of Occupational Integration	(2) Rank	(3) Measure of Marital Integration	(4) Rank	(5) Measure of Labor Force Integration	(6) Rank	(7) Sum of Individual Measures of Status Integration	(8) Rank	(9) Suicide Rate	(10) Rank
16-19	.2121	1	.8825	1	.6121	10	1.7067	1	2.0	10
20-24	.2032	3	.4897	9	.5015	11	1.1944	11	1.7	11
25-29	.2006	4	.6533	5	.6215	9	1.4754	6	3.9	9
30-34	.1768	7	.7192	3	.6851	5	1.5811	2	7.2	6
35-39	.1694	8	.7196	2	.6806	6	1.5786	3	4.1	8
40-44	.1680	9	.6899	4	.6778	7	1.5357	4	7.6	5
45-49	.1652	10	.6444	6	.6527	8	1.4623	7	6.8	7
50-54	.1647	11	.5864	7	.6863	4	1.4374	9	10.8	3
55-59	.1792	6	.5123	8	.7423	3	1.4338	10	13.7	1
60-64	.1839	5	.4350	10	.8373	2	1.4562	8	12.3	2
65+	.2089	2	.3794	11	.9360	1	1.5243	5	9.0	4
ρ with Rank of Suicide Rates		−.35		−.48		+.89		−.30		

164

SUICIDE RATES BY MARITAL STATUS

Suicide rates and measures of integration by marital status for New Zealand males are given in Table 72. According to the major theorem we should expect to find that the ranks in the table vary inversely in this Type 1 (within-column) test. The computed value of ρ is —.60.

Table 72. MEAN ANNUAL SUICIDE RATES, 1946-1951, AND MEASURES OF MARITAL INTEGRATION, 1945-1951*, FOR NON-MAORI MALES SIXTEEN YEARS AND OVER, BY MARITAL STATUS, NEW ZEALAND

Marital Status	Suicide Rate	Rank	Measure of Marital Integration	Rank
Single	15.4	4	.3150	2
Married	15.5	3	.6331	1
Widowed	41.8	1	.0418	3
Divorced	28.2	2	.0101	4

* The measure of marital integration is the proportion of males in each marital status over the years 1946-1951 as estimated from New Zealand's 1945 Census (Vol. IV, Table 14, p. 37) and 1951 Census (Vol. II, Table 12, p. 45). In computing the suicide rates and measures of marital integration, the category of "legally separated" was combined with the category of married. This combination was necessary because "legally separated" suicides are reported as married. Maoris have been excluded from the data shown in the table. Suicide rates are based on the mean of the 1945 and 1951 population.

Table 73. MEAN ANNUAL SUICIDE RATES, 1946-1951, AND MEASURES OF MARITAL INTEGRATION, 1945-1951*, FOR NON-MAORI FEMALES SIXTEEN YEARS AND OVER, BY MARITAL STATUS, NEW ZEALAND

Marital Status	Suicide Rate	Rank	Measure of Marital Integration	Rank
Single	5.6	4	.2669	2
Married	5.9	3	.6199	1
Widowed	12.0	2	.1024	3
Divorced	14.0	1	.0107	4

* For explanatory notes see Table 72.

Table 74. MEAN ANNUAL SUICIDE RATES, 1946-1951, AND MEASURES OF MARITAL INTEGRATION, 1945-1951,* FOR NON-MAORI POPULATION SIXTEEN YEARS AND OVER, BY MARITAL STATUS, NEW ZEALAND

Marital Status	Suicide Rate	Rank	Measure of Marital Integration	Rank
Single	10.8	3	.2905	2
Married	10.7	4	.6264	1
Widowed	20.4	2	.0727	3
Divorced	20.8	1	.0105	4

* For explanatory notes see Table 72.

Suicide rates and measures of integration by marital status for New Zealand females are given in Table 73. Consistent with the major theorem, the ρ between the ranks shown in this table proved to be theorem, the ρ between the ranks in this table proved to be —.80.

Suicide rates and measures of integration by marital status for both sexes in New Zealand are shown in Table 74. Consistent with the major theorem, the ρ between the ranks shown in the table is -1.00.

In these three tests, the values of ρ ($-.60$, $-.80$, -1.00) taken together provide a pattern of strong support for the major theorem.

A MORE COMPLEX PROBLEM IN PREDICTION

The major theorem anticipates that the suicide rate of any given age-marital status configuration varies inversely with the proportion of the persons in the age group who occupy the configuration. To test this, suicide rates by marital status were computed within seven age groups of New Zealand's non-Maori population. These rates are shown in Table 75, along with a measure of integration for each marital status within an age group (that is, the proportion of the persons in an age group who occupy the marital status). Because of the small number of divorced suicide victims, the widowed and divorced have been combined in Table 75 as one status.

Within each of the seven age groups shown in this table, the major theorem anticipates that the rank of the suicide rate of a marital status will vary inversely with the rank of its measure of integration. As Figure 10 shows, this is substantially true. Whereas on the basis of chance, one would expect correct prediction of the rank of the suicide rate of an age-marital status configuration in seven out of the twenty-one cases, fifteen correct predictions can be made on the basis of the integration of marital status with age. The ratio of the number of correct predictions to the number expected on the basis of chance is 2.1 to 1.

In contrast to the United States, the small number of suicide cases in New Zealand prohibits repeating the above test for males and females separately.

Marital Integration and Variables in Suicide Rates by Age Groups. It has been shown that in the United States as of 1949-1951 the suicide rates of different age groups tended to vary inversely with the degree of marital integration within each age group.[9] We now turn to New Zealand to see if the same relationship holds there.[10]

---

[9] See pp. 87-89.

[10] Two tests of the relationship between a measure of marital integration within an age group and the suicide rate of the age group have already been reported for males and females in New Zealand (Tables 69 and 71). The test now being considered will be based on both sexes combined.

Table 75. MEAN ANNUAL SUICIDE RATES BY MARITAL STATUS AND AGE, 1946-1951, AND MEASURES OF INTEGRATION OF MARITAL STATUS WITH AGE*, FOR THE NON-MAORI POPULATION, NEW ZEALAND

Age Group	Single	Married	Widowed and Divorced
16-24			
S.R.†	5.3	1.5	39.9
Rank	2	3	1
M.S.I.‡	.0864	.1917	.0032
Rank	1	2	3
25-34			
S.R.	15.1	5.7	20.2
Rank	2	3	1
M.S.I.	.2464	.7377	.0159
Rank	2	1	3
35-44			
S.R.	15.4	8.0	10.5
Rank	1	3	2
M.S.I.	.1286	.8389	.0325
Rank	2	1	3
45-54			
S.R.	21.9	14.0	23.1
Rank	2	3	1
M.S.I.	.1176	.8118	.0705
Rank	2	1	3
55-64			
S.R.	27.9	16.9	23.2
Rank	1	3	2
M.S.I.	.1191	.7291	.1518
Rank	3	1	2
65-74			
S.R.	31.0	21.7	24.4
Rank	1	3	2
M.S.I.	.1273	.5913	.2814
Rank	3	1	2
75+			
S.R.	28.2	12.6	15.7
Rank	1	3	2
M.S.I.	.1273	.3704	.5023
Rank	3	2	1

* Population figures used in computing suicide rates and measures of the integration of marital status with age were drawn from: New Zealand, *Population Census, 1945,* Vol. IV, "Ages and Marital Status," Table 20, p. 40; and New Zealand, *Population Census, 1951,* Vol. II, "Ages and Marital Status," Table 18, p. 49. Measures of the integration of marital status with age and suicide rates are based on the mean of the 1945 and 1951 population figures.
† S.R.=Suicide rate.
‡ M.S.I.=Measure of status integration.

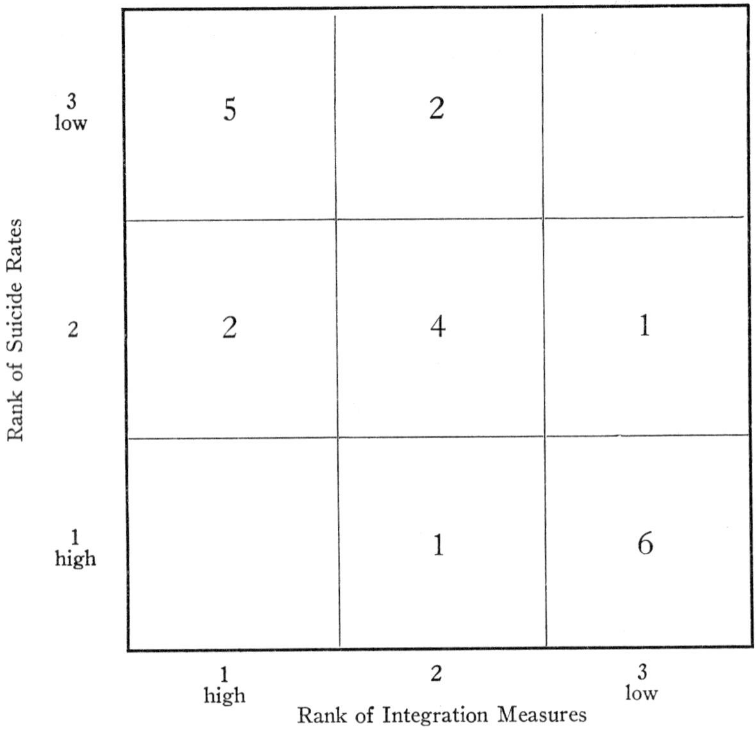

Fig. 10. RELATIONSHIP WITHIN AGE GROUPS BETWEEN RANKS OF THE MEASURES OF STATUS INTEGRATION AND RANKS OF THE SUICIDE RATES FOR 21 AGE-MARITAL STATUS CONFIGURATIONS IN NEW ZEALAND, 1946-1951.

In Table 76 suicide rates and measures of the degree of marital integration are shown for each of eight age groups.

This is a Type 2, between-columns test and the measures of marital integration shown at the bottom of each column are simply the sum of the squares of the proportions within the columns (ΣX^2). An age group with the maximum in marital integration ($\Sigma X^2 = 1.0000$) would be one in which all persons occupied the same marital status. According to the major theorem, one should expect to find that an inverse relationship holds between the ranks shown in the second and third row from the bottom in Table 76. This is substantially the case, with ρ being —.60.

A UNIQUE TEST OF THE MAJOR THEOREM

The major theorem lends itself to three different types of tests regarding differences in suicide rates. Type 1, the within-columns test, is difficult to conduct because it calls for detailed suicide statistics.[11] The only tests of this type reported up to now were based on the differences among the suicide rates of marital statuses within age groups in the United States[12] and New Zealand,[13] a somewhat simpler test made by marital statuses in Belgium,[14] and a simple test on occupational integration in Italy.[15]

Ideally, the power of the major theorem to make correct within-column predictions should be tested on occupational statuses as well as marital statuses. Because suicide rates by occupation and age are rarely reported, the New Zealand data are of considerable importance.[16] In Table 77, measures of occupational integration for eight occupational categories[17] within five age groups[18] are shown along with corresponding suicide rates.

In analyzing the data shown in this table, it is necessary to keep two points in mind. First, the measures of status integration within each age group are simply proportions. And, second, to make the suicide rate correspond to the census population it was necessary to exclude the following types of suicides: females, males with no occupation, retired males,[19] and males with occupation unknown. This is another instance where the opportunity to analyze suicide on the basis of individual cases, as opposed to aggregate statistics, proved to be of value.

According to the major theorem, we should expect that within each of the five age groups shown in Table 77 an inverse relationship will hold between the measure of integration of an occupation-age status configuration and its suicide rate. As the rank-difference correlations in

---

[11] For a discussion of this type of test, see p. 39.

[12] See pp. 90-97.

[13] See pp. 165-168.

[14] See p. 145.

[15] See pp. 145-148.

[16] Suicide rates by occupation and age can be computed for males only, however, since the occupations of females in New Zealand are not consistently recorded on the death register.

[17] Occupational categories (6) and (11) (see p. 161) have been excluded from Table 77 because the small number of suicides in the categories do not lend themselves to a breakdown by age. Occupational categories (3) and (4) have been combined because it is difficult to distinguish between the two when classifying specific occupations.

[18] All of the 13 age groups used by the New Zealand census in reporting occupation by age could not be used because of the small number of cases of suicide.

[19] The fact of being retired, as opposed to being actively engaged in an occupation, had to be determined from testimony incorporated in the report of the coroner. Since the fact that a person was retired at the time of his death may not be disclosed in testimony, this is an unsatisfactory way of excluding persons, but it is a far better way than assuming that all persons are actively engaged in the occupation that is recorded on their death certificate.

the bottom row of the table testify, this inverse relationship is present. Although the individual's ρ's are not impressively high, the consistent pattern of the findings provides firm support for the idea that the suicide rate of an occupational category within an age group is a function of the proportion of the persons in the age group who are in the occupational category. As a general rule, occupational categories with a

Table 76. MEAN ANNUAL SUICIDE RATES, 1946-1951, AND MEASURES OF MARITAL INTEGRATION WITH AGE*, 1945-1951, FOR THE NON-MAORI POPULATION, BY AGE GROUPS, NEW ZEALAND

	16-19	20-24	25-34	35-44	45-54	55-64	65-74	75+
Marital Status								
Single	.9727	.6709	.2464	.1286	.1176	.1191	.1273	.1273
Married	.0272	.3259	.7377	.8389	.8118	.7291	.5913	.3704
Widowed and Divorced	.0001	.0032	.0159	.0325	.0705	.1518	.2814	.5023
Measure of Marital Integration (ΣX^2)	.9469	.5563	.6052	.7213	.6778	.5688	.4450	.4057
Rank of Measure of Marital Integration	1	6	4	2	3	5	7	8
Rank of Suicide Rate	8	7	6	5	4	2	1	3
Suicide Rate of Age Group	3.2	5.9	8.4	9.2	15.8	19.5	23.6	16.5

* See note for Table 75.

small proportion have high suicide rates and those with a large proportion have low suicide rates. The results are particularly impressive since this test does not take into account other dimensions of status integration (such as marital, parental, or religious integration) and is based on broad occupational categories rather than specific occupations.

Table 77. MEASURES OF OCCUPATIONAL INTEGRATION, 1951, AND MEAN ANNUAL SUICIDE RATES,* 1946-1951, FOR OCCUPATION-AGE STATUS CONFIGURATIONS AMONG NON-MAORI MALES, NEW ZEALAND

Occupational Category†	16-29				30-39				40-49				50-64				65+		
	S.R.‡	Rank	M.S.I.§	Rank	S.R.	Rank	M.S.I.	Rank	S.R.	Rank	M.S.I.	Rank	S.R.	Rank	M.S.I.	Rank	Rank	M.S.I.	Rank
1	3.5	8	.0540	6	20.8	3	.0495	6	31.9	3	.0511	6	29.9	3	.0462	8	5	.0504	6
2	41.4	1	.0045	8	45.0	1	.0285	8	58.9	1	.0448	7	30.4	1	.0474	7	6	.0495	7
3 and 4	6.2	6	.1819	3	5.0	8	.1805	3	9.7	8	.1740	3	9.7	8	.1698	3	8	.1560	3
5	8.5	5	.2208	2	14.4	5	.2238	2	30.1	4	.2246	2	44.7	4	.2455	1	3	.3712	1
7	10.9	4	.0862	5	7.1	7	.0907	5	34.0	2	.0731	5	97.8	2	.0483	6	1	.0154	8
8	5.5	7	.3268	1	8.7	6	.2955	1	11.7	7	.2752	1	29.4	7	.2384	2	7	.1791	2
9	14.3	3	.1052	4	23.3	2	.0092	4	19.7	5	.1144	4	53.1	5	.1417	4	2	.1134	4
10	18.3	2	.0206	7	15.9	4	.0323	7	13.1	6	.0429	8	34.8	6	.0627	5	4	.0650	5
ρ between ranks	−.60				−.60				−.69				−.64				−.31		

* Measures of status integration and suicide rates have been computed on data drawn from *New Zealand, Population Census, 1951*, Vol. IV, "Industries, C Incomes," (Wellington: Government Printer, 1954), Table 11, p. 83.
† For occupational titles see p. 185.
‡ S.R., Suicide rate.
§ M.S.I., Measure of status integration.

PART FOUR

Differences by Sex and
Temporal Variation

CHAPTER THIRTEEN

Status Integration and the Sex Ratio of Suicides

PROBABLY EVERY searching discussion on suicide has dwelt on the almost universal tendency for males to have a higher suicide rate than females. For example, in an examination of statistics on 20 European countries for dates ranging around the middle of the nineteenth century, Morselli found that the male suicide rate was always higher. He pointed out, however, that there existed an important variation in the ratio of male to female suicides; among his countries the per cent of female suicides varied from 12.2 for Switzerland to 28.8 for Spain.[1] Without attempting to review speculation on the subject, it is clear that there are two pertinent questions: What are the conditions that lead to an almost universally higher suicide rate for males? Under what conditions does the female suicide rate approach or even surpass the male rate? No scientifically acceptable answer to these questions has been given to date.

If the theory of status integration is a general theory of variation in the suicide rate, it should be possible to predict variation in the suicide rates by sex as well as by other categories. Such variation certainly comes within the scope of the theory, which leads to the expectation that it can be predicted by differences in status integration of males

---

[1] Morselli, p. 190.

and females. Specifically, the theory suggests that in most countries females have a greater degree of status integration than males, and that in those countries in which the status integration of females approximates or drops lower than that of males, the suicide rate of females will equal or surpass that of males.

The results of a test of the proposition that sex differences in suicide rates can be predicted on the basis of differences in status integration were presented in Chapter V.[2] This test pertained to the United States, where the male suicide rate is considerably higher than the female rate. Although the findings in Chapter V support the major theorem, additional evidence may be gathered from the tables already presented that provide data on differential status integration by sex. For example, Table 5 gives occupational integration measures for males and females by color and by four age categories. Examination of the integration measures reveals that for both whites and nonwhites the occupational integration measure of females in a particular age category is without exception larger than the measure for males in the corresponding age group.

Further evidence of the greater status integration of females in the United States is presented in Tables 9, 10, and 12. Similar results are shown for England and Wales in Tables 47 and 48. In the many comparisons of occupational integration, there is only one instance in which the measure for females is not larger than that for males. On the other hand, tables pertaining to marital integration, such as Tables 24 and 25, give much less support to the idea of greater status integration for females than for males. For these two tables, summing the integration measures for the various age groups results in a total marital integration measure of 6.4832 for males and 5.6987 for females. Thus, while the available data pertaining to sex differences tend to support the major theorem, the evidence is not conclusive and additional tests are required.

AN INITIAL TEST IN BENGAL

The consistency with which males have a higher suicide rate than females makes Miner's report[3] of 177.1 female suicides per 100 male suicides in Bengal for the year 1907 truly remarkable.[4] It may be possi-

---

2 See pp. 60-61.

3 John Rice Miner, "Suicide and Its Relation to Climatic and Other Factors," *American Journal of Hygiene*, Monographic Series No. 2 (1922), p. 31.

4 It would appear that the excess of female suicides over male suicides holds throughout India, at least at the turn of the century. We have only selected Bengal as an example.

ble for us to come to some conclusions about probable differences in status integration among populations within our own society, but this does not hold for populations for which we have no first-hand knowledge. Such is the case for Bengal.

The only data than can be used to link Miner's report on Bengal with the present theory pertain to marital status. With the excess of female suicides in Bengal it would be expected that for at least one of the major families of statuses the females would have lower measures of status integration than the males. Table 78 shows measures of marital integration for males and females in Bengal for 1911.[5]

Table 78. MEASURES OF INTEGRATION OF MARITAL STATUS WITH SEX, BENGAL, 1911

Marital Status	Males	Females
Unmarried	.5112	.3357
Married	.4541	.4637
Widowed	.0347	.2006
Measure of Status Integration	.4687	.3680

The differences between the measures shown in this table are in line with what would be anticipated on the basis of the present theory. Although the differences may appear to be small, it should be noted that the measure for females is only 10 per cent above minimum (.3333), while the measure for males is 40 per cent above.

One could argue, of course, that the measures of marital integration shown in Table 78 ignore so many other statuses that the extent of marital integration is possibly masked more for the female than the male. The nature of the data precludes a complex measure of marital integration, but it has proved possible to take into account age, a variable that is very important as far as marital integration is concerned. Table 79 gives measures of the integration of marital status with age among males and females in Bengal.

When the total measure of the integration of marital status with age for males and females in Table 79 is considered, we find it to be 11.32 for males in contrast to 9.76 for females. The differences are once again in line with the major theorem, and the results indicate that the higher measures of marital integration for males in Table 78 is not a function of ignoring age.

It is most unfortunate that suicide rates by age and marital status are not available for Bengal in 1911, since the measures of integration

---

[5] *Census of India*, 1911, Vol. I: *India*, Part II (Calcutta), p. 48.

Table 79. MEASURES OF THE INTEGRATION OF MARITAL STATUS WITH AGE AMONG MALES AND FEMALES, BENGAL, 1911

Marital Status	0-4	5-9	10-14	15-19	20-24	25-29	30-34	35-39	40-44	45-49	50-54	55-59	60-64	65-69	70+
Male															
Unmarried	.9985	.9882	.9394	.7194	.3592	.1424	.0523	.0292	.0252	.0196	.0185	.0169	.0176	.0172	.0180
Married	.0015	.0115	.0589	.2745	.6246	.8299	.9097	.9233	.9060	.8906	.8596	.8297	.7923	.7571	.6957
Widowed	.0000	.0004	.0016	.0061	.0163	.0277	.0379	.0475	.0688	.0898	.1219	.1534	.1901	.2257	.2863
Measure of Status Integration	.9970	.9767	.8859	.5929	.5194	.7089	.8317	.8556	.8262	.8016	.7541	.7122	.6642	.6244	.5663
Female															
Unmarried	.9948	.8971	.3762	.0423	.0171	.0108	.0081	.0061	.0053	.0036	.0032	.0029	.0031	.0034	.0042
Married	.0046	.0984	.5997	.8967	.8858	.8347	.7386	.6207	.4732	.3522	.2352	.1730	.1087	.1019	.0651
Widowed	.0006	.0045	.0240	.0610	.0971	.1545	.2533	.3732	.5215	.6442	.7616	.8240	.8882	.8946	.9307
Measure of Status Integration	.9896	.8145	.5017	.8096	.7944	.7207	.6098	.5246	.4959	.5391	.6354	.7089	.8007	.8107	.8705

suggest that some unusual pattern of variability was present. On the basis of the integration of marital status with age, we would expect to find that the suicide rate of females tended to increase with increasing age but only up to the age period 45-49, at which point a trend of decreasing suicide would appear. Other interesting patterns are also suggested. For ages beyond 70, it would be anticipated that married males had a suicide rate lower than widowed males of the same age, but the reverse would be expected for females.

In the analysis of the relationship between marital integration by sex and the sex ratio of suicides in Bengal, an important consideration is introduced. Evidence has already been noted to suggest that occupational integration is of considerable significance in the explanation of variability in suicide rates in the United States. This cannot be taken to mean that occupational integration is the crucial variable in all societies. On the contrary, in some societies occupational specialization may not be pronounced, and this would have certain consequences as far as status integration measures are concerned. If practically all of the males in a society are farmers, the measures of the integration of occupation with age, for example, can vary little from one age group to the next. In the face of little variability in occupational integration within a society, it would be expected that marital integration would assume the position of importance that occupational integration has in a society like the United States. In short, with increasing homogeneity of occupations in a society, measures of the integration of marital status with other statuses may become the key to variability in suicide rates.

There are two qualifications that must be made explicit regarding the speculation above. First, there are obviously far more families of statuses than occupation and marital condition to be taken into account; for example, in a society where occupational homogeneity is at a maximum, parental status as well as marital status may be crucial. And, second, while occupational integration may not be as important as marital integration in accounting for variability in suicide rates within an agrarian society, it would be crucial in fixing the level of the total suicide rate. A society without a pronounced specialization of occupations would be expected on a purely chance basis[6] to have a high degree of occupational integration and a low suicide rate. But this does not mean that occupational specialization inevitably leads to low measures of occupational integration. On a probability basis, however, an increase

---

[6] With a small number of occupational statuses, the minimal level of occupational integration is higher than the minimal level with a large number of occupational statuses.

in the number of occupational statuses tends to lower measures of occupational integration, since it offers opportunities for deviant patterns of status occupancy that would otherwise not be present.

The question of occupational specialization is significant not only for differences in suicide rates among societies but also for the variation we find in the sex ratio of suicides. It would appear that in virtually all societies with a high degree of occupational specialization, males are more subject to its influence than females, the latter's position in the division of labor remaining that of housekeeper. With decreasing occupational specialization, however, males tend to concentrate in one status much like the females. This being the case, where occupational specialization is not pronounced in a society, the difference between the suicide rate of males and females is more likely to be a function of differences in marital integration. Assuming that males are generally more influenced by occupational specialization than females, the ratio of male to female suicides should be highest in societies where occupational specialization is pronounced, and the ratio of female to male suicides should be highest in societies where occupational specialization is not pronounced and measures of marital integration are lower for females than males.

There appears to be some support for this speculation. In some European countries and in the United States, males actually have a very slight edge over females as far as marital integration is concerned, but the males do not concentrate in one position in the division of labor as much as the females, and the slight edge that they hold with respect to marital integration apparently is not sufficient to compensate for their being involved in occupational specialization. We have seen in the present study how females in the labor force in the United States have higher measures of occupational integration than do the males. In Bengal, however, where the males tend to concentrate in one status (farmer) to a degree comparable to the concentration of females in one status (housekeeper), the difference between them with regard to marital integration would appear to be crucial in determining the sex ratio of suicides. It should also be noted that Bengal is not unique in having a high ratio of female to male suicides. As judged from other studies and observations, the concensus is that only among non-Europeans do we find a very high ratio of female to male suicides. There are, of course, reasons for anticipating this, since among non-European peoples males could conceivably have more marital integration than females. Also, with the increasing diffusion of the European occupational structure, there is reason to believe that a high ratio of male to female suicides will be found more frequently among non-European peoples in the future.

It must be stressed that the Bengal data do not constitute proof that the high ratio of female to male suicides is a function of differences in marital integration; the most that can be said is that the findings are in line with the theory.

SEX RATIO AND LABOR FORCE STATUS

According to the preceding line of speculation, the higher suicide rate of men is because they have less status integration than females, primarily as a consequence of their being in the labor force and being subjected to occupational specialization more than are females. If this is true, one should expect to find that the sex ratio of suicides bears a relationship to the sex ratio within the labor force; specifically, the theory of status integration provides a rationale for hypothesizing that among countries a direct relationship holds between the ratio of the male to the female suicide rate on the one hand, and the ratio of the per cent of males to the per cent of females in the labor force on the other hand. This means that in those countries where the per cent of females in the labor force is high, the suicide rate of females will tend to be more nearly equal that of males.

There are two reasons why only a moderately high relationship can be anticipated. The hypothesis does not take into account the possibility of sex differences with respect to the degree of occupational integration in the labor force; and some of the difference between the suicide rates of males and females may be caused by differences in status integration other than labor force or occupation.

A Test by States. To test the above hypothesis, the ratio of the male to the female suicide rate, 1949-1951,[7] and the ratio of the per cent of males 14 years and over in the labor force to a corresponding per cent for females was computed for each state in the United States. These data are presented in Table 80.

When a coefficient of correlation was computed between the two sets of values shown in this table, r proved to be $+.53$. Although the correlation is not particularly high, it indicates that those states with a high suicide sex ratio are predominantly states with a small per cent of females in the labor force.

A Test by Countries. It was suggested earlier that most sociological

---

[7] See note 2, p. 79, for sources of data used to compute male and female suicide rates by states.

Table 80. RATIO OF THE SUICIDE RATE OF MALES TO FEMALES, 1949-1951, AND
RATIO OF PER CENT MALES TO FEMALES FOURTEEN AND OVER
IN LABOR FORCE BY STATES, 1950, UNITED STATES

State	Ratio of Male Suicide Rate to Female Suicide Rate	Ratio of Per Cent Males in Labor Force to Per Cent Females in Labor Force*
Maine	3.41	2.73
New Hampshire	3.76	2.33
Vermont	5.64	2.74
Massachusetts	2.94	2.32
Rhode Island	2.79	2.23
Connecticut	3.06	2.30
New York	2.82	2.43
New Jersey	2.60	2.52
Pennsylvania	3.57	2.77
Ohio	3.73	2.83
Indiana	3.39	2.90
Illinois	3.47	2.57
Michigan	3.77	2.93
Wisconsin	3.67	2.79
Minnesota	4.82	2.78
Iowa	4.20	3.15
Missouri	3.67	2.78
North Dakota	5.11	3.56
South Dakota	4.90	3.41
Nebraska	5.00	3.07
Kansas	3.69	3.19
Delaware	2.50	2.63
Maryland	3.25	2.60
Virginia	3.57	2.90
West Virginia	3.92	3.80
North Carolina	5.57	2.61
South Carolina	3.75	2.40
Georgia	4.10	2.54
Florida	3.00	2.41
Kentucky	3.75	3.77
Tennessee	3.90	3.01
Alabama	5.50	2.94
Mississippi	4.43	3.17
Arkansas	5.00	3.63
Louisiana	4.43	3.07
Oklahoma	3.90	3.13
Texas	3.42	2.98
Montana	4.33	3.18
Idaho	5.00	3.35
Wyoming	4.75	3.16
Colorado	3.43	2.77
New Mexico	4.20	3.35
Arizona	3.41	2.86
Utah	4.67	3.23
Nevada	2.85	2.57
Washington	4.22	2.82
Oregon	3.60	2.74
California	3.04	2.54

* United States Bureau of the Census. *U.S. Census of Population: 1950.* Vol. II, *Characteristics
of the Population,* Part 1, United States Summary, Table 72, p. 124.

hypotheses suffer from the fact that their validity too often depends on tests conducted within one country and not on a cross-cultural or international basis. For this reason, an effort has been made with this study to test the hypothesis pertaining to the sex ratio of suicides within a universe of countries. Of the 32 countries previously used in a test of the major theorem, it was possible to obtain suicide rates for males and females separately for 24 countries.[8] These countries and the ratios relevant to the hypothesis are shown in Table 81.

Table 81. RATIO OF THE MALE TO THE FEMALE SUICIDE RATE AND THE PER CENT MALES TO FEMALES ECONOMICALLY ACTIVE, TWENTY-FOUR COUNTRIES, *circa* 1950

Country	Year of Suicide Rates*	Year of Economically Active Data	Lower Age of Economically Active†	Ratio of Male Suicide Rate to Female Suicide Rate	Ratio of Per Cent Males Economically Active to Per Cent Females‡
El Salvador	1950	1950	15	7.40	5.31
Costa Rica	1950-52	1950	15	6.29	5.50
Finland	1948-52	1950	14	4.71	1.67
Norway	1945-47	1946	15	4.25	3.22
Chile	1950-51	1952	15	4.11	3.21
France	1945-47	1946	14	3.89	1.85
Union of South Africa§	1949-53	1946	15	3.62	3.72
U.S.A.	1948-52	1950	14	3.56	2.72
Ireland	1949-53	1951	14	3.45	2.82
Canada	1949-53	1951	14	3.35	3.47
Portugal	1948-51	1950	15	3.27	4.01
Sweden	1948-52	1950	15	3.24	2.86
Belgium	1951-53	1947	15	3.08	3.40
Switzerland	1948-52	1950	15	2.83	2.63
Australia§	1946-48	1947	15	2.80	3.51
Venezuela§	1950-52	1950	15	2.76	4.61
New Zealand§	1944-46	1945	14	2.27	3.17
Austria	1949-53	1951	15	2.15	1.91
West Germany	1948-52	1950	15	2.12	2.13
Denmark	1948-52	1950	15	2.03	2.07
Ceylon	1944-47	1946	15	2.03	3.19
England and Wales	1949-53	1951	15	1.92	2.55
Netherlands	1946-48	1947	14	1.92	3.19
Japan	1948-52	1950	14	1.49	1.72

* For sources of data see notes for Table 42.
† *Demographic Yearbook, 1956,* (New York: United Nations, 1957) p. 302.
‡ Ratios based on data from *Demographic Yearbook, 1955, op. cit.,* pp. 479-509.
§ Excluding non-Europeans.

When a coefficient of correlation was computed between the values

[8] See pp. 121-124 for sources of suicide data and labor force data and their interpretation and limitations.

shown in the last two columns of this table, r proved to be $+.60$, indicating that those countries with a high sex ratio among their suicides are predominantly countries with a high ratio of males to females in the labor force.

The coefficient indicates that some countries are exceptions to the anticipated relationship; but this was not entirely unexpected, since sex differences among members of the labor force with respect to occupational integration have been ignored in the test. Table 81 shows that of the 24 countries, only France, Finland, and Venezuela fail to conform to any appreciable degree. It is anticipated that a considerable sex difference with respect to occupational integration prevails in these countries. The same may be said for the individual states in the United States which are outstanding exceptions to the rule.[9]

A TEST OF THE HYPOTHESIS IN A NON-EUROPEAN CULTURE

We have seen that the suicide rates of Bengal are particularly interesting, because they fail to show the predominance of male suicide which is characteristic of European societies. Suicide rates for males and females for the 14 districts of West Bengal for 1941-1950 were shown in Table 66; marital-age-sex-integration measures and occupation-residence-age-sex integration measures for these districts for 1951 were presented in Table 67. With these data, it is possible to conduct a test for the districts of West Bengal similar to the one reported for states and 24 countries. In this instance, however, the measures of marital integration and occupational integration for West Bengal will be used rather than the simpler labor force integration measure.

The major theorem anticipates that the greater the integration of males in comparison to females, the lower will be the male suicide rate in comparison to that of the female. The data necessary for the tests are presented in Table 82.

It may be observed that the ratios shown in column 5 of this table are in the direction anticipated by the theory. In districts with low suicide rates for males relative to females, the integration measure for males relative to females tends to be high. Only three of the 14 districts fail to conform to the prediction. However, contrary to theoretical expectations, only four districts conform for occupational integration

---

[9] The findings reported here receive additional support from Morselli. After reporting that there is no apparent relationship between the masculine preponderance and other climatic and ethnological differences, Morselli states "All the professions and trades which, by habits and muscular or psychical occupation, bring women near to men, tend to raise, and sometimes in an extraordinary degree, their inclination to suicide" (p. 245).

(column 3). The ratios shown in column 3, though not as large as expected, are still either larger than 1.00 or nearly as large. Although strictly comparable measures are not available for other countries, there is evidence to indicate less difference between males and females in occupational integration in West Bengal than in the United States. Using data already presented, the ratios of male to female occupational integration measures in the United States, 1949-1951, are as follows:

Table 82. RATIO OF THE MALE TO THE FEMALE SUICIDE RATE, 1941-1950, AND RATIO OF MALE TO FEMALE MEASURES OF OCCUPATIONAL INTEGRATION AND MARITAL INTEGRATION, 1951, FOR DISTRICTS, BENGAL

District	Suicide Rate	Rank	Ratio of Male to Female Occupational Integration	Rank	Marital Integration	Rank
Burdwan	.89	9	.96	7	1.04	6
Birbhum	1.15	3	1.20	1	1.03	8
Bankura	1.08	5	.94	9	1.12	1
Midnapur	1.00	7	.99	5.5	1.05	3.5
Hooghly	.75	13	1.04	3	1.08	2
Howrah	.88	10	.92	11	1.04	6
Twenty-four Parganas	.80	12	1.07	2	1.02	9.5
Calcutta	.68	14	.91	12	.88	14
Nadia	.81	11	.99	5.5	1.05	3.5
Murshidabad	.96	8	.89	14	1.02	9.5
Malda	1.04	6	.90	13	1.04	6
West Dinajpur	1.09	4	.95	8	.94	13
Jalpaiguri	1.39	2	.93	10	.96	12
Darjeeling	2.25	1	1.03	4	1.01	11

total male and female, .76 (Table 9); white males and white females, .71; Negro males and Negro females, .64; and other males and other females, .88 (the last three from Table 10). In contrast to these figures, the ratios shown in column 3 for West Bengal are, with one exception, .90 or higher. The data thus support the suggestion that the occupational integration of males and females is much less dissimilar in agrarian societies than in industrialized countries. On this basis, it was hypothesized that marital integration is more closely related to the sex ratio of suicides in West Bengal than in countries where sex differences in occupational integration are greater.

The test of the hypothesis was carried out by computing a coefficient of rank-difference correlation between the ratio of male to female suicide rates (column 2) and the ratio of male to female occupational integration measures (column 4). Since a negative correlation was predicted, the computed ρ of +.01 represents a failure to support the theory.[10] A similar test was made, using the ratio of male marital integration measures to female integration measures (column 6) ; ρ proved to be —.22. This value, while small, is in the predicted direction.

This is another situation in which a variety of procedures can be followed in relating male and female rates. Here, it would be just as logical to merely take the difference between the male and female figures rather than the ratio. When differences, rather than ratios, are used, both ρ's are in the anticipated direction, —.51 and —.21.

SUMMARY

In this chapter, the theory of status integration has been applied to several sets of data concerning differences in male and female suicide rates. With regard to the conditions that produce an almost universally higher suicide rate for males than for females, the theory suggests a correspondingly lower status integration for males. Examination of data indicates that this is indeed true in the United States, England and Wales, and West Bengal as far as occupational integration is concerned. On the other hand, marital integration measures tend to be higher for males than for females. This discrepancy raises questions about the possible differential influence of these two dimensions of status integration, but in general, the major theorem is supported.

Systematic tests in the United States and among countries have shown that as the proportion of females in the labor force comes to equal the proportion of males in the labor force, the more equal become their suicide rates; a finding that supports the theory of status integration. In independent tests, using two separate measures of status integration for 14 districts in West Bengal, the findings are less conclusive, although generally supporting the theory.

---

10 In evaluating these negative results, it must be borne in mind that the reliability of the suicide rates in the districts of Bengal is most questionable because of the nature of the population figures used to compute the rates. See pp. 154-155 for a fuller discussion of the problems involved.

CHAPTER FOURTEEN

The Major Theorem
Applied to
Temporal Variation

FROM Morselli and Durkheim to the present, temporal variations in the suicide rate have attracted the attention of many investigators. It has been clearly demonstrated that for any given national population, the rate of suicide varies somewhat from year to year, and that there are fairly characteristic variations by month, day of the week, and hour of the day. There have been various attempts to develop a theory which would predict such temporal variations, the most successful being the recent work of Henry and Short on the relationship between the suicide rate and the business cycle.[1] This latter work, however, is concerned with long range variation and does not treat seasonal nor shorter variation. Ideally, a theory which purports to explain variations in the rate of suicide would explain both long and short range temporal variations in addition to differences among populations. Indeed, the ability to correctly predict temporal variations would seem to be the crucial test of a theory which has already demonstrated its ability to predict other types of variation.

In contrast to those who attempt to explain temporal variations in terms of climatic fluctuations or a single variable such as the business cycle, is Durkheim, who rejects the idea that monthly or seasonal varia-

---

[1] See pp. 11-12 for discussion.

tions in suicide are the result of "cosmic factors." He says, "Above all [the physical environment] has no effect on the progression of suicide. The latter depends on social conditions" (p. 122).

In terms of the present theory, Durkheim's statement immediately suggests that the changes in "social conditions" which underlie variations in the suicide rate are actually variations in the degree of total status integration. In other words, changes in the degree of status integration over a period of time should vary inversely with changes in the suicide rate over the same period. This proposition could be restated as a series of specific hypotheses dealing with variations over different periods of time—years, months, weeks, or shorter periods. The suggestion that societies experience mensurable changes in status integration over time is consistent with what is known concerning historical changes in societal characteristics—marital, occupational, religious, age, and sex composition—as countries experience industrialization, urbanization, war, peace, prosperity, and depression. Furthermore, while variations in suicide rates from one year to the next are microscopic and hardly worthy of consideration, long range trends may be quite significant; a fact consistent with the belief that major changes in status integration typically do not occur abruptly but only over a considerable period of time.

In this connection, it must be admitted that while it is possible to set up hypotheses regarding hourly and daily variation as well as long historical periods, status integration would not be expected to experience significant variations within such periods of time; consequently, it is somewhat doubtful that the present theory can explain all forms of temporal variation in suicide. We would expect the greatest success in dealing with long range historical trends and the least success in explaining hourly variations.

A test of the theory's ability to predict long range temporal variation in suicide rates would be of great importance, but the absence of requisite data precludes it. However, we can consider the results of an even more difficult test—monthly variation in the volume of suicide. This test is more difficult, since, as explained above, it seems less likely that significant variations in status integration would occur by months than over a period of several years.

MONTHLY VARIATION IN THE SUICIDE RATE

To test the hypothesis that monthly variation in suicide is associated with monthly variation in status integration, it is necessary to have, in addition to statistics on suicide by months, data for computing a status integration measure for each month of the year. That is, ideally, data would be available for each month regarding the number of people that are single, married, widowed, and divorced; number of people in each occupation, each age group, and so on. However, no country provides such data on a monthly basis. Consequently, monthly variation in status integration can only be examined indirectly through the use of data indicating changes in status (number of marriages, deaths, and divorces as indicative of changes in marital status, and number of births indicating changes in parental status). Statistics of this type are available for several countries, although none provides all the data ideal for a test even by the indirect method. Japan was selected as a country which provides at least a minimum of data and which is almost completely outside the European-Christian tradition, thereby adding to the generality of the tests of the theory.

Nature of the Test. In preparation for testing the hypothesis, data were obtained on a limited number of vital events—births, deaths, marriages, and divorces—which would result in changes in status for one or more persons in each case. An additional set of data, estimated conceptions per month, was obtained by simply shifting the number of births by nine months, a procedure which obviously underestimates the actual number. It would be very desirable to have data on the number of people obtaining, losing, and changing jobs for each month but these were not available. The only labor force data included was the number of unemployed. Each variable is expressed as the mean number of events per day by months in Table 83.

At this point it should be noted that the mean number of suicides per day by month for the combined years 1950-1952 conforms closely to the characteristic pattern of European countries. Without exception the number of suicides increased from a low of 36.3 per day in January to a high of 54.7 in May and then decreased regularly to 35.0 in December. The number for May is thus 1.57 times greater than the number in December, a variation with a magnitude and a consistency that make it well worth investigating.

The procedure followed in testing the hypothesis was to compute a rank-difference correlation between the number of suicides per month and each of the other variables shown. The signs of the computed coefficients were expected to be different, since some of the events result in persons being placed in status configurations with a high integration measure, while other events place persons in configurations with low integration measures. For example, the number of live births is an indi-

Table 83. MEAN NUMBER OF SELECTED VITAL EVENTS PER DAY BY MONTH, JAPAN, 1950*

Month	Suicide†	Live Births§	Conceptions§	Deaths‖	Marriages**	Divorces††	Unemployed‡‡
January	36.3	8,262.3	6,272.3	3,121.8	2,065.5	179.0	12,900
February	39.7	7,843.8	5,505.1	2,787.5	2,154.3	176.8	15,400
March	45.8	6,934.3	5,395.8	2,510.0	1,647.0	185.2	14,500
April	53.5	6,272.3	5,980.0	2,284.9	1,691.0	183.1	16,300
May	54.7	5,505.1	6,152.4	2,125.2	1,117.6	168.7	13,500
June	47.5	5,395.8	6,392.6	2,040.0	409.0	147.7	15,300
July	46.3	5,980.0	6,060.1	2,121.9	267.3	155.4	15,500
August	44.6	6,152.4	6,173.1	2,088.8	256.3	166.5	17,400
September	41.2	6,392.6	5,969.1	2,121.0	284.8	132.0	15,000
October	39.2	6,060.1	8,262.3	2,026.8	712.0	100.8	13,200
November	36.1	6,173.1	7,843.8	2,093.7	588.9	65.6	12,000
December	35.0	5,969.1	6,934.3	2,286.0	272.8	34.6	11,000

* Number of events reported for month divided by number of days in month.
† Data for 1950-52, *Vital Statistics* (Japan, 1950), Part 3, pp. 276-77; 1952, Part 3, pp. 260-61.
‡ *Ibid.* (1950), Part 1, pp. 10-11.
§ Uncorrected estimate made by shifting number of births back nine months.
‖ Data for 1951, *Statistical Yearbook*, (Japan, 1953), p. 42.
** Number of marriage ceremonies, *Vital Statistics* (1950), Part 1, p. 434.
†† Divorces by month of cessation of cohabitation, *Ibid.*, pp. 528-29.
‡‡ *Statistical Yearbook* (Japan, 1951), p. 48.

cator of the extent to which an increasing number of people occupy the status parent. Since this status has a high integration measure, only a negative coefficient of correlation would support the major theorem.

Conversely, the number of divorces, an indicator of the number of people moving into a status having a low integration measure, was expected to have a direct relationship with the volume of suicide. Thus, an inverse relationship was predicted for marriages, conceptions, and births, and a direct relationship for deaths, divorces, and unemployment.

At least two factors operated to make this an imperfect test: The test did not use actual measures of status integration for each month, but only indicators of status changes; and the events occurring in any one month were linked with the suicides that occurred in that month, a procedure which ignores that the influence of status incompatibility cannot be expected to be felt immediately. We noted earlier (page 46) that it is almost inconceivable to think of the loss of social relationships that supposedly results from the occupancy of incompatible statuses as being an instantaneous consequence. This major problem notwithstanding, the test was made as described above.

Results of the First Test. The size and direction of ρ between the number of suicides and the number of other events were as follows: live births, $-.31$; conceptions, $-.47$; deaths, $-.13$; marriages, $+.10$; divorces, $+.52$, and unemployed, $+.63$. Thus, the correlations are in the anticipated direction in four instances, but in the opposite direction for deaths and marriages. The coefficients in these two unfavorable cases are much the smallest of the six. In general, the test supports the major theorem, but the results are far from conclusive.

A TIME LAG TEST

The somewhat inconclusive results obtained in the first test turned attention to the matter of the "instantaneous consequences" of changes in status. Given the monthly incidence of the events shown in Table 83, it is possible to shift any of the variables several months forward to allow the changes to have their effect on social relationships. For example, if divorce takes two months on the average to have an appreciable effect, it is entirely logical to shift the divorce figures forward so that those occurring in January are related with suicides occurring in March. The immediate question is the basis for allowing for a time lag of two months rather than more or less. Similarly, is there any obvious basis for expecting that all changes of status require two months to have an effect, or, conversely, that for one type of change it should be one month but three months for another? Obviously no such basis existed to guide the investigation.

Nature of the Test. The decision was made to shift three of the six variables forward two months in relation to suicide. No shift was made in the case of number of unemployed, since this variable, in contrast to number of births or number of divorces, refers not to the number of events occurring in a single month but to a state which may prevail for some people throughout the year. That is, there is no way of knowing how many people became unemployed in July and how many of July's unemployed held this same status in June. Thus no shift was made in number of unemployed, three months for number of deaths, six months for number of marriages, and two months for all other variables. While there is an obvious need to allow for some time lag between a change in status and the disruption of social relationships and the corresponding impact on the individual concerned, there is no particular justification for the specific shifts made. On the other hand, there is no concrete evidence to indicate that other time lags should have been used.

Results of the Second Test. Rank-difference correlations were again computed and the results, as summarized in Table 84, show marked changes in their direction and magnitude. All the coefficients are .63 or larger, and all are in the direction predicted by the theory.

Table 84. RELATIONSHIP BETWEEN MONTHLY INCIDENCE FOR SUICIDE AND OTHER SELECTED EVENTS BEFORE AND AFTER SHIFT IN TIME, JAPAN

		ρ	
Independent Variable	Shift in Months	Before Shift	After Shift
Live births	2	−.31	−.68
Conceptions	2	−.47	−.65
Deaths	3	−.13	+.84
Marriages	6	+.10	−.59
Divorces	2	+.52	+.83
Unemployed	0	+.63	+.63

As a final test of the hypothesis that monthly changes in the number of suicides are linked to changes in status integration, or more precisely, to the number of changes in statuses, the following procedure was adopted. After the six variables were shifted as described above, the ranks of all six were summed for each month. In doing this, it was necessary, of course, to invert the ranks of the three variables inversely correlated with suicide. The sums of ranks by months are as follows: January, 21; February, 34; March, 50; April, 61; May, 56; June, 56; July, 39; August, 37; September, 33; October, 36; November, 25; December, 20. When these sums were themselves ranked and related to the rank of the incidence of suicide, the computed ρ proved to be $+.95$.

CONCLUSION

The tests reported in this chapter were made without actual measures of temporal variation in status integration. The advisability of attempting to test the major theorem through the use of indirect measures, such as used here, may be questioned; but it is desirable to bring the theory to bear as much as possible on all major types of variation in suicide rates.

In addition to being limited to a single country and relying on crude, indirect measures, the tests, in contrast to the others reported in this volume, involve shifting the variables on a purely intuitive basis. Consequently, the analysis in this case is characterized by all the weaknesses usually associated with the intuitive approach, including leaving the writers open to the possible charge that the variables were juggled or otherwise manipulated. In recognition of these problems, we stress that we are under no illusion that we have demonstrated the ability of the theory to predict all temporal variations in suicide rates. On the other hand, the outcome clearly suggests that the theory does not fall hopelessly short when applied to temporal variation. Although it does not provide conclusive evidence against the popular idea of a connection between suicide and climatic conditions, the test does give support to the idea that variations in suicide rates are directly the result of changes in social conditions, just as Durkheim asserted. Furthermore, it points the way for future, more rigorous tests of the theory as an explanation of temporal variation.

PART FIVE

Evaluation

CHAPTER FIFTEEN

The Predictive Power of the Major Theorem

IMPORTANT though other considerations may be, the acid test of a theory is its predictive power. With this in mind we shall consider a summary of the results of the tests of the major theorem. For it is these results that offer the most suitable basis for deciding whether the theory warrants future consideration. The distinction between an evaluation of a theory as being worthy of further consideration and accepting it as valid should be obvious.

SUMMARY OF THE TESTS OF THE MAJOR THEOREM

Predictive Tests. All in all, the major theorem was subjected to 197 separate tests, not counting duplicate tests using alternative measures of status integration, and not counting the first series of tests made with the Japanese data. Thus, while not all the tests included in this count are strictly independent, the obvious duplications have been omitted. Of the 197 tests, 22 involved problems of predicting the rank order of suicide rates from the known rank order of measures of status integration, or vice versa. A total of 676 predictions were made, of which 392 or 58.0 per cent were correct, and the ratio of the correct number of predictions to the number of errors is thus 392 to 284 or 1.38 to 1. On a chance basis, 172 correct predictions would have been expected in these 22 tests. The ratio of the number of correct predictions to the number expected on the basis of chance is 392 to 172 or 2.3 to 1. That the theory led to more than twice as many correct predictions as expected on a chance basis is made even more impressive by the fact that most of the errors in prediction failed to be correct by a small margin.

Coefficients of Correlation. In most of the tests the relationship between measures of status integration and suicide rates was expressed in terms of a coefficient of correlation. These coefficients of correlation can be evaluated in two ways—in terms of direction and of magnitude.

A theory should at a minimum be capable of anticipating, well beyond chance expectancy, the direction of the relationship between the variables to which it pertains. The theory of status integration meets this requirement satisfactorily, with 160 of a total of 175 coefficients (91.4 per cent) being in the direction anticipated by the major theorem. If the true correlation between status integration and the rate of suicide were zero, the coefficients should be equally divided as to positive and negative. The question is, do the 160 negative coefficients represent a significant deviation from the 87.5 that would be expected on a 50-50 basis? If the total 175 coefficients are considered as a random sample of independent observations of a universe of correlation coefficients, it is possible to state the 95 per cent confidence limits of the obtained proportion (.914) that were negative. That is, given the assumptions of random sampling and the empirical finding that 91.4 per cent of the coefficients are negative, it can be expected that if similar studies were repeated a great many times, the figures .84 and .93 would enclose the proportion of negative coefficients in 95 times out of 100.[1] Thus, it is extremely unlikely that the true correlation between status integration and the suicide rate is zero or positive.

The data used in the tests of the major theorem were not drawn from a random sample in a single instance. In each case, the findings apply to a specified universe of countries, states, races, occupations, or ages, some of which are quite inclusive in scope while others are simply unrepresentative fragments of larger universes. For this reason, we have not provided measures of statistical significance, although we have stressed the extremely small number of cases involved in many tests. Our major goal has not been to develop generalizations based upon representative samples, since the nature of the data make this impossible, but rather to demonstrate the predictive power of the major theorem whatever the universe or fragment of universe under consideration.

---

[1] C. J. Clopper and E. S. Pearson, "The Use of Confidence or Fiducial Limits Illustrated in the Case of the Binomial," *Biometrika*, XXVI (1934), 404-413.

In evaluating the magnitude of the total number of coefficients of correlation, however, the coefficients were tabulated not only by magnitude but also by the level of significance[2] that would hold if the data had been drawn from random samples. The concept of statistical significance is meaningful here, of course, only if one treats the data as representative of some hypothetical universe to which one wishes to generalize. Nevertheless, in a study reporting a rather large number of coefficients of considerable magnitude but based on a very small number of cases, it is desirable that the reader be kept aware of the numbers involved. It is hoped that the presentation in Table 85 will serve this purpose.

It was pointed out that 160 of the 175 coefficients are in the direction predicted by the major theorem. If only those 59 that are shown as statistically significant at the .01 level are considered, 57 (96.6 per cent) are in the direction predicted by the major theorem. If, on the other hand, the 99 coefficients shown as significant at the .05 or .01 levels are considered, 97 (98.0 per cent) are in the anticipated direction. Even among the 76 coefficients listed as statistically insignificant, 63 (82.9 per cent) are in the direction predicted by the major theorem. Expressed differently, if they were computed for data drawn from random samples, 97 of the 160 coefficients (60.6 per cent) that support the major theorem would be expected to occur by chance less than 5 times in 100 observations, while among the coefficients not providing support, only 2 of 15 or 13.3 per cent meet this criterion.

APPRAISAL

There are other standards that could be employed in an analysis of the results of the tests of the major theorem. From a practical point of view, however, the summary is sufficient to indicate that the theory is worthy of being retained for future consideration. First, the predictive power of the major theorem, while not perfect, is well beyond chance expectancy. Second, the consistency with which the relationship between measures of status integration and suicide rates are in the direction anticipated by the major theorem can hardly be termed accidental. Third, in the majority of cases, the coefficients of correlation are of a

---

[2] Since the hypotheses all specify the direction of the relationship, the values of p and τ are all taken from a one-tailed sampling distribution. The source for the product-moment coefficients of correlation is Ronald A. Fisher, *Statistical Methods for Research Workers* (London, 1954), table VA, p. 209; for the coefficient of rank-difference correlation, the source is Sidney Siegel, *Nonparametric Statistics for the Behavioral Sciences* (New York, 1956), table P, p. 284.

sufficient magnitude to be regarded as denoting a substantial relationship.

Table 85. SUMMARY OF COEFFICIENTS OF CORRELATION* BY DIRECTION, MAGNITUDE, AND DEGREE OF STATISTICAL SIGNIFICANCE

Magnitude of Coefficient	Number of Coefficients	Coefficients by Degree of Statistical Significance		
		$P > .05$	$.05 > P > .01$	$P < .01$
In Direction Anticipated				
0-9	5	5	....	....
10-19	7	7	....	....
20-29	9	9	....	....
30-39	12	12	....	....
40-49	12	12	....	....
50-59	18	8	6	4
60-69	25	4	16	5
70-79	18	....	9	9
80-89	25	6	1	18
90-99	22	....	1	21
100	7	....	7	....
Total	160	63	40	57
Not In Direction Anticipated				
0-9	4	4	....	....
10-19	1	1	....	....
20-29	1	1	....	....
30-39	1	1	....	....
40-49	5	5	....	....
50-59	1	1	....	....
60-69	....	....	....	....
70-79	....	....	....	....
80-89	2	....	....	2
90-99	....	....	....	....
100	....	....	....	....
Total	15	13	....	2

* Includes both coefficients of product-moment correlation and coefficients of rank-difference correlation.

In passing judgment on the theory, we note two factors that warrant consideration beyond the *de facto* nature of the findings. Of greatest importance, as stressed throughout the report, the data used in the tests of the major theorem are inadequate in many respects. If the data had not been of such nature, cases of clearly negative results would deserve serious consideration as grounds for rejecting the theory. Given the fact of the inadequate data, however, negative results cannot be so interpreted without running the risk of failing to retain a theory that is actually valid. One should also consider that, even if the results had proved far less positive, the theory would warrant retention from a purely pragmatic point of view, because there is no other that equals its predictive power.

CHAPTER SIXTEEN

Alternative Explanatory Variables

W E BELIEVE that the validity of a theory rests primarily on empirical evidence. Rigorous logical and conceptual analysis are obviously important in evaluating a theory, but, in the end, its validity must be judged mainly on the results of the tests of hypotheses derived from it. Though we have adhered to this belief in the explication and testing of the theory of status integration, we well recognize that for many reasons, including the inevitable problems of deduction, it is impossible to make an evaluation in absolute terms. Validity is always a relative matter. One of the difficulties inherent in evaluation is the matter of negative evidence; positive empirical evidence can never validate a theory in the absolute sense, but must it follow that a single instance of negative evidence may be taken as conclusive proof of nonvalidity? Such a point of view provides an absolute standard, but it is an oversimplification of a complex matter. A specific negative event may be the product of factors extraneous to the theory proper, such as inadequate or unreliable data.

Another problem involved is the extent to which the data examined support not only the theory in question, but also opposing ones. The history of science is replete with examples of opposing theories, both of which draw some support from the empirical data. Eventually, one theory becomes ascendant over another, not because it is satisfactory in an absolute sense, but because in the competitive world of science it establishes relatively more order than the other. Once one accepts a fundamental order in the fluctuations of suicide rates, the problem is the governing factor; status integration is the theory which we advance, but many other variables have been suggested. An evaluation of the theory would be incomplete without a consideration of other factors which might have an even more consistent relationship with suicide rates.

Several problems are encountered in the consideration of alternative explanations. In some cases, it is difficult to establish where speculation ends and formal theory begins; and even when theories are explicit and formal, they may fail to designate a specific explanatory variable. Anything approaching exhaustive tests of all possible alternative theories and suggested variables is precluded as beyond the scope of this study. And, even if these problems did not exist, the fallacy involved in argument by elimination makes it impossible to obtain conclusive evidence regarding the position of the theory in relation to other possible explanations. Regardless of how many different variables are considered, there will always be the possibility that one yet to be considered will bear a closer relationship to suicide rates than does status integration.

We have deliberately limited comparative analysis to the more formal and explicit theories concerning variability in suicide rates, and have restricted the tests to spatial variability in suicide rates and variability by age. In this sense, then, the demands placed upon the alternative variables are not nearly so rigorous as those placed upon status integration.

SOCIAL DISORGANIZATION AND POPULATION MOBILITY

The study of suicide by American sociologists, and European sociologists under their influence, has been dominated by one particular concept—social disorganization. If one seeks to find a general theory in the works of Mowrer, Elliott and Merrill, Faris, Cavan, Schmid, and Sainsbury,[1] it boils down to a statement that suicide is in some way linked to social disorganization.

---

[1] Ruth S. Cavan, *Suicide* (Chicago, 1928); Mabel A. Elliott and Francis E. Merrill, *Social Disorganization* (New York, 1941); Robert E. L. Faris, *Social Disorganization* (New York, 1948); Earnest R. Mowrer, *Disorganization, Personal and Social* (New York, 1942); Peter Sainsbury, *Suicide in London* (New York, 1955); Calvin F. Schmid, "Suicides in Seattle, 1914-1925: An Ecological and Behavioristic Study," *University of Washington Publications in the Social Sciences*, V (October, 1928), 1-94; "Suicide in Minneapolis, Minnesota: 1928-1932," *American Journal of Sociology*, XXXIX (July, 1933), 30-48; and *A Social Saga of Two Cities, An Ecological and Statistical Study of Social Trends in Minneapolis and St. Paul* (Minneapolis, 1937).

One of the more important questions regarding an assertion of a link between social disorganization and suicide pertains to the nature of the connection—is the relationship conceptual or empirical? The question is crucial, for if social disorganization is defined in terms of suicide, it is meaningless to assert a causal connection between the two. All too often, one encounters statements which would indicate that social disorganization does not produce suicide but is defined in terms of it. Mowrer, for example, at one time refers to suicide as a "form" of social disorganization.[2]

Some of the more abstract definitions of social disorganization seem at first glance to indicate that the concept may be defined independently of its alleged effects—suicide, crime, or other forms of deviant behavior: "Social disorganization," says Cavan, "is the loss of control of the mores over the members of the group."[3] But this does not suggest empirical referents for the concept, nor does it escape the characteristic problem of social disorganization theory—the failure to distinguish the phenomenon from its alleged effects.[4]

It appears that a case for the relationship between social disorganization and variability in suicide rates rests not on actual empirical correlations between the two, but on observations which connect the postulated effects of social disorganization. If variability in the amounts of suicide, alcoholism, drug addition, homicide, robbery, illegitimacy, and juvenile delinquency is attributed to the degree of social disorganization in a population, then a certain relationship should hold among these forms of deviant behavior. Thus, if suicide rates show a consistently high positive correlation with the other alleged effects of social disorganization, the theory is supported indirectly.

Although Cavan's study in Chicago and Schmid's in Seattle and Minneapolis[5] demonstrated that suicide was found most frequently in those areas of the city that abounded in other forms of socially undesirable behavior and thereby implied that the amount of suicide and other alleged effects of social disorganization vary directly, other observations have been made to the contrary. Porterfield, in a series of works involving the incidence of several forms of deviant behavior in

---

[2] Mowrer, p. 19.

[3] Cavan, p. 330.

[4] Similar problems arise in other definitions of social disorganization; see, for example, Elliott and Merrill, p. 26; Faris, p. 19; Mowrer, p. 26; and Ralph H. Turner, "Value Conflict in Social Disorganization," *Sociology and Social Research*, XXXVIII (1954), 302.

[5] See Cavan, pp. 81-105; see also, Schmid, "Suicides in Seattle," pp. 4-23, and *Social Saga*, pp. 370-380.

American cities and states, has demonstrated that the amount of suicide in a population may be unrelated to or actually vary inversely with other alleged effects of social disorganization.[6] Of particular importance is his demonstration of an inverse relationship between homicide and suicide rates by states. In commenting on this inverse relationship, Porterfield points out the negative results which arise when one seeks to indirectly validate the postulated direct relationship between social disorganization and suicide: "Social disorganization cannot account for variations in opposite directions by states and cities of the designated responses, both of which are supposed to be correlated positively with it."[7]

A methodologically unacceptable way of dealing with the failure of suicide rates to vary directly with other alleged effects of social disorganization is found in Sainsbury's study of suicide in London. Sainsbury took three factors to be indicative of social disorganization—the incidence of divorce, illegitimacy, and juvenile delinquency. By boroughs of London, the suicide rate correlated +.56 with the incidence of divorce, +.57 with illegitimacy, but only +.07 with juvenile delinquency.[8] Sainsbury regards the correlations as support of the hypothesis, and concludes that juvenile delinquency is not indicative of social disorganization. According to this procedure, the empirical referents for social disorganization are those variables which prove to vary directly with suicide, which makes the assertion of a direct relationship tautological.

At the present state of our knowledge, social disorganization, whatever it is and however it be operationally defined, cannot have all the effects attributed to it, since the effects it is supposed to produce may vary independently of each other, if not inversely. Although the postulated direct relationship between social disorganization and suicide is not refuted, it cannot be validated indirectly by correlating the incidence of suicide in a population with other forms of deviant behavior. A

---

[6] Austin L. Porterfield, "Indices of Suicide and Homicide by States and Cities," *American Sociological Review*, XIV (August, 1949), 481-490; "Suicide and Crime in Folk and Secular Society," *American Journal of Sociology*, LVII (January, 1952), 331-338; "Suicide and Crime in the Social Structure of Urban Setting: Fort Worth, 1930-1950," *American Sociological Review*, XVII (June, 1952), 341-349.

Austin L. Porterfield and Robert H. Talbert, *Crime, Suicide, and Social Well-Being in Your State and City*, (Fort Worth, Texas, 1948); see especially, pp. 95-108; also, *Mid-Century Crime in Our Culture* (Fort Worth, Texas, 1954).

[7] Porterfield, "Indices of Suicide and Homicide," p. 489.

[8] Sainsbury, p. 41.

relationship between the two can only be demonstrated by the correlation of direct measures.

To arrive at the empirical referents of social disorganization, one must turn from conceptual analysis and consider research on the subject. Although descriptions by Schmid, Cavan, and Sainsbury of urban areas that are presumably socially disorganized suggest a number of empirical referents for the concept, most of them appear to be relative to certain cultures. Cavan, for instance, cites the presence of lodging-houses and pawnshops as being indicative of social disorganization for certain areas of the city of Chicago,[9] but it is unlikely that Cavan or anyone would maintain that the absence of lodging-houses and pawnshops means that social disorganization is nonexistent.

If one seeks a universal common denominator among various suggested empirical referents for the concept of social disorganization, it would appear to be population mobility—generally, residential mobility on the individual level as contrasted with vertical mobility or the collective migration of groups such as nomadic tribes.

It has been clearly shown by a number of studies of urban life that a high rate of mobility is indicative of social disorganization, the degree of disorganization varying more or less directly with the amount of instability of the population.[10]

Population mobility has a degree of specificity necessary for measuring its prevalence in a population and also may be defined independently of suicide and other alleged effects of social disorganization.

If the degree of social disorganization is gauged by the extent of population mobility, there is some evidence to support the postulated direct relationship between social disorganization and suicide, and, as far as we know, there is no clear-cut negative evidence. Schmid found a correlation of +.60 between the percentage of the residents of cities who were born in some other state and the suicide rate of the cities.[11] Porterfield has reported a correlation of +.66 between a similar index and suicide rates by states.[12] Sainsbury, using three measures of mobility, found the suicide rates of London boroughs to be positively correlated with all three measures to a degree of statistical significance.[13] On the basis of this evidence, the prevalence of mobility is accepted as being potentially capable of accounting for spatial variability in suicide rates. The major remaining question is the ability of population mobility to account for variability in suicide rates by age.

---

[9] Cavan, pp. 90-95.
[10] Schmid, "Suicides in Seattle," p. 12.
[11] Schmid, "Suicide in Minneapolis," p. 30.
[12] Porterfield, "Suicide and Crime in Folk and Secular Society," p. 35.
[13] Sainsbury, p. 41.

In attempting to gauge the extent of mobility in a population, it is desirable to use several different measures so as to include as many types of spatial movement as possible. Thus, with reference to distance, the possibility is always present that suicide varies directly only with changes in residence that involve a certain amount of distance. The use of several different measures rather than one is particularly desirable when attempting to compare the extent of mobility among age groups. It is likely that certain age groups in a society have a great deal of mobility of one type but not of another. Since the social disorganization theory does not specify the types of mobility crucial to variability in suicide rates, we must include as many types as possible in making a test of the theory.

Table 86 gives six measures of the extent of mobility in nine age groups in the United States between 1949 and 1950.[14] The percentages in this table shown for the age group, 14-19, represent an average of the percentages for age groups, 14-17 and 18-19; and the suicide rate for the age group, 15-19, is used as the best approximation of that of the 14-19 group.[15]

Contrary to the theory of social disorganization and the findings of a direct relationship between population mobility and spatial variability in suicide rates, the data in Table 86 demonstrate that population mobility varies inversely with suicide rates by age to a remarkable degree. All six measures show the extent of mobility to decrease uniformly with age, while the suicide rate is shown to increase uniformly with age. Though only this single test was made, the results indicate that population mobility is not a general explanation of variability in suicide rates.

CIVILIZATION OR SOCIOCULTURAL COMPLEXITY AND VARIABILITY
IN SUICIDE RATES

A particular theoretical controversy closely bound up with anthropological observations on suicide has raged for at least three-quarters of a century. The controversy involves the relationship between civilization and suicide. Morselli was led to this conclusion after analyzing secular trends in the rates of European countries, which he interpreted as showing signs of a constant increase in suicide during the nineteenth

---

[14] *U. S. Census of Population, 1950.* Vol. IV, *Special Reports,* Part 4, Chapter B, Population Mobility—States and State Economic Areas, Table 2 (Washington, D.C.), p. 13.

[15] See Chapter IV, note 7, for sources of data used in computing the rates in Table 85.

Table 86. PLACE OF RESIDENCE IN 1949 BY AGE GROUPS, 1950, AND MEAN ANNUAL SUICIDE RATE, 1949-1951, BY AGE GROUPS, UNITED STATES

| Age Group | Suicide Rate Rate | Suicide Rate Rank | Different House in the United States (Movers) and Different County (Migrants) | | | | | | | | | | | | | Mobility Status Not Reported % |
			Same House (non-movers) %	Rank	Same County %	Rank	Total Migrants %	Rank	Same State Economic Area %	Rank	Different State Economic Area %	Rank	Abroad in 1949 %	Rank	
14-19	2.6	9	78.0	6	11.7	4	8.0	3	1.3	3.5	6.8	3	0.5	3.5	1.9
20-24	6.2	8	64.8	9	20.2	1	11.2	1	1.8	1	9.4	2	0.7	1	2.8
25-29	7.9	7	70.0	8	17.9	2	9.3	2	1.7	2	7.7	1	1.0	2	2.1
30-34	9.7	6	77.4	7	13.6	3	6.7	4	1.3	3.5	5.4	4	0.5	3.5	1.8
35-39	12.6	5	82.0	5	10.8	5	5.1	5	1.0	5	4.1	5	0.4	5	1.7
40-44	16.0	4	85.0	4	9.0	6	4.1	6	0.8	6	3.3	6	0.3	6	1.6
45-54	20.2	3	87.4	3	7.4	7	3.3	7	0.7	7	2.6	7	0.2	7	1.7
55-64	26.0	2	89.4	2	6.2	8	2.7	8	0.5	8.5	2.2	8	0.1	8.5	1.6
65+	28.8	1	89.6	1	6.0	9	2.6	9	0.5	8.5	2.1	9	0.1	8.5	1.8
Coefficient of correlation (ρ) with suicide rate			+.90		−.90		−.95		−.91		−.95		−.95		−.91

century: "It is not possible to explain it otherwise than as an effect of that universal and complex influence to which we give the name civilization."[16]

Some fifty years later, Morselli's theory was countered with Zilboorg's claim that civilization is correlated inversely with suicide.[17]

Evaluation of these conflicting positions is difficult, both because of the nebulous nature of "civilization," which is the basic concept of these exchanges, and because writers on both sides appear to have ignored available data which did not support their position. For example, Morselli's statistics should have given him pause, since they show that Norway's suicide rate began to decrease uniformly after 1851, while England's suicide rate remained remarkably constant from 1831 to 1875, at the very time that the more commonly accepted indicators of increasing civilization were present in both countries.[18] Zilboorg rested his position on Steinmetz' observations on primitive peoples, which he interpreted as substantiating an inverse relationship between civilization and suicide; but Steinmetz' study only indicates that self-destruction was not uncommon among primitive peoples. Zilboorg overlooked not only Westermarck's reports of suicide being unknown among some peoples,[19] but also Steinmetz' three instances of the absence of suicide among primitive peoples.[20] The apparent variability in the prevalence of suicide among the Indians of the western part of North America, as described by Benedict [21] and Hrdlicka,[22] casts little light on either side of the argument.

Because of the nebulous quality of the concepts of "civilization" and "sociocultural complexity," it is difficult to test any theory that postulates a direct relationship between one of the two and the volume of suicide. Although there are many specific empirical variables that may be taken to be indicative of the level of civilization or sociocultural complexity, only a few of these are generally regarded as fundamental. The level of formal education is the one considered here. For, from an impressionistic point of view, there seems to be a definite relationship

---

[16] Morselli, p. 16.

[17] Zilboorg, p. 1361.

[18] Morselli, p. 22.

[19] Edward Westermarck, *Origin and Development of the Moral Ideas*, Vol. II (London, 1908), pp. 229-230.

[20] S. R. Steinmetz, "Suicide Among Primitive People," *American Anthropologist*, VII (January, 1894), 53-60.

[21] Benedict, *Patterns of Culture*, pp. 117, 118, and 219.

[22] Ales Hrdlicka "Physiological and Medical Observations Among the Indians of the Southwestern United States and Northern Mexico," U. S. Bureau of American Ethnology Bulletin No. 34 (Washington, D.C., 1908), 171.

on an intersocietal level between suicide rates and the level of formal education. This relationship is confirmed by systematic examination of the relationship between the two variables for states. For the thirty states used in previous tests,[23] the coefficient of rank-difference correlation between median years of school completed for persons 25 years of age and over as of 1950[24] proved to be +.83.

Thus, in at least one universe of observation, it would appear that the level of formal education accounts for spatial variability in suicide rates even better than does status integration. When one turns to nonspatial forms of variability in suicide rates, however, there is some very convincing evidence that the level of formal education is an unsatisfactory variable for a general explanation. Table 87 gives median years of school completed by persons 25 years of age and over in the United States as of 1950[26] and mean annual suicide rates, 1949-1950,[27] by age groups.

The coefficient of rank-difference correlation between the ranks given in Table 87 proved to be —.99, indicating that, almost without exceptions, as the level of formal education decreases by age groups, suicide increases. There is, perhaps, in this finding even more conclusive evidence against formal education than was produced by Durkheim. For nations and provinces in Europe, Durkheim found that the suicide rate varies directly with the level of formal education or related variables, but he refuted the explanatory significance of this by pointing to the Jews in Europe as constituting a singular exception to the rule (pages 162-167).

PSYCHOPATHOLOGY AND VARIABILITY IN SUICIDE RATES

Attempts to account for variability in suicide rates have been characterized by a fundamental conflict between a sociological and a psychological orientation to the problem. Insofar as one purports to compare formal theories in terms of empirical evidence, however, there are at least two possible reasons why it is questionable to consider psychological observations. In the first place, there is no formal psychological theory of suicide, either in regards to individual cases or variability in suicide rates; and numerous problems are created when one treats as a formal theory the general belief that the two are connected with

---

[23] See Chapter IV, Table 6.

[24] *U. S. Census of Population: 1950*. Vol. II, *Characteristics of the Population,* Part 1, United States Summary, Table 67, p. 118.

[25] See Chapter VII, note 2, for sources of data used in computing rates.

[26] *U. S. Census of Population: 1950*. Vol. II, *Characteristics of the Population,* Part 1, United States Summary, Table 115.

[27] See Chapter IV, note 7, for sources of data used in computing rates in Table 87.

psychopathology. One problem lies in the fact that psychopathology is a concept applied to some quite heterogeneous forms of behavior, and there is some argument as to which forms of it account for suicide. The present study uses several different measures presumed to be indicative of the prevalence of all forms of psychopathology (the total number of persons in a population afflicted with any mental disorder other than mental deficiency or epilepsy), but not all of the possible individual forms could be considered separately.

Table 87. MEDIAN NUMBER OF YEARS OF SCHOOL COMPLETED BY AGE GROUPS, 1950, AND MEAN ANNUAL SUICIDE RATES, 1949-1951, BY AGE GROUPS, UNITED STATES

Age Group	Suicide Rate	Rank of Rate	Median Years of School Completed	Rank of Median
25-29	7.9	11	12.1	1
30-34	9.7	10	11.6	2
35-39	12.6	9	10.7	3
40-44	16.0	8	9.8	4
45-49	18.8	7	8.9	5
50-54	21.7	6	8.7	6
55-59	24.8	5	8.5	7
60-64	27.5	4	8.4	8
65-69	28.2	3	8.2	9.5
70-74	28.6	2	8.2	9.5
75+	29.9	1	8.1	11

The second reason for questioning the need for an examination of psychological observations on suicide is the possibility that the negative evidence marshalled by Durkheim against the "psychopathology theory" is conclusive. His findings regarding the relationship between suicide rates and the prevalence of psychopathology for European nations and provinces during the nineteenth century are: (1) Although there was a slight excess of females in insane asylums, the ratio of male to female suicides was on the average of four to one; (2) the proportion of persons in insane asylums and suicide rates by religious denominations varied inversely, not directly; (3) the incidence of insanity and suicide varied independently by age groups; and (4) the incidence of insanity did not bear a direct relationship to the suicide rates, the relationship tending to be, if anything, inverse (pages 70-77).

Although these findings are very suggestive, present-day knowledge poses some serious questions about the adequacy and reliability of Durkheim's measures of the prevalence of psychopathology, questions that are sufficiently important to keep the issue open for further investigation. There is always the possibility that other data will reveal a direct relationship between suicide rates and the incidence of psychopathology.

In examining the relationship between suicide rates and the prevalence of psychopathology in the United States, we lay no claim to possessing data superior to Durkheim's in reliability and validity. For one thing, like Durkheim, we found it necessary to treat statistics on patients in mental hospitals as the best approximation of the prevalence or incidence of psychopathology. The statistics we use, however, are probably better than Durkheim's because of advances in standardization of diagnosis, admission practices, and reporting of admissions to mental hospitals. Also, since the present data have been drawn from one source within one country, they are probably more comparable than those employed by Durkheim.

A First Test of the Relationship. The findings reported in this chapter regarding population mobility and formal education indicate that accounting for variability in suicide rates by age is a major obstacle for alternative explanations. This being true, it is perhaps most appropriate to first examine the relationship that holds between suicide rates[28] and the percentage of persons in sixteen age groups in the United States who were reported by the Bureau of the Census as being mental hospital patients at a particular date in 1950.[29] The following description indicates the scope of the data incorporated in the report:

Mental hospitals.—The figures for mental hospitals presented here cover, in general, patients in hospitals devoted in large part to the care of psychiatric patients. These hospitals are classified by type of control into *federal hospitals*, comprising, by and large, neuropsychiatric hospitals operated by the Veterans Administration; *State, county, and city hospitals*, comprising, in large part, State mental hospitals; and *private hospitals*, comprising proprietary and nonprofit establishments providing care for psychiatric patients.

Some difficulty in discriminating between mental hospitals on one hand and homes and schools for the mentally handicapped (that is, institutions for mental defectives, or feeble-minded, and epileptics) was encountered in establishing this general category, particularly with reference to private hospitals. Thus, it is quite possible that statistics for mental hospitals cover some few institutions which might more properly fall in the category of institutions for the mentally handicapped.

In addition, some attempt was made to cover patients in the psychiatric services of large general hospitals. This attempt was not altogether successful so that although some such patients are included under federal and under State, county, and city hospitals, the number is relatively small.[30]

The percentages shown in Table 88 are based on the number of patients in mental hospitals of all types of control. The value of p be-

---

[28] See Chapter IV, note 7, for sources of data used in computing rates by age.
[29] *U. S. Census of Population: 1950.* Vol. IV, *Special Reports*, Part 2, Chapter C, Institutional Population, Table 5, p. 16.
[30] *Ibid.*, p. 5.

tween the ranks given in the table proved to be $+.99$. It would thus appear that the prevalence of psychopathology is capable of accounting for variability in suicide rate by age in the United States.

Table 88. PERCENTAGE OF PERSONS IN MENTAL HOSPITALS, 1950, AND SUICIDE RATES, 1949-1951, BY AGE GROUPS, UNITED STATES

Age Group	Percentage in Mental Hospitals	Rank of Percentage	Mean Annual Suicide Rate	Rank of Rate
Under 14	.01	16	0.1	16
15-19	.07	15	2.6	15
20-24	.16	14	6.2	14
25-29	.28	13	7.9	13
30-34	.38	12	9.7	12
35-39	.48	11	12.6	11
40-44	.57	10	16.0	10
45-49	.68	9	18.8	9
50-54	.80	8	21.7	8
55-59	.91	7	24.8	7
60-64	.98	5	27.5	6
65-69	.97	6	28.2	5
70-74	1.11	4	28.6	4
75-79	1.31	3	28.8	3
80-84	1.48	2	31.5	1
85+	1.73	1	30.9	2

Notice that, although a particular measure of the prevalence of psychopathology can account for variability in suicide rates by age, it seems as incapable of accounting for such variability among nonwhite females as status integration proved to be (see Table 89). Nine age groups have been employed to make the test comparable to the examination of the relationship by age groups between measures of status integration and suicide rates. The value of ρ between the ranks proved to $+.10$.

Table 89. PERCENTAGE OF PERSONS IN MENTAL HOSPITALS, 1950, AND MEAN ANNUAL SUICIDE RATES, 1949-1951, NONWHITE FEMALES BY AGE GROUPS, UNITED STATES

Age Group	Percentage in Mental Hospitals	Rank of Percentage	Suicide Rate	Rank of Rate
15-19	.09	9	1.4	9
20-24	.19	8	2.5	4.5
25-29	.33	7	2.1	6
30-34	.48	6	3.2	1
35-44	.63	5	2.5	4.5
45-54	.87	4	2.8	2
55-59	1.09	2	2.6	3
60-64	1.17	1	1.8	8
65+	1.03	3	2.0	7

No other tests of the relationship between the prevalence of psychopathology and variability in suicide rates by age were conducted. On the basis of the relationship shown in Table 88 alone, the ability of the prevalence of psychopathology to account for variability in suicide rates by age is accepted.

A Second Test. A somewhat comprehensive report by the Bureau of the Census on the number of mental hospital patients in each of the 48 states at a particular date in 1950[31] has made it possible to examine the relationship between a measure of the prevalence of psychopathology and suicide rates on an intersocietal level. The measure employed is based on the total number of residents in each state who were patients in a federal, state, county, city, or private hospital. This number was divided by the total resident population of the state as of 1950, and the quotient was multiplied by 100,000. When this rate was correlated with suicide rates by states, ρ proved to be $+.02$. The statistics employed in this test represent perhaps the most comprehensive coverage to date regarding patients in mental hospitals by states.

A Third Test. In attempting to obtain a reliable measure of the incidence of psychopathology, one must take into account that many persons who are afflicted with some form of mental illness may not be patients in a hospital. One of several reasons for this is a purely administrative one. It is a common practice for mental hospitals to release a patient to family care or other forms of extramural care. Even though a person is not a resident patient, he may be carried on the books of a hospital. Because of this, the number of patients on the books provides a wider coverage of persons in a state who have been afflicted with some form of mental illness.

For the years 1949 and 1950-1951, statistics pertaining to the number of patients on the books of mental hospitals by states are provided by the Public Health Service. The figures for 1949 are based on reports from 199 state hospitals, eight Ohio receiving hospitals, and 225 of 272 known private hospitals.[32] For the years 1950-1951, corresponding figures are based on the reports of 201 state hospitals, and 228 of 270 known private hospitals in 1950, and 228 of 275 known private hospitals in 1951.[33] To obtain the number of patients on the books of mental

---

[31] *Ibid.*, Table 37, pp. 80-90.

[32] U. S. Federal Security Agency, *Patients in Mental Institutions, 1949* (Washington, D.C.). See Table 3, p. 25, and Table 5, pp. 31-34.

[33] U. S. Department of Health, Education and Welfare, *Patients in Mental Institutions, 1950-1951* (Washington, D.C.). See Tables 3 and 4, pp. 36-41, and Tables 11 and 12, pp. 34-59.

hospitals in each state over the period 1949-1951, the figures for state and private hospitals for each of the three years were combined. This total number was then divided by the population of the state as of 1950 and the quotient multiplied by 100,000. When this rate was correlated with the suicide rates by states, ρ proved to $+.12$.

A Fourth Test. In consideration of the fact that administrative policies and differential rates of release from mental hospitals may operate to create differences among states in the number of resident patients and patients on the books, a third set of statistics on pyschopathology by states was employed. This third measure, which pertains more to incidence than prevalence, is based on the combined numbers of first admissions to state and private mental hospitals for the years 1949[34] and the years 1950-1951[35] per 100,000 population. When this rate of first admissions was correlated with suicide rates by states, ρ proved to be $+.12$.

A Fifth Test. The rates described above take into account patients in private mental hospitals, but they have not exhausted all the possibilities. Rates that are based only on state and private hospitals fail to take into account the county and city psychopathic mental hospitals, and general hospitals with psychiatric facilities. When these types are ignored, rates for certain states are influenced more by their omission than are rates for others. New Jersey and Wisconsin, for example, have large county hospital systems that care for patients who, in other states, would be cared for in state hospitals.

For the years 1949[36] and the years 1950-1951,[37] the number of first admissions to mental hospitals other than state or private are reported separately. When the number of first admissions to these types of hospitals are combined with the number of state and private hospitals, the result is the most inclusive statistic on the incidence of psychopathology that can be obtained. This over-all number of first admissions in each state was divided by the 1950 population of the state and the quotient multiplied by 100,000. When this rate was correlated with suicide rates, ρ proved to be $+.09$.

---

[34] *Patients in Mental Health Institutions, 1949,* Table 2, p. 24, and Table 5, pp. 31-34.

[35] *Patients in Mental Institutions, 1950-1951,* Table 5, pp. 42-46; Table 6, pp. 47-50; Table 13, pp. 60-63; and Table 14, pp. 64-67.

[36] *Patients in Mental Institutions, 1949,* Table 4, p. 30; Table 6, p. 35; and Table 7, p. 37.

[37] *Patients in Mental Institutions, 1950-1951,* Table 9, p. 52; Table 10, p. 53; Table 17, p. 69; Table 18, p. 70; Table 19, pp. 71-73; and Table 20, pp. 74-76.

Reliability of the Statistics. Insofar as the statistics on patients in mental hospitals are taken to be indicative of either the prevalence or the incidence of psychopathology, it is appropriate to consider, even if briefly, reasons for questioning their reliability.

Variations in resident patient and first admission rates provide, in theory, a basis for inference as to variations in the prevalence and incidence of serious mental disorder among the several States.

However, there are certain reasons why such inferences cannot be made for this purpose in our present state of knowledge. These reasons are as follows:

(1) The relationship between the number of persons with a specific disorder who are hospitalized and the number of persons with a similar disorder in the population who are not hospitalized is not known.

(2) Not all persons who are seriously mentally ill, mentally defective, or epileptics are institutionalized. The inability to gain admittance may be related to the degree of overcrowding which, in turn, varies with the adequacy of facilities for the care of mental patients. Those states with more extensive facilities of various types are more apt to show greater numbers of hospitalized patients.

(3) In a given State, either the expansion of facilities or a sudden increase in discharges will provide empty beds and thus permit an upswing in admission of some patients who, because of insufficient hospital space, were unable to gain admittance in previous years. This means that the sudden increased admission rates does not reflect increased numbers of *new* mentally ill but rather an accumulation of patients who would ordinarily have been included in the admission figures of previous years. Similar considerations also apply to the concept of resident patients as an indication of prevalence.[38]

Although this statement takes into account only general considerations regarding the data used in the tests,[39] it is sufficient to indicate a need for caution in interpreting the results. As is often true in investigations of this kind, there is no way of demonstrating with any degree of certainty that one is justified in using rates of hospitalization as estimates of the true prevalence or incidence of psychopathology. Some observations may be made, however. For one thing, rates of hospitalization appear to vary independently of the proportion of known mental hospitals in each state which submitted reports. It should also be noted that the absence of extensive psychiatric facilities in certain states may not necessarily lower the correlation; on the contrary, those states that have limited psychiatric facilities, notably the southern states, are characterized by low suicide rates. If the low rates of hospitalization found

---

[38] *Patients in Mental Institutions, 1949*, p. 9.

[39] For a more complete analysis of specific problems and questions regarding the data, see *Patients in Mental Institutions, 1949*, pp. 9-10, and *Patients in Mental Institutions, 1950-1951*, pp. 7-9.

in these states are a function of limited psychiatric facilities, this operates to increase the correlation. However, such observations are not grounds for declaring the results of the tests as conclusive evidence against the psychopathology theory. We can only conclude, with Durkheim, that rates of the hospitalization of mental patients are incapable of accounting for a variability in suicide rates by states.

Other Considerations. It could be argued, of course, as it was earlier, that the tests reported above are not complete because all of the specific forms of psychopathology have not been considered separately. Because of the necessity of imposing limitations on this part of the study, no attempt was made to correlate suicide rates with rates of hospitalization for specific forms of psychopathology. Moreover, any such attempt would be confronted with even more serious problems regarding the reliability of the data than is true for total mental disorders. Even if a particular form of psychopathology should prove capable of accounting for spatial variability in suicide rates, it must also account for variability by age. From what is known about the incidence of specific forms of psychopathology by age, it is not likely that any one form can account for variability in suicide rates by age. During 1949, rates of first admissions by age to state mental hospitals with a diagnosis of schizophrenia, involutional psychoses, and manic-depressive psychoses reached their maximum, respectively, in the age groups 25-34, 35-44, and 45-54; and all three rates declined sharply for age groups beyond the maximum.[40] In contrast to this, as has been seen, suicide rates by age in the United States continue to increase long after first admissions for these three forms of psychopathology have started to decline. Only first admission rates for mental diseases of the senium show an increase with age parallel with suicide rates;[41] and these are mental disorders that, in addition to being seldom if ever mentioned in observations on the psychodynamics of self-destruction, are least capable of accounting for suicide among the young.

The remarkable relationship between the prevalence of psychopathology and suicide rates by age shown in Table 88, must be subjected to careful interpretation, because the statistics are not based on the age of the onset of mental illness. Consequently, the high percentage of old persons in mental hospitals is probably caused in large part by an accumulation of patients over the years.

---

[40] R. H. Felix and Morton Kramer, "Extent of the Problem of Mental Disorders," *The Annals*, CCLXXXVI (March, 1953), pp. 10, 11.
[41] *Ibid.*

The resident population consists largely of a slowly accumulated core of schizophrenic patients who are admitted during youth or early maturity and stay, in many cases, for the rest of their lives.[42]

Even when rates of first admissions to hospitals for mental disorders of all types show a close correlation with suicide rates by age, it is probably the result of a composite effect.

In the age range of 15-44 years, schizophrenia and manic-depressive psychoses predominate. During the next decade of life the involutional psychoses, general paresis, and alcoholic psychoses attain considerable importance. In the sixties, psychoses with cerebral arteriosclerosis and senile psychoses assume prominence, and these mental diseases of the senium continue to rise until the end of the life span.[43]

This suggests that no particular form of psychopathology accounts for increasing rates of hospitalization with increasing age; it is a sequence of different forms that keep the rate rising. Thus, the only possible way to explain the increase in suicide with increasing age is in terms of the amount of mental disorders of all types; but this category does not appear to be capable of accounting for spatial variability in suicide rates.

SUMMARY AND CONCLUSIONS

In this chapter, three variables were subjected to empirical tests in a comparison of their ability with that of status integration to account for variability in suicide rates. These variables are population mobility, formal education, and rates of hospitalization for mental disorders, corresponding respectively to the social disorganization, the sociocultural complexity, and the psychopathology theories of suicide. None of the three variables proved to be capable of accounting for both spatial variability in suicide rates and variability by age.

Although consideration could be given to only a few of several specific variables that could be used to test the three theories, the tests served their purpose by providing a basis for judging whether or not these alternate theories are superior to the theory of status integration in accounting for variation in suicide rates. The results clearly suggest that they are not.

---

42 *Ibid.*
43 *Ibid.*

CHAPTER SEVENTEEN

Further Research and Speculation

A SERIES of tests seldom provides conclusive results. In view of this, a very important part of the evaluation of a theory is the possibilities for continued research. This is particularly true in sociology, where doubts about particular tests appear to be inevitable.

Three types of theories have defects insofar as future research is concerned: those which do not lend themselves to empirical tests and should, therefore, receive a negative evaluation; those, found rarely, which have already exhausted the available data; and those which have limited possibilities for international or cross-cultural tests. The theory of status integration, we believe, while not entirely free of these defects, holds forth numerous potentialities for future research, some of which will be considered in this chapter.

Another aspect of the evaluation of the theory pertains to general observations, which, while of an empirical nature, do not constitute systematic tests. For want of a better term, we have seen fit to refer to such observations as speculation.

GENERAL PROPOSALS REGARDING FUTURE RESEARCH

In all tests of the theory, the data employed were inadequate in that the available data were either unsatisfactory or not fully exploited. Truly definitive tests would have entailed enormous expense, feasible neither then nor now. In retrospect, this is not altogether unfortunate. Although immediately available data are crude and inadequate, they have a strategic function, in that they may be exploited to determine whether the theory deserves the expenditure required for a series of tests under ideal conditions.

Exploitation of Available Data. Before discussing costly and time-consuming research projects, it should be emphasized that all of the available data have not been exhausted. Data pertaining to status integration in the United States, as we have seen, have not been fully used because of limitations imposed on the study. In some cases, the data provide a basis for computing measures of status integration beyond those considered.[1] In others, an opportunity is presented for the refinement and fuller exploitation of data that were actually used in the present study. As an example of this, the reports of the Bureau of the Census make it possible to use specific occupational statuses rather than broad categories. Several possibilities are presented for the fuller use of the data by states, many of which have been noted already. Also, in other countries a considerable amount of data could be used to test hypotheses derived from the theory.

Beyond Immediately Available Data. If the full exploitation of available data results in evidence that supports the theory, then (and only then) will an extensive research project be justified. Such a project should endeavor to subject the theory to a series of crucial tests involving populations that represent not only cultural diversity but also a wide range in suicide rates.

The test of the major theorem in such a universe of observation would require that the project—in addition to gathering data necessary for computing suicide rates—design and execute a census for the purposes of measuring status integration in each of the populations. Herein lies a crucial question regarding the evaluation of the theory in terms of the possibilities for future research: can the theory actually be tested? While the tests reported point to an answer in the affirmative, the question nevertheless calls for some consideration.

For all practical purposes, apart from the availability of data, the only serious methodological problem in a test of the theory is that of identifying statuses. While recognizing that linking an abstract concept such as status to its empirical referents is a complex matter, there are several reasons to believe that the theory can be tested in any population. The anthropologist, Linton, analyzing patterns of status occupancy among the Tanala and the Comanche, expressed no difficulties in identifying

---

[1] The substitution of marital status for occupational status is an example.

status configurations, and his conclusion suggests that it is possible in any population.[2]

Still another important consideration is that the theory does not call for each population to have the same number of types or statuses. Also, granting their somewhat arbitrary nature, there are in any society certain obvious and discernible categories that provide a means of getting at status integration, even if indirectly. Finally, in virtually any population there are certain universal status families (age, sex, race, marital condition, occupation, religious affiliation, and parental status) that in themselves yield a comprehensive measure of integration. It is true that attempts to establish categories that have the attributes of statuses will be confronted with numerous technical problems in any population, but the obstacles are not insurmountable. An ideal point of departure would be an anthropological field study devoted to the isolation of categories to be treated as statuses.

Though invaluable as a means of providing evidence for the evaluation of the theory, the results of cross-cultural tests could not be considered conclusive. The evaluation of the theory will not be complete until the temporal relationship between status integration and suicide rates have been examined under a variety of conditions. Observations of this nature call for an enormous expenditure, since measures of status integration would have to be established at several points in time for a number of societies. Here, particularly, one finds that available data have little to offer.

Beyond the Major Theorem. In describing the prospects for further evaluation of the theory, only tests of the major theorem have been considered. However, in the future it may prove possible to test other theorems that can be derived from the set of postulates. As an example, if and when it becomes possible to measure the extent of the durability and stability of social relationships in populations, such a measure would be expected to bear a direct relationship with status integration. If this relationship does not hold, then the connection between status integration and suicide rates, while still accepted as empirically valid, would be subject to reinterpretation on a theoretical level.

DEVELOPMENT OF THE THEORY

We have discussed future development of the theory in terms of additional tests, but there are at least four considerations beyond the compiling of empirical evidence:

---

[2] Ralph Linton, "A Neglected Aspect of Social Organization," *American Journal of Sociology*, XLV (May, 1940), 870-886.

(1) There will continue to be a need for further conceptual analysis of status integration independent of its relationship to suicide rates. The central task should be to determine what is left implicit in the concept. For example, status integration should be analyzed in terms of its connection to the concept of social control, its applicability to certain types of statuses (with particular reference to the distinctions between ascribed and achieved statuses), its connection with the division of labor and the concept of consensus, and the possibility that it does not reflect certain types of role conflicts that are disruptive insofar as social relationships are concerned. The observations that were made in this direction throughout Chapter II have only scratched the surface.

(2) The limitations of conceptual analysis are recognized; therefore, there is some justification for purely exploratory work of an empirical nature. Status integration may be linked to far more phenomena than suicide; and it is through observation on such relationships that the nature of the concept will come to be better understood.[3] For one thing, it should be correlated with the incidence of forms of deviant behavior other than suicide, to ascertain if its consequences are general or specific. Though exploratory in nature, observations on relationships with other phenomena should not be based purely on trial and error; they should be guided by hypotheses developed in conceptual analysis.

(3) Without doubt, the most pressing need is for a rigorous analysis of the mathematical operations performed in the measurement of status integration, including experimentation along these lines with different sets of operations. As we have remarked, the method of measurement employed in the tests represents only one of several possible approaches, and the study suffers from the limited experimentation along these lines. There are also certain problems involved that are not purely mathematical in nature; for example, that of the temporal dimension of status occupancy. The element of time may not only condition the consequences of status occupancy, but may also in itself be indicative of status compatibility.

(4) Testing the major theorem on inadequate data presents more than one problem. It is possible that such tests could lead to a premature rejection of the theory, but what amounts to the reverse is also true. That is, the inadequate data could by its very inadequacy produce positive results. As yet, we have found no evidence to suggest that

---

[3] Work is currently in progress, linking status integration to other types of deviant behavior, adjustment in old age, and various characteristics of social structure.

this is true for the tests reported here. Granted that a particular bias in the data could have operated to produce positive results in a few tests, it is difficult to see how such a bias could operate the same way in a series of nearly two hundred tests. It would appear far more likely that inadequate data operate to produce negative results, but it must be concluded that little is known about the consequences of using inadequate data, and insufficient exploration of the possibilities is one of the shortcomings of the study.

SPECULATION

In comparison to systematic tests of hypotheses derived from a theory, the method of illustration is obviously an inferior means of validation. However, once the results of tests of hypotheses have been considered, it is justifiable, and perhaps even profitable, to take into account isolated instances of the phenomenon in question and more general considerations of a speculative nature. In this connection, we shall consider here some of the more remarkable characteristics of suicide rates, both the unique and the common. Since the analysis is based for the most part on general observations, no claim is made that it provides strong support for the theory. The observations at best may be regarded only as impressions that are consistent with the theory.

An Instance of Pronounced Immunity to Suicide. Virtually all observations on suicide rates indicate that suicide is extremely rare among children. In the United States, for example, of over 50,000 suicides reported in the three-year period, 1949-1951, only four of the cases were less than ten years of age.[4] The significance of this remarkable immunity lies in the fact that, of all social groups, children are likely to have the most status integration, as it is in this period of life that measures of the integration of marital and occupational statuses with age most closely approximates the maximum.

Sociocultural Change and Suicide. It has been frequently noted that pronounced increases in the volume of suicide are often found to be associated with countries or civilizations undergoing sociocultural changes on a grand scale. Cavan has concluded that suicide increased in Greece during the period of decline in power, in Rome during the fall of the Empire, and in the Renaissance period in Europe;[5] and reliable estimates suggest that the volume of suicide in Europe increased sharply during the Industrial Revolution.

---

[4] For sources, see Chapter IV, note 6.
[5] Cavan, p. 106.

Although it is true that status integration can increase or decrease in a society without the introduction of new statuses, it would appear that their introduction would tend, at least over a period of time, to decrease integration. Consequently, assuming that most periods of sweeping sociocultural changes give rise to new statuses, it is not unexpected that the volume of suicide apparently tends to increase in such periods. The assumption that social change on a grand scale gives rise to new statuses is not without historical support. Also, although it cannot be demonstrated statistically, periods of marked sociocultural change probably witness a considerable change in the patterns of status occupancy independent of new statuses. Though the introduction of a new status would be more conspicuous than changes in the pattern of status occupancy, the latter could be as important as the former.

The above observations obviously do not prove that suicide increases in periods of sociocultural change because of the introduction of new statuses or modification of the prevailing pattern of status occupancy. For that matter, one can hardly speak with certainty regarding the alleged increases in the volume of suicide. However, on the basis of a probable connection between sociocultural change and the introduction of new statuses, there is reason to hold that evidence of increased suicide does not constitute negative evidence as far as the theory is concerned.

Ritual Suicide and Status Integration. Several studies have stressed the prevalence of ritual suicide among certain non-European peoples.[6] Although the present theory purports to account for variability in suicide rates, and not individual cases, insofar as ritual suicides could conceivably produce a high suicide rate, they do warrant consideration.

Although ritual suicide has undoubtedly prevailed with slight variations and different names in many places, it appeared in classical form in India and Japan as the customs of *suttee* and *hara-kiri*. We are not concerned with individual instances of *suttee* and *hara-kiri*, but the existence of the two customs is not negative evidence as far as the theory of status integration is concerned. Throughout observations made on *suttee* and *hara-kiri* one is struck by the fact that both types of suicide share one characteristic: in the typical case, a change in status is the initial event in the complex of behavior leading to self-destruction. One cannot jump to the conclusion that this change always leads to the occupancy of incompatible statuses, but the apparent status change

---

[6] This should not be understood to mean that ritual suicide has never occurred among Europeans. The fact remains, however, that observations on ritual suicide have tended to associate it more with non-Europeans.

involved suggests that the classical forms of ritual suicide are not inconsistent with the theory.

Although there is a need to stress repeatedly that the theory does not stand or fall on its ability to predict or otherwise account for individual cases, there is something of particular interest in ritual suicide. Assuming that the typical case of ritual suicide involves the occupancy of a status configuration with a low measure of integration, one would then be in a position to ask a significant question pertaining to the origin of the custom. It could be that a history of a high suicide rate for a certain status configuration precedes the development of ceremonial suicide for persons who occupy that configuration, meaning that the custom evolved from an already established behavior pattern.

The above observations represent, of course, nothing more than sheer speculation. The essential point is that while the present theory does not have to account for individual cases of ritual suicide, the apparent association of the custom with a change in status is not inconsistent with the theory.

Wars and Economic Depressions. As numerous investigations have shown, the suicide rates of nations appear to react in a fairly consistent way to wars and economic depressions. Generally, at least among countries populated by Europeans, suicide rates increase in times of economic depressions and decrease in times of war. These characteristics of variability in suicide rates deserve particular consideration. What makes their interpretation difficult is the fact that there is actually very little known regarding the impact of war and economic depressions on the social structure of a society. However, even on an impressionistic basis it appears obvious that both wars and economic depressions are normally accompanied by changes in status for a considerable proportion of the population. Once again, however, it is true that a change in the pattern of status occupancy can lead to increased status integration. Thus, it is possible that in a period of economic depression measures of status integration tend to increase, while in war they decrease. If such should prove to be true, the present theory would be subject to some serious questions. However, the fundamental point to be made is that a change in statuses for a large proportion of the population is consistent with a change in the suicide rate; whether the changes result in increased status integration during a war and decreased status integration in an economic depression remains to be seen.

Although the over-all influence of war and economic depression on status integration remains unknown, there is some evidence to suggest that the occupancy of at least one status tends to vary in a manner consistent with the assumption of increased status integration during war and decreased status integration in economic depressions. It can be demonstrated by measures of integration that the status of unemployed is a very incompatible one, be the period one of war, economic depression, or normalcy. It can further be demonstrated that in periods of war there are few unemployed persons, while the reverse is true for a period of economic depression. This probably lowers integration measures in a period of economic depression and increases them during a war.

It should be noted that exceptions to the general rule of increased suicide in economic depressions and decreased suicide in time of war are not unexpected. It is not inconceivable to think of a war as being so devastating that one consequence is unemployment. Further, an economic depression may not have the consequences of a change in status for a large proportion of the population but rather a simple decrease in material well-being. In short, it is doubtful that all wars and economic depressions have a uniform effect on status integration. Consequently, there are reasons for anticipating exceptions to the rule of increased suicide during economic depressions and a decrease in times of war.

This final chapter adds no new evidence toward the evaluation of the major theorem. Rather, its function has been to indicate briefly the range and variability of research that flows from the theory of status integration. Obviously, much remains to be done before a final evaluation can be made of the theory's ability to account for variations in suicide rates. In the meantime, other theories and other applications also deserve attention.